The Tragic Drama of

William Butler Yeats

Figures in a Dance

The Tragic Drama of
William Butler Yeats

Figures in a Dance

by LEONARD E. NATHAN

Columbia University Press *New York and London*

1965

Leonard E. Nathan is Assistant Professor of Speech at the University of California, Berkeley. He has published a number of volumes of verse.

Copyright © 1965 Columbia University Press
First published in book form 1965
Library of Congress Catalog Card Number: 65-16513
Manufactured in the United States of America

Preface and Acknowledgments

Any serious discussion of W. B. Yeats's work involves problems in terminology partly because Yeats sometimes used traditional terms in an eccentric way, partly because he imported so many terms from other disciplines (like that of the occult) into literary discourse, and partly because he was not always consistent in his usage. This book is, in fact, mainly the outcome of an attempt to define the special senses in which Yeats used the word "tragedy." I believe that this term, as well as some others that offer problems to the critic, takes on precision in the context of the following chapters.

A catalogue of debts does not pay them, but no one to my knowledge has invented a better way to indicate that an author has no heady illusions about his "independence of judgment." Professor Ian Watt saw the manuscript through its primitive stages. I can think of no words gracious enough for his support and guidance. Professors Josephine Miles and Thomas Parkinson gave lavish help when it was needed; so too did Professors Thomas Flanagan, William Brandt, Will C. Jumper, and Elroy

Bundy. My assistants, Mrs. Susan Mazurski and Carroll and Beverly Selph, know how much I am obliged to them. It was pure good luck that this book had Mrs. Beatrix Dinitz of Columbia University Press as its editor. And for everything already printed about Yeats's work I can only show gratitude by trying to write up to the best of it. The book is dedicated to my wife, but less as a gift than as an acknowledgment only two can understand.

For permission to quote from the works of Yeats and from the works about Yeats, grateful acknowledgment is made to the following: The Clarendon Press, for lines from *The Oxford Book of Modern Verse,* ed. by W. B. Yeats, 1937. Harvard University Press, for lines from *Letters to the New Island,* by W. B. Yeats, 1934, and for *Yeats's "Vision" and the Later Plays,* by Helen H. Vendler, 1963. Macmillan and Co. Ltd., London, for passages from *W. B. Yeats,* by Joseph Hone, 1943, and from *Yeats: The Man and the Mask,* by Richard Ellmann, 1949. Macmillan Co., New York, for passages from *Yeat's Iconography,* by F. A. C. Wilson, 1960, and from *The Permanence of Yeats,* ed. by James Hall and Martin Steinmann, 1950, and for lines from *The Unicorn,* by Virginia Moore, 1954. Macmillan Co., New York, and A. P. Watt and Son, London, for lines from *The Collected Plays of W. B. Yeats,* 1952; *The Collected Poems of W. B. Yeats,* 1950; *The Collected Works of W. B. Yeats,* 1908; and also for lines from the following works by W. B. Yeats: *Responsibilities,* 1916; *A Vision,* 1937; *Wheels and Butterflies,* 1934; as well as for passages from *The Autobiography of W. B. Yeats,* 1938; *The Cutting of an Agate,* 1912; *Essays,* 1924; *Essays and Introductions,* 1961; *Plays and Controversies,* 1923. New Directions and Mr. Arthur V. Moore, for passages from *The Classic Noh Theatre of Japan,* by Ernest Fenollosa and Ezra Pound, 1959, originally published in 1916 as *'Noh' or Accomplishment.* Oxford University Press, A. P. Watt and Son, and Professor Richard Ellmann, for passages from *The Identity of Yeats,* by Richard Ellmann, 1954. Thomas Parkinson, for lines from his unpublished essay "Later Plays of W. B. Yeats." Princeton University Press, for passages from *The Japanese Tradition in British and American Literature,* by Earl Miner, 1958. Routledge and Kegan Paul Ltd., and Barnes and Noble Inc., for passages from *Yeats the Playwright,* by Peter Ure, 1963. Rupert Hart-Davis Limited for passages from *A Bibliography of the Writings of W. B. Yeats,* by Allan Wade, 1958, and *Letters of W. B. Yeats,* ed. by Allan Wade, 1954. University of California Press, for passages from *W. B. Yeats, Self Critic,* by Thomas Parkinson, 1951. *Victorian Studies,* for passages from "W. B. Yeats' Experiment With an Influence," by Leonard E. Nathan, 1962. Mrs. W. B. Yeats, for passages and lines from all the above works by W. B. Yeats.

Contents

The Tragic Drama of

William Butler Yeats

Figures in a Dance

Tragic and happy circumstance alike
offer an intellectual ecstasy at the
revelation of truth, and the most
horrible tragedy in the end can but seem
a figure in a dance.

YEATS, A Vision

Drama and the Dynamics of Reality

What set William Butler Yeats apart from other writers of the 1880s and 1890s was his philosophical seriousness. This quality goes a long way toward explaining both the trouble he had in finding a viable dramatic form and the eccentricity of the forms he ultimately came to. Neither traditional drama nor the realism of the new Ibsenite theatre was much help to him because neither allowed for what he thought the most significant experience possible to man, that of supernatural reality. To define the human condition without reference to the supernatural was to reduce man's stature in both life and art. In Yeats's eyes, this was precisely the sin of the realists who, with the help of that sinister enemy of human wholeness, "modern" science, had measured man and found him natural.

But man's passionate aspiration to what lay beyond the natural seemed to Yeats sufficient proof for the existence of the supernatural. And serious literature of the past, he was convinced, showed that human greatness was always bound up with intense passion and that passion linked man to the gods. Thus, the artist who would restore to life and art their proper greatness must, before all, comprehend passion and its relation to supernatural reality. This line of reasoning provided the conscious motive for Yeats's early interest in myth and legend. In *The Celtic Twilight* he insisted that folklore is "not a criticism of life but rather an extension" and praised a tale of Douglas Hyde's for its refusal to stay within the bounds set by "an age of realism. . . . Here at last is a universe where all is large and intense enough to almost satisfy the emotions of man." [1] Though his equivocation here would hardly have offended any Ibsenite, the drift of Yeats's thought is clear: he rejected the universe understood through scientific measurement in favor of a mysterious one understood through the direct apprehension of personal feeling.

But the metaphysical view that Yeats developed over these two decades was not simply an answer to naturalism and a substitute for what he regarded as an exhausted Christian orthodoxy; it also created possibilities and imposed limits within which Yeats had to seek a satisfactory dramatic form.

THE WAR OF ORDERS

In his dedication to *The Secret Rose*, Yeats declared that "these stories . . . have but one subject, the war of spiritual with natural order." [2] It is this conception of a "war" of orders that suggests why Yeats necessarily looked for intellectual support among heterodox philosophic traditions and why he turned to the highly personal transcendentalism of Shelley, the eccentric and mystical Christianity of Blake, and the growing movements of theosophy and occultism. These provided him with materials for a synthesis that, with other later "discoveries," would culminate in *A Vision*. But at this early period he was still laboring to bring them into line with his own uninformed feelings about the nature and extent of reality.

The conception of a war between supernatural and natural is intrinsic to Christian thought, and is traditionally conceived as the ancient struggle between spirit and flesh. But Yeats did not envisage so orthodox a conflict. The ingredients of his own conception combined, instead, to make something far more complex and far less susceptible to precise definition. Particularly from his work on Blake he received ideas that defined the war of orders in most unorthodox terms. In Yeats's interpretation, Blake's cosmic view involved a conflict between the individual and the universal; man reacts against God and God against man.[3] This conflict arises out of the shattering of the original oneness of the universal, and continues until, with the restoration of the Golden Age, the fragmented individual is once more joined to the universal. Neither of the participants in this struggle is evil in any ordinary sense. The inherent evil of the situation is the unhappy separation. Yet the separation is not hopeless, for, in Yeats's view, Blake thought that the individual contained an element of the universal and that this element (which constituted the godhead) was "mood"[4] or emotion and was the very root of man's being. Blake regarded passions and emotions, because they derived from infinite and universal experience, as holy. Man's emotional life is actually a longing for union with the divine. Emotion, then, is associated with the good and with the supernatural, while reason is associated with the evil and the natural.

However, to this interpretation of Blake's ontological theory Yeats brought another idea. He derived this somewhat sinister addition to the great and mainly optimistic cosmic drama that he saw in Blake from his study of Irish myth, legend, and poetry, all of which seemed preoccupied with a great conflict: "[The] thought of war of immortal upon mortal life has been the moving thought of much Irish poetry."[5] It is this momentous conflict that puts a tragic color on the war of orders. Man, propelled by his emotions to achieve identity with the infinite, wages a bold war to compass the supernatural. But the supernatural is, in its turn, cruelly indifferent to man. The result of this conflict is devastating for human life and without any evident reward of ultimate unity with divine being.

In Yeats's cosmos, man strives with the gods to his great peril. The gentle, mildly hedonistic hero of Yeats's short story "The Tables of the Law" describes the dreadful consequences of contact with the mysteries of divine being:

I am not among those for whom Christ died, and this is why I must be hidden. I have a leprosy that even eternity cannot cure. I have seen the whole, and how can I come again to believe that a part is the whole? I have lost my soul because I have looked out of the eyes of the angels.[6]

Man's tragic plight is defined in the framework of a cosmic struggle in which the odds are inevitably against him because of his mortal limits. Human nature, ironically and fatally, partakes of emotion, of divine being, that seeking to rejoin the universal and infinite which brings man to grief or death. For, as the divine ruler in the short story "The Wisdom of the King" menacingly asserts:

Law was made by man for the welfare of man, but wisdom the gods have made, and no man shall live by its light, for it and the hail and the rain and the thunder follow a way that is deadly to mortal things.[7]

The man who seeks to follow "wisdom the gods have made," and whose emotion is sufficiently passionate to call into play his whole human nature, is the hero. As such, he, like Costello in the short story "Of Costello the Proud," is bound to a tragic fate:

He was of those ascetics of passion who keep their hearts pure for love or for hatred as other men for God, for Mary and for the saints, and who, when the hour of their visitation arrives, come to the Divine Essence by the bitter tumult, the Garden of Gethsemane, and the desolate Rood ordained for immortal passions in mortal hearts.[8]

The phrase "immortal passions in mortal hearts" is Yeats's most concise definition, in this period, of the tragic state of human existence. Driven by ungovernable desire, a "love" or "hatred" that leads ruinously beyond human limits, man finds his heroic stature and a tragic destiny.

Concerning the qualities of the supernatural, Yeats is not so explicit. Unquestionably, his obscurity on this subject came in part from intellectual immaturity and the lack of a systematic terminology, but also in part from his desire at this period to represent the supernatural as he understood it—essentially ambiguous, mysterious, and even sinister from the human point of view. He never defined the supernatural, preferring rather to approach it through metaphor and to call it by many poetic names: "divine ecstasy," [9] "immortal fire," [10] "secret rose," [11] "infinite," [12] "great memory," [13] "universal imagination," [14] among others.

The most marked characteristic in Yeats's attitude toward the supernatural was his belief in its impersonal cruelty toward the fragmentary, limited beings who attempted to attain unity with it. In this belief Yeats differed from the occult view of his times as embodied in the doctrine of theosophy. The theosophists laid heavy stress upon man's ethical nature and the ethical nature of the divine source of all being.[15] But to Yeats the supernatural order was no ethical wellspring of existence and no Platonic heaven:

Everything in heaven or earth has its association, momentous or trivial, in the great memory, and one never knows what forgotten events may have plunged it, like the toadstool and the ragweed, into the great passions.[16]

The "great memory" is both the source of strength and the foe of the individual human identity that has a primal need to return to it even at the risk of losing identity.

Beyond its inhumanity (in both senses), its infiniteness, and its power to make mortals seek to attain it through some great passion—such as hopeless love—the supernatural remained, for Yeats, mysterious. No matter how he embodied it in his early work, it carried with it an ambiguity which emerged from and returned to shadows. While escaping the dangers of romantic allegory with this approach, Yeats's early work carried a burden of characteristic vagueness.

Vagueness notwithstanding, the outlines of the cosmic drama stand fairly clear, which is a remarkable achievement, especially for a youth in his twenties with no intellectual training beyond high school except what his father intermittently provided. It should not, of course, be assumed that this philosophical structure or vision was a complete doctrine or was built quickly. The greater part of the theory of the war of orders was probably conceived during Yeats's work on the Blake edition from 1889 to 1893, although he had attempted to express the concept of the war of orders in plays written before he was twenty. He had discovered unusually early the beginnings of a broad and serious philosophical outlook by which to interpret his times. And this outlook was clearly religious, a fact which had obvious implications for his art.

Holding the view that man was engaged in constant and uneven battle with a mysterious, hostile, and magnetic spiritual or supernatural order, Yeats was clearly heterodox. This fact determined his assessment of both the traditional and the realistic drama, as well as the philosophies out of which they grew.

THE INITIAL ALTERNATIVES FOR A DRAMATIC FORM

A serious dramatist beginning to write in the early eighties would have had obvious alternatives as models for his first efforts: either the Victorian version of the Elizabethan form or the realistic form then enjoying its first notoriety in England. Toward the traditional alternative, Yeats's objections would have been twofold: first, the traditional model, even at its best, assumed a world view opposed to his own; second, it was so far from being at its best that even an inexperienced young dramatist might have doubted his capacity to restore it to its past vitality.

Yeats showed great respect for the ability of Elizabethan dramatists to bring to the theatre immense variety and plenitude; they "knew all the gamut of unhappy love from the deep bass notes of realism to the highest and most intense cry of lyric passion." [17] Yeats was to return again and again to Shakespeare's plays and characters for fresh understanding of his own thought and art. But for his attempt to create a "new drama of wisdom" characterized by its "lyrical and meditative ecstasies," [18] the length, variety, and plenitude of traditional plays would seem to have been leading away from his purpose. Moreover, Yeats rightly regarded such drama as essentially concerned with the working out of man's fate in the natural world; the supernatural, even in *Macbeth,* hardly suggests the war of orders that is central to Yeats's conception of reality. Whenever, in fact, he did write traditional drama he discovered that its form undercut his intentions by leading him away from what he thought to be a religious art.

For, believing that the "theatre began in ritual," he declared that it could not "come to its greatness again without recalling words to their ancient sovereignty." [19] This implied a poetic drama, but one, unlike the Elizabethan, that approximated ceremony. And, if the Elizabethan theatre was too secular for his taste, its Victorian descendant was plainly a vulgar parody of that secularism, consisting of melodramatic action, fustian dialogue, and scenes of "verisimilitude, [and] reportorial exactness." [20] When the supernatural entered such work, it did so for melodramatic effect, as the inexplicable voice in Tennyson's *Becket* which cries helpfully, "Becket, beware of the knife." [21] Or it appeared as an allegorical device, as in Henry Arthur Jones's *The Tempter* in which the supernatural devil is a crude symbol of brute fate.[22] William Archer complained in 1882 that on the modern stage the supernatural was "being vulgarized" and was "becoming a matter of science rather than of imagination." [23] The supernatural had, in Victorian versions of traditional form, become chiefly a device to create mystery and sensation but its use was not based upon any conviction of ontological import. Plays like W. B. Wills's *Vanderdecken* (performed in 1878) [24] treated the supernatural with no more seriousness than had the Gothic novel.

Characterization and diction in Victorian traditional drama suffered from the same exaggerations as other elements of the form. At best, the dramatist aimed at psychological portraiture, as in Tennyson's *Queen Mary* (1875); at worst, as in Michael Field's *The Tragic Mary* (1890), the aim was grandiloquent personification. Dialogue ranged from metrical prose to bombast, from Tom Taylor to Stephen Phillips. Yeats later disparaged John Todhunter's poetic *Helena in Troas* (performed 1886) for being "an oratorical Swinburnian play . . . as unactable as it was unreadable." [25] Shelley and Tennyson he regarded as having been corrupted by the weight of tradition:

When Shelley wrote *The Cenci* . . . when Tennyson wrote *Beckett* [sic], they were . . . deliberately oratorical; instead of creating drama in the mood of *The Lotos Eaters* or of *Epipsychidion* they had tried to escape their characteristics, had thought of the theatre as outside the general movement of literature.[26]

The monumental quality of the best Elizabethan drama was overpowering, and Shakespeare, according to Yeats, had become "one of our superstitions." [27] And Yeats clearly wished to avoid falling under the spell of that superstition. Moreover, his philosophic outlook and impulse to write plays that would escape the dying English tradition compelled him to seek a formal expression other than that offered by the five-act verse drama.

It was perfectly clear to Yeats from the beginning that the other alternative, as exemplified by the drama of Ibsen, was un-

acceptable. At least, traditional verse drama, even in its vulgarized form, had imaginative action, splendid scenes, high character, and style. The new theatre, representing a clean break
with such qualities, aimed at middle-class subject matter and
social "problems," and was written in prose dialogue. If the
Victorian verse drama emphasized the natural order at the expense of the spiritual, the new drama gave total and oppressive
attention to the natural. And though Yeats's characters often
rebelled against society, like their counterparts in the new
drama, the rebellion was far different in quality. Yeats's protagonists were engaged in a cosmic war whose divine context
transcended the limits of any society. The rebellion of protagonists in the new drama was usually no more than the symp-
tom of poor adjustment between an oppressive society and its
members; the frank aim of dramatists like Jones and Pinero was
to instruct individuals for their proper role in society or to
create an impulse for social reform that would relax irrational
and unduly severe restraints for those unable to bear them well.

The very power of the new form, its ability to mirror
middle-class life accurately, was precisely its most devastating
shortcoming in Yeats's view: "When an atmosphere of modern
reality has to be built up . . . and the tendency, or fate, or society
has to be shown as it is about ourselves, the characters grow
fainter. . . ." [28] So much the worse for man's heroic passions
and godlike affinities.

His condemnation of the new drama was almost total. He
judged it with all the unfairness of youth and its unjustified
optimism, and prophesied concerning realistic drama and his
own ideal:

We may again—for genius can never be exhausted—experience
dramatic movements mighty as the last agony of Faustus . . . where
now real fire engines driven by real firemen find worthy setting in
absurd plays. When things are at their worst, philosophy, popular
and otherwise, assures us they begin to mend, and realism has had

rope enough to hang itself these latter years, and we have still some coils left if it wants to do it decoratively.[29]

It is true that he found some value in the best realists; for example, he found Ibsen to a certain degree worthy of admiration because the latter understood perfectly the nature and limits of his own dramatic genre and had, therefore, something to teach other dramatists.[30] But it was plain to Yeats very early that to create plays of "heroic passion and lofty diction" he would have to find some form other than the realistic.

If any form of drama then being written pleased Yeats, it was closet drama: Todhunter's "A Sicilian Idyll" [31] and later Robert Bridges' "The Return of Ulysses." [32] But, unlike Todhunter and Bridges, Yeats was not satisfied with a one-shot *succès d'estime* or a polite literary appreciation.

His deep desire to write poetic plays fit for a living stage kept him from the preciousness characteristic of the time, and carried him in the next years through many experiments with dramatic form until he found what he needed. These experiments and what he learned from them constitute the subject of this book.

1

The First Stage

Though they hardly compose a coherent theory, Yeats's early comments on the drama suggest a fairly consistent view of what good drama and theatre should be. Naturally, these comments emphasize what drama and theatre should not be, because Yeats was engaged for the most part in polemics against both the old-fashioned Philistinism and the new fashion of Ibsen. These polemical assertions, mostly found in his letters to American newspapers from 1889 to 1891,[1] must, however, be read with some of his other writings in mind. His public remarks on the drama usually have to do with formal literary and theatrical matters. But for matters of subject and of philosophical context one must turn to essays such as those found in *The Celtic Twilight,* for these essays derive from the same motive as his letters on the drama: the desire to make total and coherent sense out of all his experiences. A standard rule Yeats's critics come to abide by, sooner or later, is that nothing he did or wrote is random; everything has its role in what seems to have been a life-long program to make everything in and around him significant, or Yeatsian.

For this reason, too, it is wise to pay some attention to his earliest drama (almost *juvenilia*) because, read along with his other work of this time, it provides a fairly clear picture of his first efforts as a dramatist; and in those first efforts, as it will more and more appear, his later development is incipient.

A POETIC THEATRE: THE "THEORY"

In his brief appreciation of Todhunter's verse drama *Helena in Troas,* Yeats, drawing hope from the success of its performance, asserted:

We may see once more the work of poets put upon the stage as a matter of regular business, and have plays of heroic passion and lofty diction, instead of commonplace sentiments uttered in words which have at the very best no merit but successful mimicry of the trivial and unbeautiful phraseology of the streets and the tea table.

(New Island, p. 217)

Here Yeats declares two necessities for his kind of drama: the style must be high, that is, poetic; the tone must be heroic, that is, intense with elevated passions. In another appreciation of Todhunter, this time "A Sicilian Idyll," Yeats's praise goes further in defining the formal qualities of the ideal theatre: "Its sonorous verse, united to the rhythmical motion of the white-robed chorus, and the solemnity of burning incense produced a semi-religious effect new to the modern stage" (pp. 113–14). Underlying this judgment is the idea that theatre is essentially defined by a ceremoniousness profoundly akin to religious ritual; the identification of theatre with religious verse is one of those deeply held ideas that links Yeats's work from first to last. The mingling of art and religion was in vogue among Yeats's contemporaries whose aestheticism was chiefly a weapon against the Philistines and realism and a justification of a rather precious glorying in the bizarre and impressionistic. Yeats was far more serious; behind his identification of the dramatic performance with the religious ceremony lay the philosophical vision that would make the act of writing for the theatre as momentous as the most solemn religious experience.

This vision, though mainly found in his work on Blake, appears also in apparently random stories and essays of this period. He discovered in his search through folklore intimations of cosmic mysteries, for the folk imagination was still close to basic human impulses and emotions, close, therefore, to supernatural reality. Thus, legends and tales were a symbolic expression of the peasant's sense of a greater-than-natural presence and his way of accounting for the strangeness that he felt surrounded his life: "Only let it be quite plain that the peasant's vision meant much more than the mere atmospheric allegory of the learned." [2] This portentous "peasant's vision" related in a very specific way, as we shall see, to the outlook so central to Yeats's earliest dramas. For he noted in "The Queen and the Fool" that there "is a war between the living and the dead, and the Irish stories keep harping upon it." [3] Hence in these stories the Yeatsian theme of the war between natural and supernatural realities has its affirming analogue with the instinctive and, therefore, trustworthy imagination of the folk.

This war between the dead and the living, the spiritual and the natural order, involves man in a heroic inner struggle; for he participates through his passions in the spiritual or immortal but is after all a creature bound by his natural limits. The war forces upon him an agonizing choice between two mutually antagonistic worlds, two ways of life, two sets of values. He cannot have both; by choosing one he falls victim to the other. Thus man was, for Yeats, the center of cosmic tension. Born into a world in which mortal limits and natural needs demand his allegiance to the temporal and local reality of a particular social order, man yet feels the impulse to attain another and transcendent reality. As hero he is impelled to choose between the orders and sees his fate bound up with striving for the spiritual reality. The hero is, therefore, one of those who bear "immortal pas-

sions in mortal hearts." His passionate desire, his emotional nature (as distinct from common-sense reason that links him with
the natural order), involves him in an effort to transcend circumstance. The consequences of this heroic effort, for Yeats,
partake of tragedy: the hero becomes the victim of his own
mortal limits. Yet man's suffering and defeat are illuminated
by the possibility that he can know and experience (even if only
for a brief moment) a passionate harmony with the essential
spirit behind all limitations and appearances. The greatness
and dignity of man hinge upon his ability to transcend his own
limitations, to transform his mortality into a passionate essence
of superhuman selfhood, to achieve, in short, a spiritual identity. Because the limits of both the natural world and human
nature represent obstacles to such dignity, the struggle to transcend them is a heroic and ultimately tragic drama.

Yeats gave a central place to emotion in his conception of
life as a tragic drama. It is through emotion, intensified and
purified to passion, that the hero transcends himself. From his
occult studies, Yeats had learned to regard the passions as the
connecting link between supernatural and natural, an emanation of spirit into matter: "Every emotion is, in its hidden
essence, an unfallen angel of God, a being of uncorruptible
flame." [4] From Blake, Yeats had learned to connect emotion,
in its passionate state, with creative imagination whose function
was to reveal the divine:

He [Blake] had learned from Jacob Boehme and from old alchemist
writers that imagination was the first emanation of divinity, "the
body of God," "the Divine members," and he drew the deduction,
which they did not draw, that the imaginative arts were therefore
the greatest of Divine revelations. . . . Passions, because most living,
are most holy . . . and man shall enter eternity borne upon their
wings.[5]

In this view the obligation of the serious artist was to express
spiritual or supernatural reality. If intense and pure emotion

was an emanation of supernatural reality, the dramatist, as an imaginative artist, must bend his efforts to evoke such a passion. The truly "realistic" dramatist then, for Yeats, was one who could represent on the stage emotion elevated to passionate intensity. Yeats, in this sense, wished to be a "realistic" dramatist.

The significant place accorded to the emotions in his philosophical and literary cosmology led Yeats to adopt stylistic effects that would enable him to evoke a purified and heightened emotion in his drama. It was not unnatural that he should turn to poets—chiefly romantic and Victorian—who themselves had strongly emphasized human emotion in their work. More particularly, he modeled himself on poets whose verse was sustained by emotional suggestiveness rather than by abstract statement and whose techniques of evocation were based on an exotic, somewhat archaic, diction. They sought the stylized image placed in a cloudy atmosphere of half-lights and shadows and the rhapsodic or elegiac tone. In short, it was the lyric poets, Shelley, Morris, and Rossetti, to whom Yeats turned when he was searching for a dramatic style.

But for one whose experience with the stage was as yet virtually nonexistent, it was perhaps a natural failing not to recognize what, from hindsight, appears to be perfectly obvious: that the lyric, no matter how intense, is not necessarily dramatic and can, indeed, lead to the blurred and ambiguous expression fatal to the drama. Especially the static, shadowy style of Rossetti's lyrics would seem hostile to the dynamic clarity required for adequate delineation of character and action. Yet Yeats's misjudgment concerning appropriate dramatic style is understandable in the light of his philosophical outlook. Though intrinsically dramatic, this outlook put far more emphasis on emotion, conceived as the isolated "mood," than on the actions and motives that inspired the emotion. Indeed, to attain the ecstatic elevation that characterized the transcendental experience of "hidden essence," emotion had to be purified of the

common circumstances of life. Emotion, seen from this view-
point, lends itself to a static rather than dynamic presentation.
Moreover, because Yeats viewed the nature of divine reality as
mysterious and not subject to logic, the style that led to an orderly presentation of clearly outlined ideas or events would have
seemed to him inappropriate.

For these reasons Yeats was drawn to the belief that presenting the supernatural on the stage meant presenting the
rhapsodic or the dreamy lyric in an appropriate context, one
free of the circumstantial characteristics of realism. The difficulties and failures of all his dramas of this period are in large
measure the result of this view and the contradiction which it
contained: that an inherently dramatic view can be embodied
effectively by an inherently nondramatic style.

EMERGENCE OF A THEME: PLAYS 1884–1886

Yeats's first published plays are without exception poor
things, hardly stageable (though intended for the stage), unhap-
pily echoing other men's styles, feeble in grasp of character and
action, literary in the worst senses—in short, amateur closet
drama. And yet almost without exception they foreshadow
both what his idea of the true tragic theme would be in his
mature plays and the kind of difficulties that theme would cause
him in his search for a living theatre. Each of the plays, aside
from *Mosada,* is concerned with the war of orders, and each of
the plays, including *Mosada,* presents that war in a manner
that is singularly unconvincing. To understand Yeats's development as a serious dramatist, one must see clearly that to Yeats
the problem of how to embody in a persuasive dramatic form
the war of orders is always of first importance, and it is prefigured in these earliest plays.[6]

Of these early dramas, *Love and Death* [7] and, according to
Ellmann, a tragedy variously entitled *The Blindness, The Epic
of the Forest,* and *The Equator of Wild Olives* [8] were not pub-

lished. The remainder of the plays were published and included the following: *Vivien and Time, Mosada, The Island of Statues,* and *The Seeker.*[9] Almost without exception, these plays, published and unpublished, are variations on one theme: the calamitous relationship of mortal to immortal, natural to supernatural.

Ellmann's summary of the plot of *Love and Death* reveals this typical Yeatsian theme:

A god and a mortal are twin brothers; the secondary plot which deals with the mortal is ill-conceived, but in the primary plot the daughter of a king falls in love with the god and, to make herself queen and thereby worthy of him, kills her father. The god at last appears, but, since no mortal can behold his glory and live, the queen is destroyed by her own love.[10]

In *The Seeker* the same fate awaits a mortal who strives for something beyond natural limits. The protagonist of this wooden little allegory, an old knight, sacrifices earthly comfort and honor for the sake of a quest urged on him by a mysterious voice. Instead of the miraculous spiritual vision and "joys inhuman" that he had expected to find at his quest's end, the knight is confronted by the bearded witch, Infamy.

A quest also constitutes the significant action of *The Island of Statues.* This quest, in a Spenserian pastoral setting, is for a magic flower, the possession of which the hero believes will demonstrate the depth of his passion for his beloved. Far from achieving his aim, he falls under an enchantment and is only rescued when his beloved finds the flower and with it saves him. The seeming victory of mortal love over the supernatural is canceled by an ominous final stage direction: "Naschina [the heroine] is standing shadowless." The "goblin flower of joy" rewards its finder with the dubious "burden of the infinite." [11] While it gives mortals eternal life, this ambiguous gift of supernatural power will leave Naschina alone in a perpetually strange world, always to survive lovers and friends. The sombre conclusion, however, is belied by the fairy-tale props, the archaic pastoral style, and the improbability of the action. The presence of the supernatural, necessary to the theme of the war of orders, is reminiscent of the machinery of Victorian melodrama.

The two remaining plays of this group reveal typical characteristics in theme and form. In *Time and the Witch Vivien,* the heroine attempts to achieve immortality by playing dice and chess with Time. She is beaten in both the realms of chance and choice by the limitations of her own mortality (her temporal nature) though as a witch she has access to special supernatural powers. The theme is typical, and the formal treatment is also typical in that it reduces the theme to trite and heavy-handed allegory. Yet in its often pedestrian simplicity, *Time and the Witch Vivien* is more fit for acting than the more lyrical dramas of this group because its action and motive are not blurred or ill-defined. But by any standards the play is bad, for its commonplace qualities take it out of the realm of a serious attempt to grasp the larger reality implied by the war of orders.

In *Mosada,* which is perhaps the least typical of this early group, the Moorish heroine, in trying by witchcraft to call back her lost lover, Ebremar, falls afoul of the Inquisition. Too late, after taking poison, she discovers her lover to be the chief inquisitor. The theme of the play involves the irony that a genuinely passionate love must end in death; but this love is for a mortal man and, therefore, the play is the more or less conventional romantic melodrama of frustrated passion and does not involve any more of the supernatural than is necessary to make Mosada a conjurer. Yet even in this play suggestions of the typical theme appear. Mosada attempts to regain her lover through magic, as did the hero of *The Island of Statues.* And her spell succeeds in effecting a reunion, but, through a dramatic irony, he has become her judge and executioner. Although the characteristic calamity resulting from contact with the supernatural is present, the tragic implications of such a theme for both Mosada and Ebremar are never realized.

Stylistically, the old influences are in evidence and weaken the work as a play.[12] Mosada, like other of Yeats's heroines in these plays, is a creature insufficiently developed to justify the passion that she exhibits; her intense lyricism seems factitious rhetoric. Thus the play, except that the supernatural does not receive significant attention, belongs in spirit to the early group and, like all the others, is weakened by an inappropriately lyrical style, although less so perhaps than the others. Basically, the theme is far more conventional than that of the others, and *Mosada* is, therefore, much less damaged by a conventional, if awkwardly managed, style.

A summary of the chief characteristics shared by these very early plays must include both their single, significantly dominant theme and Yeats's ineptitude in investing this theme with any dramatic effectiveness. The seriousness of this theme—the profound and mysterious forces of passion that drive men beyond mortal limits and bring them ultimate defeat or ruin—is everywhere undermined by weakness of form. The melodramatic plot, the oversimple or obscure motivation of character, the unconvincingly fairy-tale settings, the rhapsodic and derivative style of verse—all these indicate a lack of comprehension of the dramatic requirements of his own theme, which, at this point apparently, Yeats had felt rather than thought out. His inadequate grasp both of his own vision and of dramatic form led him to the false assumption that the rhapsodic or elegiac lyric was an appropriate style for the drama. Obviously, his youth and inexperience lay at the bottom of his ineptitude at this first stage, and it is hardly to be wondered at that these early plays seemed to Yeats not to have solved any basic dramatic problems. His judgment of the group is admirably summed up by his rejection of *The Island of Statues,* which Joseph Hone asserts "was cast away as a work too much influenced by the romantic vocabulary of *Prometheus* and as weak in the handling of the longer metres." [13] These plays are from what might be called (in all but theme) Yeats's Pre-Raphaelite period. In "The Trembling of the Veil," he asserted of this time and a little after (1887–91): "I was in all things pre-Raphaelite. When I was fifteen or sixteen my father had told me about Rossetti and Blake [three years before the first of the plays discussed] and given me their poetry to read." [14] Add to this comment his great love of Shelley's verse, and most of Yeats's poetic characteristics of the time can be seen as imitations of lyrical voices that proved to be of no great assistance in helping him create an effective dramatic style. [15] His first major effort was to come a few years after these crude tries. Like these, *The Countess Kathleen* would reveal both the Yeatsian tragic theme and the problems it produced. The play also exhibits Yeats's first serious effort to find a solution for those problems.

THE COUNTESS KATHLEEN (1892)

In several letters in the year 1889, Yeats indicated his desire to write a poetic drama based upon the tale of Countess Kathleen O'Shea. In April he informed Katharine Tynan that the "new poem" would be "in all ways quite dramatic" and that it would consist of "five scenes" and be "full of action." In the same letter he expressed his interest in the possibility of a drama about St. Angus. [16] This interest, coupled with the fact that *The Countess Kathleen,* when produced in 1899, was subtitled *A Miracle Play,* [17] and the further fact that, in 1890, he asked Katharine Tynan to collaborate with him on a miracle play based upon the adoration of the Magi, [18] suggests clearly the direction which he had at this time mapped out for himself as a dramatist. With the exception of the Magi theme, the plays would concern Irish figures and these figures would give coherence to his vision. The lives of the saints would provide a link between natural and supernatural, and would thus serve as a possible means to embody dramatically the relationship between the two orders of reality. The question arises, however, why, when Yeats was not an orthodox Christian, let alone a Catholic, he should be drawn to figures best suiting orthodox views of natural and supernatural. One answer might be that the lives of saints were seldom, except in pious legends for the instruction of the young, orthodox. Unorthodox writers, near contemporaries of Yeats like Flaubert and Shaw, found in such religious figures subject matter worthy of their most serious literary efforts.

Another answer arises out of the requirements of dramatic form as Yeats then saw it:

The Christian cycle being mainly concerned with contending moods and moral motives needed, I thought, a dramatic vehicle. The tumultuous and heroic Pagan cycle, on the other hand, having to do with vast and shadowy activities and with the great impersonal emotions, expressed itself naturally—or so I imagined—in epic and epic-lyric measures. No epic method seemed sufficiently minute and subtle for the one, and no dramatic method elastic and all-containing enough for the other.[19]

But underlying the surface clarity of the "contending moods and moral motives" and the "perfectly simple" style that he aimed for [20] was the philosophical impulse which was a basic influence in the genesis of *The Countess Kathleen*. For philosophical outlook was, Yeats believed, the ground of all his literary expression. The relationship between philosophy and dramatic form is best revealed in a letter to John O'Leary, dated July of 1892. In this letter Yeats defended his occult activities against the disapproval of his friend:

If I had not made magic my constant study I would not have written a single word of my Blake book, nor would *The Countess Kathleen* have ever come to exist. The mystical life is the center of all that I do and all that I think and all that I write. It holds to my work the same relation that the philosophy of Godwin held to the work of Shelley and I have always considered myself a voice of what I believe to be a greater renaissance—the revolt of the soul against the intellect—now beginning in the world.[21]

Here, by an analogy of Godwin's philosophy and Shelley's poetry, Yeats made the connection between his metaphysical speculation (magic) and his literary expression perfectly clear. Speculation made possible and informed the literary expression. That is, philosophy provided the way of looking at a subject or delineated the theme; aesthetic form provided the viable structure for the subject or gave it an effective dramatic embodiment.[22]

Scrutiny of *The Countess Kathleen* should reveal, then, a hidden but controlling intention based upon Yeats's occult studies: the heterodox conception of reality in which natural and supernatural engage in a war that demands a fatal but ennobling choice by the hero. This conception prevailed in the earliest drama, and there is no reason that it should have radically changed and that the "magic, mystical life" that he claimed to be at the root of his art should have persuaded him suddenly to turn toward orthodox metaphysical views. Insofar as his characteristic view of reality is missing and the play falls back on philosophical and formal orthodoxy, it would fail by Yeats's standards at that time. And in fact the play fails precisely because of its heavy dependence upon orthodox perceptions and conventions. Again, as in *Time and the Witch Vivien,* Yeats retreats from the problems posed by his own difficult vision when he adopts a conventional form.

The plot is based upon a simple legend concerning an Irish noblewoman who sells her soul to save her peasantry from the ravages of a famine.[23] Yeats kept close to the original line of action, but extended character beyond the sketchy figures that people the legend. The play is laid in sixteenth-century Ireland, and it opens at the inn of a peasant, Shemus Rua; "a wood of oak, hazel and quicken trees is seen through the window, half hidden in vapour and twilight." [24]

Shemus' son, Teig, and his wife, Mary, are discussing the terrible famine, when Shemus returns bringing the carcass of a wolf that he has killed. His first act is to blaspheme by calling upon the devil and offering to burn the holy quicken wood. His invocation is answered when two demon merchants enter; making themselves at home, they persuade Shemus to burn the quicken wood, get him and Teig drunk, and announce that their mission is to buy souls.

The second scene takes place in a great hall of the Countess Kathleen's castle. The action hinges on a series of discoveries: the Countess' serfs, arriving one by one, announce to Kathleen that her crops and herds have been plundered by starving peasants. Already deeply worried by the famine, Kathleen begins to despair, wishing for escape to fairyland, but she immediately regrets such feelings and blames them on the bard, Kevin, who is constantly singing of love and the beautiful supernatural beings, the shee. Another and more terrifying discovery drives the Countess to radical action. Her steward has brought in peasants who repay what they have stolen with money received by selling their souls. Kathleen promptly sells her property and, using the gold to relieve the famine, she invites all to the castle to partake of her largesse.

The third scene also takes place in the castle. The merchants enter and discuss the various successes of their mission, and one notes that while Kathleen prayed he was powerless. Now while she sleeps, they steal her remaining money, calling on unwilling water fairies to help them carry away the gold. The demons also call up other more or less supernatural creatures to assist them, this time creatures associated with "decay/Ill longings, madness, lightning, hail and drouth," (*Kathleen,* p. 55). Even these creatures, out of pity for the Countess, are unwilling laborers. When Kathleen awakens, the demons lie to her about the goods that she has purchased from distant places, asserting that these have been either delayed or lost. Kathleen suspects them, but they depart before her servant and nurse,

Oona, discovers that the treasure room has been broken into and looted. After the news of this last robbery is reported, Kathleen resolves to sell her own soul in order to save those of the peasants.

Scene four is once more at Shemus' inn, where the demons are doing a brisk business. Peasants come forward and bargain for the highest price they can get, but they are often forced to take far less than they had hoped for since the demons have access to the secret sins of the bargainers. The bard, Kevin, in despair over the sadness in the Countess' face, tries to sell his soul, but, after deeply disturbing the demons, he is refused and taken away by force. He returns as Kathleen attempts to sell her soul and interrupts by crying out his vision, but is once more taken away and the final bargain is sealed.

The last scene takes place in the castle again. The peasants hear a strange noise at dawn and Oona discovers an owl's (demon's) feathers in the oratory and sees angels carrying off the body of the Countess. A spirit announces that Kathleen is in heaven and that Oona will soon follow her there. The curtain falls on peasants keening.

The play is a fairly straightforward extension and dramatization of the old legend, kept structurally simple. The plot is built on scenes alternating between antagonists and protagonist, who are brought together in scene three, in which the high point of the action is the dramatic irony of Kathleen's near-recognition of her enemies. Tension is built to the climactic fourth scene, in which the Countess sells her soul to save the peasantry; and the final scene is equivalent to the Greek "Epiphany or Resurrection in glory." [25]

The play represents a great advance over the earlier plays in every way. Plot and action are more clearly realized, character is more sharply defined and distinctive, scenes are more dramatically relevant, and style less clogged by awkwardness and callow imitation. However, Yeats has not yet solved his major dramatic problem: how to present his unorthodox theme on the stage, how, in short, to embody effectively the war of orders. Furthermore, these improvements do not bear out Yeats's own assertion to O'Leary that magic, the study of the supernatural, is the foundation of the play.

Surface faults of the play are numerous, but these do not explain the fundamental failure; they are only manifestations of it. For instance, the plot suffers from wrong emphasis. Presumably, the main conflict is in Kathleen and involves the awful choice she must make between her own salvation and the salvation of the peasantry; and yet Yeats, showing relatively little of Kathleen, gives equal share to the agents of evil whose presence ought to be important only to the extent of their effect on the protagonist. If the play were as rich in theme as *King Lear,* then a divided emphasis might be understandable; but *The Countess Kathleen* is based simply on the heroine's dramatic choice between two evils.

Characterization also is weak. The allegorical simplicity of the characters is best illustrated by Kathleen, who represents no very deep exploration of individual or type and whose innocence and goodness seem given facts, never truly tested and evidently incapable of change. Kevin is essentially the embodiment of passionate imagination whose close affinity to the pagan supernatural seems to be outside the conflict between the demonic forces (who are, for no evident reason, unnerved by his presence) and the forces of God. The demons are creatures from a morality play, simply evil figures poorly disguised as merchants; Shemus and Teig are unregenerate and greedy low characters; Mary is a pious peasant; Oona is the loyal old nurse; and the other figures are either devoted serfs or "realistic" types mildly humorous when confronted by demons who know every man's sins. Though each character has a particular voice, the voices tend to be monolithic and thin, except, perhaps, where there are what Henn calls "superb flashes of lyricism which are never wholly assimilated to the action." [26]

This unassimilated lyricism bears upon the stylistic faults

of the play, the chief of which is a scrappy eclectism: the dialogue of the play is written in blank verse that is occasionally prosaic, as

> He [God] does not forsake the world,
> But stands before it modelling in the clay
> And moulding there His image.   (*Kathleen*, p. 65)

occasionally consists of dictional and rhetorical archaisms, as "How yon dog bays" (p. 14); occasionally, as Ellmann notes,[27] swells to Tennysonian orotundity, as "Gilding your tongue with the calamitous times" (p. 16); and occasionally reflects the romantic or Pre-Raphaelite spirit, as

> Would that like Adene my first forbear's daughter,
> Who followed once a twilight piercing tune,
> I could go down and dwell among the shee
> In their old ever-busy honeyed land.   (p. 39)

Moreover, one looks in vain for a serious treatment of the supernatural in the context of a conventional natural scene. Both demons and angels belong to orthodox theology and orthodox morality drama. Besides being moral puppets, figures with no ability to act on their own, both demons and angels are peripheral agents to the action, not centrally significant to Kathleen's choice. The vague fairy folk and the sowlths and tavishes (lost souls of men) are even more on the fringes of the action than the demons and angels. The scenery itself, though it has qualities suggesting supernatural or occult significance, functions as a backdrop or atmosphere for the action. The trees outside Shemus' inn are associated with mystical or symbolical significance: the oak, besides being the object of pagan worship, is associated with the druidic ceremony of cutting the mistletoe;[28] the hazel in Yeats's own words is regarded as the "Tree of Life . . . under its common Irish form";[29] the berries of the quicken (or rowan) tree "are said to be the food of the gods."[30] Yeats's selection of particular trees indicates a growing concern

with the possibilities of scenery. Yet the presence of these trees
has no particular significance to theme or action; it merely suggests to the initiated deeper, but not necessarily dramatically
relevant, meanings. To those who do not recognize their symbolic significance, oak and hazel are merely part of the dark
and mysterious atmosphere of the play, but are hardly crucial to
the play's structure. These trees, like other elements in the play,
secure only minor effects, for all their portentous suggestiveness.

It is evident, therefore, that Yeats's claim in his letter to
O'Leary that the "mystical life is the center of all that . . . I
write" does not apply to *The Countess Kathleen.* The intention
controlling the play does not arise out of the unorthodox vision
of a cosmic struggle between natural and supernatural, but
rather out of a mildly unorthodox, but hardly heretical, view
of the Christian war between divine and satanic wills, the latter
losing in the traditional fashion. The only hint Yeats gives of
an alternative world, Kevin's world of fairy folk, is in a brief
exchange between Kathleen and Oona in the second scene. Oona
sings Kevin's songs which portray the strange Pre-Raphaelite
country of *The Wanderings of Oisin,* where peace, immortality,
love, mystery, and beauty dimly mingle, and Kathleen, tempted
by this pagan vision, cries out, "The horn is calling, calling."
But this momentary movement toward unorthodoxy is abruptly
halted by the action of the play, when men enter one by one to
tell of desperate peasants robbing the Countess' lands. Thus, the
vision of fairyland is only brief and feeble when compared with
the struggle between God and the devil. However, the theme of
a superior soul surrendering "what is eternal for what is temporary" could have led to a more daring play had not Yeats permitted that soul to regain the eternal by renouncing it out of
goodness.[31]

The presence of the bard, Kevin, in the play attests strongly
to the play's unfortunate (from Yeats's point of view) orthodoxy.
Kevin has little genuine relationship to the central action; yet

surely he is Yeats's spokesman and the only figure who suggests the possibility of a less conventional theme—the mysterious and calamitous relationship of mortal to immortal in a pagan setting. Yet Kevin's efforts to draw Kathleen from the edge of disaster and his final attempts to sell his soul do not penetrate to the central issues of the play. His language is the unassimilated lyricism which Henn sees as giving the play its "Celtic-pre-Raphaelitism," [32] that stylized utterance, found in the earlier plays, that tended in almost every instance to work against dramatic structure. Thus, as a participant in the action, or at least as one who speaks for a point of view important to the play's outcome, Kevin has a role so close to being dramatically irrelevant that he often seems a mere intrusion into the world of the play. True, Kevin's role is symbolic of Yeats's world view, and both have an equally tangential position to the main concerns of the drama.

Though Yeats himself claimed later that he had begun *The Countess Kathleen* "avoiding every oratorical phrase and cadence," [33] oratory did creep in. The simplicity he aimed at Ellmann calls, correctly, a "rather lack-lustre" if "honest attempt to represent speech." [34] However, the lyricism, found mostly in Kevin's songs, harks back to the language of the earlier plays. And this lyricism—mainly an effort to create images of remote, exotic, shadowed, or fantastic regions—has no direct relationship to the action of the play. No matter how lovely, the following, a fair example of the lyrical passages, serves no dramatic function:

> Who will go drive with Fergus now,
> And pierce the deep wood's woven shade,
> And dance upon the level shore?
>
> Young man, lift up your russet brow,
> And lift your tender eyelids, maid,
> And brood on hopes and fears no more. (*Kathleen*, p. 36)

In two accurate and revealing comments spaced about two

decades apart, Yeats measured the gap between his intention and his performance in writing the play. In 1904 he asserted:

When I wrote my *Countess Cathleen,* I thought, of course, chiefly of the actual picture that was forming before me, but there was a secondary meaning that came into my mind continuously. "It is the soul of one that loves Ireland," I thought, "plunging into unrest, seeming to lose itself, to bargain itself away to the very wickedness of the world, and to surrender what is eternal for what is temporary." [35]

In "Dramatis Personae," (1935), he said:

The play itself [*The Countess Cathleen*] was ill-constructed, the dialogue turning aside at the lure of word or metaphor. . . . It was not, nor is it now, more than a piece of tapestry. The Countess sells her soul, but she is not transformed. If I were to think out that scene today, she would, the moment her hand has signed, burst into loud laughter, mock at all she has held holy, horrify the peasants in the midst of their temptations.[36]

The first comment is a statement of theme, the second, a judgment on the inadequacy of the dramatic perception. The theme is more or less orthodox: extreme self-sacrifice and the added convention of *deus ex machina* intervening at the end, so that the self-sacrifice is adequately rewarded with supreme happiness. The fact that the self-sacrifice is based upon a humanity not very convincingly established in the play and not perceivable in the peasantry that she is saving makes the Countess' act seem all the more to be taking place in a moral vacuum. The happy ending by fiat further removes the action from the realm of serious insight into character and into reality, either natural or supernatural. It is plain why Yeats felt later that the play was mere tapestry.

Virginia Moore suggests that the reason the 1899 performance of *The Countess Kathleen* was subtitled *A Miracle Play* was "that it proclaimed the central Druidic belief in an invisible, all-motivating world." [37] This opinion surely must be re-

garded as erroneous, since whatever druidic belief exists in the
play is buried under more orthodox beliefs and is accessible
only to a very few. Yeats himself revealed as much in his own
comments on the relationship of the conventional intentions that
are either dramatically subordinate or irrelevant to the main action. In a letter, to the newspaper, *Morning Leader,* published
May 13, 1899, Yeats defended *The Countess Kathleen* against the
charges of blasphemy in the following fashion:

> The play is symbolic: the two demons who go hither and thither
> buying souls are the world, and their gold is the pride of the eye.
> The Countess herself is a soul which is always, in all laborious and
> self-denying persons, selling itself into captivity and unrest that it
> may redeem "God's children," and finding the peace it has not
> sought because all high motives are of the substance of peace. The
> symbols have other meanings, but they have this principal meaning.[38]

Perhaps Yeats exaggerated his orthodoxy a trifle for the sake
of making a point, but, by and large, his judgment in this instance was a fair one and disclosed how far he was from a restoration of druidic belief or from a stage built on his unique spiritual perception of life. For the major theme in his own vision
was subordinated to a traditional theme that showed itself in
subject matter, plot, characterization, and style. So, surely, he
could not claim that he had produced a significant effort worthy
of the renaissance that he saw beginning in the world, the renaissance characterized by the "revolt of the soul against the
intellect." Even in the first version of *The Countess Kathleen*
he demonstrated remarkable improvement as a playwright but
had not yet found an embodiment for his vision; instead, he had
fallen back upon a dramatic tradition that had lost its viability,
and he had, in the process, betrayed his difficult theme to an
orthodoxy that he felt must be transcended before reality could
again be brought to the stage.

Nor did his revision of the play for the 1895 edition of
Poems amend the basic faults of the play.[39] However, some

radical changes in the structure of the new version were made (prompted in part by the experience of watching a performance of *The Land of Heart's Desire* in 1894),[40] but they were not extensive; on the most superficial level they involved only an occasional tightening up of verse. For instance, "May he bring better food than yesterday;/ No one dines merrily on a carrion crow" (p. 51) was naturalized in the second version to "May he bring better food/ Than the lean crow he brought us yesterday." [41] Yeats also subdued his early tendency toward archaisms, substituting "your" for "thy." The scene was shifted from sixteenth-century Ireland to a more generalized Ireland of olden times; a few names underwent changes (of the important characters, Mary became Maire, Kevin became Aleel, and Kathleen became Cathleen); and musicians were added (tympanists and harpists).

More important, however, are the following changes: Cathleen, attended by Aleel, Oona, and the musicians, appears in the first scene (now "act") at Shemus Rua's cabin after his return from hunting and before the entrance of the demon merchants. This change not only slightly increases tension by immediately setting the Countess in dramatic contrast to the demons, but it also extends the role of Aleel. By extending this role, Yeats introduces the possibility of expanding his unorthodox views. However, Aleel's chief function is to augment by his first speech the immediate "terrors to come" and to suggest a contrast with these terrors by his song, "Impetuous heart, be still, be still" (*Cathleen*, pp. 76–7). Beyond this, he does not enter the action. The other important change is the combining of scenes four and five of the first version into Act IV of the second. Whereas in the first version the merchants' buying of souls occupies a whole scene and includes the Countess' climactic dealing with them, the second continues the action without break after the merchants' departure, building to the climax of Cathleen's death and the coming of the angels.

Two other basic differences in the versions go beyond the combining and tightening of scenes. In the second version, Cathleen is brought back to the stage to die, and the role of Aleel is much expanded after the soul-selling scene and during the final action at Cathleen's death. When the merchants depart, Aleel, who has been thrown to the floor (Kevin was simply removed) after trying to prevent Cathleen from bartering her soul, crawls to the middle of the room and describes his vision of Hell, in which figures from Irish mythology and legend take the part of the damned: Balor, "leader of the hosts of darkness at the great battle of good and evil . . . fought out on the strands of Moytura, near Sligo" (p. 281); Barach, a traitor; and Cailitin, the evil druid who opposed the hero, Cuchulain. The chief sins of these damned, however, could just as well be regarded as having been against pagan morality as against Christian morality: "When they lived they warred on beauty and peace" (p. 147). As Oona enters the scene to announce Cathleen's illness and disappearance, Aleel continues describing his vision. He cries:

> Cathleen has chosen other friends than us,
> And they are rising through the hollow world.
> >   *(He points downwards)*
> First Orchil . . .   (p. 148)

who is a sorceress of the Fomorians, the gods of night, death, and cold and the ancestors of evil fairies.

After this, Cathleen is brought on stage in a swoon, recovering only to give proper orders concerning the distribution of the fatal gold and to utter a few loving words of farewell to Oona and Aleel. When Cathleen dies, Oona calls for a looking glass (an act reminiscent of Lear's) to find out if there is any reason to hope that the Countess has breath left. There is none, and Aleel smashes the mirror, addressing it with great bitterness. He curses "Time and Fate and Change"; hard upon his curse, he sees a vision of angels clashing with devils. The angels then appear on the scene in battle formation. Aleel seizes one and demands word of Cathleen. He is told that "she is passing to the floor of peace." It is then that Oona utters a wish to follow her mistress and the vision fades, leaving all but the faint forms of kneeling peasants in darkness.

In both the major changes of the play, in the first and last sections, the aim was obviously to give Kevin-Aleel a larger part in the action. Yeats was surely aware that in the first version this character had no dramatic justification whatsoever; he was, indeed, the author's beloved lyricist, wandering aimlessly through the play. The theme was still the orthodox one, the war of angels and devils; Aleel's presence in no way affected the action or its outcome. Through a vision of love and peace, vague though it might be, he offers an alternative pagan world to the one for which Cathleen sacrifices herself. Yeats, as usual, was careful to subsume this world under the larger one of traditional good and evil by putting the pagan gods in Aleel's visional Hell. Moreover, the possibility of Cathleen's escape to the fairy world can never be taken seriously because that world is so peripheral, so dim in relation to the central issues of the play. Thus, even with a larger part, the bard has no vital function in the play and is merely part of the atmosphere. He is even rather conventional in his habit of seeing pagan values nicely compassed by a Christian world view.

It seems as if in this drama Yeats was willing to compromise the supernatural reality that he took so seriously in theory. Perhaps he feared the consequences of an unqualified challenge to orthodoxy. It is revealing that Yeats, as he grew more confident in his powers, revised *The Countess Cathleen* to give Aleel an even larger role, until finally the latter overtly declares his love and attempts to take Cathleen away from the mundane, natural, orthodox world. In 1895, however, Yeats was still not accomplished enough to be utterly confident, and he was aware, too, of how dangerous his views might appear to some.

Not only was Yeats's philosophical position still obscure; it also constituted rather explosive matter and had to be handled within the limits of what was socially acceptable. Surely, then, both Yeats's inability as yet to find embodiment for his own views and the fact that such embodiment might damage his career militated against unorthodoxy or any full-bodied uniqueness in *The Countess Cathleen*. As a result, the secret world of deeper reality that Yeats had promised O'Leary, if actually present in either the first or second version, is similar to the ancient tapestry in the hall of Cathleen's castle, ornamental rather than functional. Like that tapestry, the hidden intention in no way affects the play. Occult vision cannot be regarded as a serious influence on the play, either as an atmospheric part of the setting or as unassimilated lyricism.

Yeats's own comment on the history of his play is perhaps a most fitting summary:

> My "Countess Cathleen" . . . was once the moral question, may a soul sacrifice itself for a good end? but gradually philosophy is eliminated until at last the only philosophy audible, if there is even that, is the mere expression of one character or another.[42]

Christian moralism was not a satisfactory dramatic framework; something far more personal and far less orthodox was Yeats's aim which, with a growing perception and craft, came more and more to manifest itself in his drama, as is amply demonstrated in the continual revisions of *The Countess Cathleen*.

THE LAND OF HEART'S DESIRE (1894)

Following closely upon the completion of *The Countess Cathleen*, *The Land of Heart's Desire* was, like its predecessor, styled a miracle play.[43] Not so ambitious as *The Countess*, the new play cost Yeats much less effort, and it is doubtful that he regarded it at any time as a major work to be judged against his most austere ideals about the drama. In some ways, however, it more nearly approached his own view of serious theatre than the earlier, more difficult play. But, like *The Countess*, although it was a step forward in the craft of dramaturgy, *The Land of Heart's Desire* represented no very profound or enduring solution to the problem of bringing an effective embodiment of the supernatural to bear upon the natural world represented on the stage. In this new play, he made an attempt to deal directly with the supernatural order on the stage, but undercut this attempt by a withdrawal into equivocal fantasy.

The plot is based upon a traditional legend: the human soul or mind stolen by fairy folk who leave behind a dead body or a mentally vacant one. Yeats plotted this legendary material simply, confining the action to one scene in one place over a short space of time. The scene is the Irish countryside; in their cabin a peasant family and their priest, Father Hart, are gathered around the fire on May Eve, a time when the fairy folk are given great power to do evil or good to men. The family consists of old Maurteen Bruine and his wife, Bridget, their son, Shawn, and his new bride, Maire. The family tries to distract the bored Maire from reading in a strange book; it is obvious that her dreamy, poetic character does not accord well with the humdrum commonplaces of peasant life. Her boredom grows to discontent and, finally, to defiance in the form of a call to the "good people" to take her away. Several times strangers come to the door and ask her for something: these are the fairy folk, who, given anything by mortals, gain power over them. Finally one of the fairy people enters—a small, beautiful girl, who quickly wins everyone's heart and even succeeds in making the priest remove the crucifix that hangs in the room. She then begs Maire to leave with her, and nothing the family or priest can say or do is powerful enough to make the offer less attractive—even Maire's evident love for Shawn is not strong enough to thwart the Faery Child's efforts. Maire "dies," and the priest declares that such occurrences are daily becoming more and more frequent. The play concludes with a triumphant song of the fairy folk who have won another mortal for the Land of Heart's Desire.

In so short a play, characters are mainly suggested types. Thus, Maurteen and Bridget are typical peasants: the good-hearted, fond, but practical husband and the shrewish, unsympathetic wife. Father Hart and the Faery Child embody the opposing "philosophic" positions of the play, he, the responsible man of staid orthodoxy and she, the wild, irresponsible creature of a power outside the realm of orthodoxy. Shawn is something more than a simple peasant, being on occasion able to speak with the rhapsodic Pre-Raphaelite lyricism characteristic of the earlier dramas:

> Sun and moon
> Must fade and heaven be rolled up like a scroll;
> But your white spirit still walk by my spirit [44]

He is thus somewhat closer to the bard, Kevin, and yet, because he represents the domestic, mortal order—no matter how rapturously lyricized—he is on the side of Father Hart and his own parents in the fight for Maire's soul. Maire, herself, is certainly akin to Kevin in her affinity for the fairy folk, and somewhat resembles Kathleen in that she, like the Countess, is made of finer stuff than the peasants, and is therefore more sensitive. Her dilemma arises out of her unusual nature. However, that nature must be mainly taken on faith because she exhibits no depth of character; she shows only a childish impatience with the limits of her world and its four distinct and too human voices, that of Maurteen: "A tongue that is too crafty and too wise," of Father Hart: "A tongue that is too godly and too grave," of Bridget: "A tongue that is more bitter than the tide," and of Shawn: A tongue that is "too full of drowsy love,/ O drowsy love and my captivity" (p. 21). She longs instead for that

> Land of Heart's Desire
> Where beauty has no ebb, decay no flood,
> But joy is wisdom, Time an endless song.
>
> (*Heart's Desire*, pp. 36–37)

Her feelings are summed up in the climactic "Dear, I would stay and yet and yet—" (p. 41). And she surrenders finally to the vision of eternal youth, loveliness, and gaiety.

Like the play's plot and characters, the scene is simple. The place is county Sligo at the end of the eighteenth century, the house as simple as the inn of *The Countess Cathleen*. It is against this generalized and simple setting that the lyrical intensity and sophistication of some of the dialogue seems obtrusive, especially Shawn's Rossettian praise for Maire. Even Maurteen's and Bridget's speeches tend to the literary, though Yeats, avoiding the stilted and turgid Victorian oratory that occasionally cropped up in *The Countess Cathleen*, managed with some success to achieve a simple, convincing blank verse, as with Bridget's:

> Before you married you were idle and fine,
> And went about with ribbons on your head:
> And now you are a good-for-nothing wife.   (p. 19)

But a characteristic and dramatically unassimilated lyricism dominates the tone of the play. Years later, in 1923, Yeats commented on this quality:

Somebody, Dr. Todhunter, the dramatic poet, I think, had said in my hearing that dramatic poetry must be oratorical, and I think that I wrote "The Land of Heart's Desire" to prove that false; but every now and then I lost courage, as it seems, and remembering that I had some reputation as a lyric poet wrote for the reader of lyrics.[45]

Loss of courage is not sufficient to account for the persistent attempts that Yeats made to introduce lyric intensity into the drama. But Yeats's judgment that excessive lyricism was a dramatic weakness in *The Land of Heart's Desire* is sound and equally applicable to the speeches of Kevin in *The Countess Kathleen*. Indeed, the lyrical style had the general effect of obscuring his basic theme in a misty, undramatic verse, derived from the Pre-Raphaelite version of the world. Yeats's essentially dramatic theme, then, far from appearing as a moving discovery both of a fuller reality and a man's tragic dignity, seems a rather dim and rhapsodical echo out of romantic and Victorian lyric poetry.

In *The Land of Heart's Desire* the theme of the war of orders dwindled to a pleasant fantasy, no more serious than *The Island of Statues,* although superior by conventional dramatic standards. The conflict in Maire took the typical shape of mortal against immortal, "the excellent old way through love/ And through the care of children" (*Heart's Desire,* p. 18) as against that way "Where beauty has no ebb, decay no flood,/ But joy is wisdom, Time an endless song" (p. 37). But two weaknesses reduce the scope of the conflict to something less than tragic seriousness: the character of Maire and the quality of the supernatural.

Maire is hardly heroic in stature, surely much less so than Cathleen. The conflict occurs in her, it is true, but she is not in any sense an active agent; rather, she acts in a half-hypnotic state, almost in a stupor. Arguments pour in on her consciousness from both sides; her mind simply receives them, and there is no evidence that anything more happens. Yeats shows no genuine struggle in her. Maire is simply unresponsive to other wills. Father Hart's orthodoxy, Shawn's love, Maurteen's common sense are helpless in a situation in which the mind that they try to influence is already lyrically wrapped up in itself. In this situation there is only the faintest conflict of realities or ideas.

However, the feebleness of the conflict might not have been a flaw in the play if the supernatural had been represented as a serious force. But the fairy people in *The Land of Heart's Desire* are the embodiment of a mild, if irresponsible, felicity, and hardly offer the sort of opposition that might dignify the "war between the living and the dead" to the point of arousing tragic emotions.[46] Indeed, the fairyland of *The Land of Heart's Desire* is a child's charming dream of eternal and harmless pleasure, and the offer of a journey to it requires no heroic effort to resist or to accept. The heroine in her choice has to undergo no deep suffering or spiritual change and revelation. Moreover, the ambiguity of *The Land of Heart's Desire* is sufficient to accord with any orthodox interpretation, for the heroine's choice leads to fantasy, and Yeats is forced to make no judgment on the heroine or her choice. The childlike amoral carefreeness of the fairy folk is not actually a dramatic alternative to pious and loving domesticity. Both fairy folk and mortals are simply the elements of a contrast between the lyrical temper and the prosaic.

Yeats's own judgment on *The Land of Heart's Desire* was severe but, in the light of his own high standards and his abiding desire to write a serious poetic drama on noble and tragic themes, entirely just. In a letter to George Russell, dated April, 1900, he wrote:

In my "Land of Heart's Desire" . . . there is an exaggeration of sentiment and sentimental beauty which I have come to think unmanly. The popularity of "The Land of Heart's Desire" seems to me to come not from its merits but because of this weakness.[47]

Ellmann declares that Yeats at this time intended to present a series of miracle plays, by which he meant plays not necessarily Christian but manifesting in one way or another the existence of an invisible world.[48] But to assert on the stage the existence of an invisible world does not necessarily mean to embody it successfully in poetic drama that "lifts us into a world of knowledge and beauty and serenity." [49] Yeats had not yet achieved anything like such an ideal, though in *The Land of Heart's Desire* the charming shadow of the ideal is present. But, so far, he had failed to produce a serious dramatic embodiment of his world view and to create an intense lyrical drama.

Yet this first stage in his dramatic career is by no means to be counted as a loss. It provided him with much needed experience and taught him much about his own shortcomings. If he still had to learn that the style he had adopted for his plays was essentially nondramatic, he progressed remarkably far in making that style express some aspects of his vision. In the next period Yeats pushed the Pre-Raphaelite lyric style further and discovered the limits of its application to the dramatic form. This earlier period gave him the technique for such a venture, even though, in it, he produced no plays that gave effective form to his intentions.

Aestheticism and *The Shadowy Waters*

Of all Yeats's plays written before the turn of the century, *The Shadowy Waters* (published in 1900) most nearly represents a serious and plenary dramatization of the war of orders. Yet, as his own later versions of the play were amply to demonstrate, *The Shadowy Waters* proved to be no more successful an embodiment of his theme than the earlier plays had been. The faults of the play, however, taught him perhaps more about his own shortcomings as a playwright and about his particular dramatic problems than any other single effort. Chiefly, he was finally made aware that assimilation of lyric intensity into dramatic structure resulted in damaging contradictions. *The Shadowy Waters* was a proving ground for his conviction that lyric intensity was the answer to the problem of creating a noble and passionate dramatic embodiment of his tragic outlook. The stylistic habits (for convenience termed Pre-Raphaelite) that had influenced him earlier were intensified by new but related influences and came to a head in this important play. The failure to dramatize his theme by means of these influences taught him that he had to seek alternative methods.

Thomas Parkinson asserts that *The Shadowy Waters,* in its "use of occult and Irish symbols and its general theme and movement . . . participated in the qualities that characterized Yeats's early verse from 1889 to 1901." [1] Indeed, the play represented, both thematically and stylistically, a kind of summation of these qualities, and also incorporated new qualities that had the effect of intensifying those found in earlier dramas.

The Pre-Raphaelitism that played so significant a role in Yeats's verse during the eighties was in great part the result of his general philosophic position and was characterized by distinct stylistic traits, chiefly the dreamlike lyrical state of mind conveyed through exotic, shadowy imagery and diction and "wavering, meditative, organic rhythms." [2] It may seem paradoxical that Yeats, seeking to embody purified passion, should choose a style that lent itself to conveying dreams instead of motivated actions associated with tragedy. However, during this phase of his work, he thought of the passions as ideally remote, purified of excitement, and contemplative.[3] Thus stylistic traits are the result of his effort to embody the "higher reality" of the passions in a purely lyric form. With his introduction, in the nineties, to influences related to Pre-Raphaelitism but far more overtly programmatic in nature, Yeats turned his own version of Pre-Raphaelite style into something more positive, which he attempted to bring into line with his vision, since for him style necessarily and consciously grew out of philosophic outlook.

These new influences, chiefly the work of Pater and of the French symbolists, may for convenience be summed up by the term "aestheticism." The aesthetic position was based on at least three assumptions: first, that art is the supreme manifestation of civilization; second, that art is radically independent of the rest of life; and third, that the best artistic expression, as distinguished from the constructions of practical common sense or the reasoning of abstract logic, is the embodiment of purified emotion. Aestheticism, though hardly as carefully elaborated a doctrine as, say, Hegel's, was surely a more serious and thorough-going movement than R. P. Blackmur indicates when he calls it "as rootless in the realm of poetic import and authority as the dominant conventions."[4] In England, its most philosophic representative, Walter Pater, aimed at establishing—if no rational system—at least a consistent point of view, an aim recognized by Yeats in his *Autobiography:* "If Rossetti was a subconscious influence, and perhaps the most powerful of all, we looked consciously to Pater for our philosophy."[5] This comment reveals not only the kind of significance that Pater's outlook had for Yeats but also the relationship of Rossetti's influence on that of the later aesthetic one; that is, Rossetti's style held an emotional, though not deeply explored, attraction for the youthful Yeats. Pater's thought offered a positive program, and the influences, including Pater's, that actively entered Yeats's career at this time—chiefly those deriving from his introduction to French symbolism through Arthur Symons—were all programmatic insofar as they provided Yeats with an aesthetic rationale and were not merely random and sympathetic insights, or benefits accruing from a half-aware apprenticeship to another's style.

However, Blackmur is on firmer ground when he asserts that poets influenced by "the dominant aesthetics" were expected, and expected themselves "to produce either exotic and ornamental mysteries or lyrics of mood."[6] Setting aside Blackmur's condemnation of such a phenomenon, one must look for reasons why Pater and the outlook generally connected with his name held so much appeal for the poets of the nineties. Louis MacNeice suggests that, for Yeats at any rate, the aesthetic position was a defense against what might be termed a vulgarizing or secularizing of the arts.[7] Yeats, long after the event, was to claim that the

revolt against Victorianism meant to the young poet a revolt against irrelevant descriptions of nature, the scientific and moral discursiveness of *In Memoriam* . . . the political eloquence of Swinburne, the psychological curiosity of Browning. . . . Poetry was a tradition like religion and liable to corruption.

The answer, then, was to write "lyrics technically perfect, their emotion pitched high, and as Pater offered instead of moral earnestness life lived as 'a pure gem-like flame' all accepted him for master." [8]

Yeats's continual insistence upon the significance of Pater's influence requires that this influence be treated as more than a mere extension of Pre-Raphaelite exoticism or as a view "rootless in the realm of poetic import." Pater's writings had an impact on Yeats's work that did not cease even after the turn of the century, and this influence is visible in Yeats's work long past the time of its immediate effect.

At the center of Pater's position was the notion that human knowledge is rooted in and defined by human feeling. Thus he could assert that "our knowledge is limited to what we feel . . . we need no proof that we feel." [9] Not only is feeling in and of itself the basis of knowledge, but pure and intense feeling or passion, as manifested in poetry, gives the purest knowledge:

Great passions may give us this quickened sense of life, ecstasy and sorrow of love, the various forms of enthusiastic activity, disinterested or otherwise, which come naturally to many of us. Only be sure it is passion—that it does yield you this fruit of a quickened, multiplied consciousness. Of such wisdom, the poetic passion, the desire of beauty, the love of art for its own sake, has most.[10]

Comments such as this—no exception in Pater's writings —would mean much to Yeats. They reinforced his own conviction that intense emotions and true knowledge or vision were bound together and made one by lyrical poetry. It was, therefore, no mere casual exercise when Yeats emulated Pater's elaborate prose style in *The Secret Rose;* [11] the emulation was based upon a strong affinity, one that went far beyond Yeats's conscious discipleship, and extended, in fact, into his later prose work, especially *Per Amica Silentia Lunae* and *The Autobiog-*

raphy. But the connection between Pater's writings and Yeats's went beyond imitation based on sympathy and affinity. Though Yeats's head, as Joseph Hone asserts, may have been full of the "Animula Vagula" chapter of *Marius the Epicurean* during his early trials with Maude Gonne,[12] he obviously gave just as close attention to Pater's remarks on the drama, chiefly those found in "Shakespeare's English Kings," an essay in *Appreciations* (1889). That Yeats knew it well is indicated by his strong reliance upon its views in his own essay, "At Stratford-on-Avon" (1901).[13]

Yeats could not have failed to perceive the implications for his own dramatic approach of the following remarks from Pater's essay:

A play attains artistic perfection just in proportion as it approaches that unity of lyrical effect, as if a song or ballad were still lying at the root of it, all the various expression of the conflict of character and circumstance falling at last into the compass of a single melody, or musical theme. As, historically, the earliest classic drama arose out of the chorus, from which this or that person, this or that episode, detached itself, so, into the unity of a choric song the perfect drama ever tends to return, its intellectual scope deepened, complicated, enlarged, but still with an unmistakable singleness, or identity, in its impression on the mind. Just there, in that vivid single impression left on the mind when all is over, not in any mechanical limitation of time and place, is the secret of the "unities"—the true imaginative unity—of the drama.[14]

The "single impression" that drama ideally gave was based upon the drama's nearness to "the unity of lyrical effect," the coherent expression of some one of the "great passions." This standard of dramatic excellence was not altogether unfamiliar to Yeats, for it had already been implied in his "discovery" of Blake's doctrine that the "higher reality"—the eternal mood—was most truly expressed in the arts. And, discussing poetic drama in 1891, he had spoken of the need for plays of "heroic passion and lofty diction." [15] But certainly Pater, as no one else before, gave

Yeats a thoughtful and authoritative rationale for the lyrical drama. That rationale is to be found underlying Yeats's own criticism of other playwrights. Of some of Maeterlinck's plays he said (and in Pateresque phrasing), "they have not the crowning glory of great plays, that continual revery about destiny that is, as it were, the perfect raiment of beautiful emotions." [16] Praising Robert Bridges' *The Return of Ulysses,* he concluded: "The more a poet rids his verses of heterogeneous knowledge and irrelevant analysis, and purifies his mind with elaborate art, the more does the little ritual of his verse resemble the great ritual of Nature." [17]

Some years later, discussing his program of dramatic reform for the Irish theatre, Yeats carried into the realm of practical staging this view so eloquently voiced by Pater:

We must simplify acting, especially in poetical drama, and in prose drama that is remote from real life. . . . We must get rid of everything that is restless, everything that draws the attention away from the sound of the voice, or from the few moments of intense expression.

But to this comment he added another, which suggests a firm limit to the extent to which he could make Pater's thought his own:

We must from time to time substitute for the movements that the eye sees the nobler movements that the heart sees, the rhythmical movements that seem to flow up into the imagination from some deeper life than that of the individual soul.[18]

Between the two kinds of "movements," that of physical action and that of emotion, is a distinction that can be easily enough translated into Pater's terms; the latter, the "nobler movements that the heart sees," is what leads to "the unity of lyrical effect." The "movements that the eye sees" pertain to a drama full of action and variety like that, say, of Tennyson's *Becket.* But Yeats's reference to "some deeper life than that of the individual soul" added a new element to Pater's criterion for an ideal drama. For Yeats, the element essential to serious drama was the spiritual order of reality and the attendant presence, the objective existence, of something beyond private human emotion. This new element was surely alien to the thought of Pater, for he was basically naturalistic in his assumptions about reality.

That Pater opposed the Philistinism of a materialistic culture, and that he regarded art with a reverence usually consistent with religious worship, does not alter the fact that his aestheticism was based upon the ontological view that Yeats rebelled against in other sympathetic naturalists like his own father, who was outspokenly sceptical of transcendental reality; indeed, Pater was more strictly naturalistic than the elder Yeats, for Pater did not assume that any knowledge was possible beyond subjective experience, and he thought that objective reality, by implication, was simply a matter of individual dreaming: "Every one of those impressions is the impression of the individual in his isolation, each mind keeping as a solitary prisoner its own dream of a world." [19]

The individual personality itself was, in Pater's view, only given coherence by the classical moral and intellectual disciplines and by the traditional canons of good taste.[20] Moreover, the end of being was selective and sensitive hedonism. But intense personal experience, no matter how refined, and the doctrine of *"life as the end of life,"* [21] could not possibly satisfy one who had as early as 1888 laid down the following maxim, which served as a guide to his own intellectual and artistic activity: "To the greater poets everything they see has its relation to the national life, and through that to the universal and divine life: nothing is an isolated artistic moment; there is a unity everywhere." [22] Nor did Pater's tendency to isolate the individual to the privacy of his own reality sort well with a view that put man in dramatic relationship with the natural and supernatural forces around him. Thus Yeats, in 1900, reflecting on the characteristic themes of much of Irish verse, asserted that the "thought of the war of immortal upon mortal life has been the moving thought of much Irish Poetry." [23]

It was typical of Yeats that he had to go beyond intellectual criticism to locate his differences with Pater and rejected that part of the latter's view which was contrary or irrelevant to his own. For Yeats, philosophic vision and literary form were so interrelated that he was impelled to embody his own reaction to Pater's hedonism in a creative act, the short story, "Rosa Alchemica." This story, when its relation to Pater's attitudes is perceived, is a remarkable experiment in that it literally tests an idea: the validity of the Paterian man's response to a reality so great and demanding that it cannot be experienced with merely passive appreciation, no matter how sensitive.[24]

The hero of "Rosa Alchemica" is a thorough disciple of Pater with characteristics strongly resembling Marius, the Epicurean: "I had gathered about me all gods because I believed in none, and experienced every pleasure because I gave myself to none, but held myself apart, individual, indissoluble, a mirror of polished steel." [25] An ominous unrest, however, divides the hero's mind; he becomes aware of the possibility that his experience, limited by his uncommitted response, prevents him from achieving something beyond the natural order of things:

Every experience, however profound, every perception, however exquisite, would bring me the bitter dream of a limitless energy I could never know, and even in my most perfect moment I would be two selves, the one watching with heavy eyes the other's moment of content.   (*Secret Rose*, p. 225)

Momentously confronted by the personality of Michael Robartes, an embodiment of the "pride of the imagination," [26] and by the "limitless energy" of the spiritual world (in the form of an occult and almost Dionysian ritual dance), the hero takes refuge in the Catholic Church and the precarious solace of the rosary.[27] In short, for Yeats the Paterian man fails to achieve the tragic passions that might raise him to heroic stature because he cannot comprehend the larger realities represented by Robartes and his mystic cult. Retreat into the protection of the orthodox church lessens the opportunity for, or the danger of, tragic experience of the "higher reality" in the Yeatsian sense, and is no better a position than the near solipsism recommended by Pater.

"Rosa Alchemica" tests the Paterian man and finds him wanting; and thus the story, as an experiment in aestheticism, also provides the best reasons why Pater's attitudes proved to be severely limited in their value to Yeats in his effort to clarify his own tragic vision. For though Pater eloquently defined the primacy of emotion in art, and provided a clear justification for a drama unified by lyrical mood, he offered no fundamentally different grounds or terms for a larger view of man from those of any other philosophic naturalist to whom Yeats had access.

Pater's attitudes proved enormously fruitful to Yeats in the nineties within the severe limits imposed by Yeats's remarkably shrewd experimentation with them. Indeed, those experiments in themselves constitute some of the most penetrating revelations regarding the inherent weakness of Pater's aestheticism, and it is to Yeats's immense credit that, unlike his fellow poets of the nineties, he had the courage and energy not only to carry to their limits his master's views, but also, as far as it was in his power to do so, to benefit from the conclusions reached. Perhaps this ability to test and learn is precisely what enabled Yeats to grow continually as a poet and dramatist.

The Paterian elements that best fit into Yeats's larger philosophic vision had to do with the quality, not with the philosophic sources and implications, of human experience, and with the style (in the largest sense) that should govern the arts. Pater affirmed for Yeats that human experience has the greatest value when it is most pure and intense, and that art should be made to approach the purity and elevation of religious ritual. These

Paterian maxims deeply affected Yeats's literary practice. But Yeats was compelled by his own convictions to go beyond what Pater offered; and, indeed, he was to find many years later, that personal disaster awaited those of Pater's disciples who could not go beyond their master:

Three or four years ago I re-read *Marius the Epicurean,* expecting to find I cared for it no longer, but it still seemed to me, as I think it seemed to us all, the only great prose in modern English, and yet I began to wonder if it, or the attitude of mind of which it was the noblest expression, had not caused the disaster of my friends. It taught us to walk upon a rope, tightly stretched through serene air, and we were left to keep our feet upon a swaying rope in a storm.[28]

YEATS AND SYMBOLISM

Speaking of Arthur Symons' translations of Mallarmé, Yeats said that they "may have given elaborate form to my verses of those years, to the latter poems of *The Wind Among the Reeds,* to *The Shadowy Waters,* while Villiers de l'Isle-Adam had shaped whatever in my *Rosa Alchemica* Pater had not shaped" (*Autobiography,* p. 273). The conjunction of names here is not fortuitous. In the late nineties Yeats tended to see these names as part of a general movement of which he had more or less recently come to be a conscious part. In "The Celtic Element" (1897), he concluded:

The imagination of the world is as ready, as it was at the coming of the tales of Arthur and of the Grail, for a new intoxication. The reaction against the rationalism of the eighteenth century . . . and the symbolical movement which has come to perfection in Germany in Wagner, in England in the Pre-Raphaelites, and in France in Villiers de L'Isle Adam, and Mallarmé and Maeterlinck, and has stirred the imagination of Ibsen and D'Annunzio, is certainly the only movement that is saying new things. The arts by brooding upon their own intensity have become religious.[29]

Yeats, besides the characteristic reference to Pater's standards for the arts—intensity and religiosity—defined here his own relationship to this movement which was aiming for a more spiritual artistic expression. Here, too, he was able to describe the Pre-Raphaelites, who had earlier influenced him, as part of a general aesthetic program; his devotion to Pre-Raphaelitism, heretofore, had been more or less instinctive; it has been based upon youthful and tentative sympathy rather than on reasoned commitment.

Yeats began to feel close to a philosophy that seemed to have both freshness and the makings of an authoritative tradition that gave him distinguished allies in unorthodoxy. He now elaborated the theory of symbolism he had begun during his Blake studies, bringing into his theory some of what he had learned from French writers loosely connected under the title *symbolistes,* particularly from Maeterlinck and Villiers de l'Isle-Adam, the dramatists mentioned in the quoted passage. Yet it should be remembered that Yeats was not being freshly introduced to the nature and function of the literary symbol by his new contacts; his study of magic, his work on Blake, and his natural literary inclination had already brought symbols into his early works. *The Wanderings of Oisin* is sufficient evidence. In a letter to Katharine Tynan, written toward the end of 1888, he spoke of the poem as saying several things "under disguise of symbolism." [30] William Tindall seems unanswerable in his attack on those critics, like C. M. Bowra and Edward Wilson, who assert that Yeats's symbolism is derived simply and unequivocally from the French.[31] For not only did Yeats use the symbolic method before he became acquainted with the work of the French *symbolistes,* but his direct contact with the French was at best a precarious one; his knowledge of the language was rudimentary, and those among his friends who were acquainted with contemporary French literature—Arthur Symons, George Moore, and later, J. M. Synge—seem to have had only vague or distorted notions of what the French school had actually achieved. While there is no doubt that Yeats's attitudes in many

ways resembled those of French writers associated with the
symboliste movement, such a resemblance is mostly the result
of parallel interests. Thus, it is best to view the French influence
as the consequence of Yeats's discussions on the subject, chiefly
with Arthur Symons, and of his reading the available translated
works of the *symbolistes*. It was during the period of his friendship with Symons, which began about 1895, that his series of
essays on symbolism in the arts was written.[32]

In Symons' own discussions of symbolism much is found
that could be attributed to a devout reading of Pater, for instance, the antimaterialistic fervor for the higher nature of art
as "a kind of religion with all the duties and responsibilities of
the sacred ritual." [33] Like Pater, Symons regarded the lyric as
the perfect form for symbolic art, though significantly he did not
regard it so on Pater's solipsistic grounds:

A lyric, then, is an embodied ecstasy, and an ecstasy so profoundly
personal that it loses the accidental qualities of personality, and
becomes part of the universal consciousness. Itself, in its first, merely
personal stage, a symbol, it can be expressed only by a symbol.[34]

Symons' definition of the symbolic process is a significant key
to Yeats's conception of dramatic character. This definition provided him with a connection, far better than Pater's views permitted, between philosophy and form, a connection which would
allow him to encompass a degree of reality that he, as yet, had
not been able to bring into the drama. The symbol was such a
connection; for the symbol was the means by which Yeats could
formulate or embody a vision that, presented directly, would
seem to lose seriousness or be smothered beneath the ortho-
doxies of traditional drama. As Symons indicated, the symbol
works precisely by detaching itself from the limitations and acci-
dents of personality, such as psychological peculiarity or physical
oddness, and can then free the deeper reality, the emotions, and
lift them out of the constraining bonds of circumstance.

This theory applied perfectly to Yeats's dramatic aims. He was at this time attempting to create a pure drama with the lyrical unity suggested by Pater as a substitute for the unities of psychological and physical probability. The symbol would be the means of achieving the pure drama by calling up with ritual patterns the "infinite emotion" that is "a part of the Divine Essence." [35] When the dramatist has purified his subject to the point at which it achieves symbolic status, then his "little ritual" resembles "the great ritual of Nature."

As Yeats saw it, the aesthetic function of the literary symbol was identical to the function of the occult symbol of his studies: both evoke through ritual patterns spiritual reality. Symbolic function is not rational, but ritual: an "arrangement of colours and sounds and forms" (*Essays*, p. 191), which evokes an infinite emotion. Thus, in any symbolic activity, rhythm and pattern become all important; action and realistic representation lose their central significance. When applied to the drama, symbolic activity implies a meditative, slow-moving intensity; a play that secures its effects by subtle variations and repetitions in rhythms rather than by clear action. In such a drama the aesthetic relationship of actor, scene, costume, and speech must be based upon the playwright's intention of arousing a subdued, but powerful ecstasy. Yeats found this intention successfully achieved in a play by Robert Bridges: "His *Return of Ulysses* is admirable in beauty, because its classical gravity of speech, which does not, like Shakespeare's verse, desire the vivacity of common life, purifies and subdues all passion into lyrical and meditative ecstasies." [36]

Though he did not radically change the direction of Yeats's thought, Symons helped establish a rationale for feelings and random ideas that had been with Yeats from the beginning of his literary career.[37] Though subsequently Yeats would find Symons "curiously vague" as a philosopher,[38] discussions with this friend helped him clarify his thought and build, along with what he had learned from Pater, a dramatic theory that at once justified and expanded his own views. If the symbolism that Yeats's occult studies had taught him was a magical method of evoking supernatural reality for himself, the symbolism that Symons helped him develop was a literary method of evoking supernatural reality for others; and both methods were made one and the same in his mind. All symbol was formed by an arrangement of words or images that had lyrical unity and intensity. In the essay, "The Symbolism of Poetry," Yeats summed up his view in the following fashion:

All sounds, all colours, all forms, either because of their pre-ordained energies or because of long association, evoke indefinable and yet precise emotions, or, as I prefer to think, call down among us certain disembodied powers, whose foot-steps over our hearts we call emotions; and when sound, and colour, and form are in a musical relation, a beautiful relation to one another, they become as it were one sound, one colour, one form, and evoke an emotion that is made out of their distinct evocations and yet is one emotion. The same relation exists between all portions of every work of art, whether it be an epic or a song, and the more perfect it is, and the more various and numerous the elements that have flowed into its perfection, the more powerful will be the emotion, the power, the god it calls among us.[39]

Here the literary symbol takes on a serious, magical function; just as in occult ritual, symbol calls "down among us certain disembodied powers" and does so by arousing emotion with beautiful and effective patterns that have a unity like that of music—all parts, as Pater might wish, in strict relation and working toward one intense impression.[40]

But Symons not only was of significant help to Yeats's developing thought; he also encouraged Yeats's interest in the plays of dramatists who were practicing some of the theory that Yeats now found so illuminating. The names of Maurice Maeterlinck and Villiers de l'Isle-Adam appeared frequently in Yeats's writings at this time, and it is evident that both lent substance to the views that Pater's and Symons' works had encouraged in Yeats.

Maurice Maeterlinck, as both dramatist and theorist, had certain obvious attractions for Yeats. Maeterlinck was influenced, as his *The Treasure of the Humble* indicates, by some of the same unorthodox traditions as Yeats: the mysticism of Swedenborg and the occult tradition.[41] His drama in many respects conformed to a theory very near that adhered to by Yeats; this theory Maeterlinck had clearly advanced in his essay "The Star":

We are in the hands of strange powers, whose intentions we are on the eve of divining. . . . It was the *nature* of disaster with which the earliest tragic writers were, all unconsciously, preoccupied, and this it was that . . . threw a solemn shadow round the hard and violent gestures of external death; and it is this, too, that has become the rallying-point of the most recent dramas, the centre of light with strange flames gleaming, about which revolve the souls of women and of men; [42]

and in "The Tragical in Daily Life": "I do not know whether it be true that a static theatre is impossible. Indeed, to me it seems to exist already. Most of the tragedies of Aeschylus are tragedies without movement." [43] In the same essay Maeterlinck described the Greek drama as

life that is almost motionless. In most cases, indeed, you will find that psychological action—infinitely loftier in itself than mere material action, and truly, one might think, well-nigh indispensable—that psychological action even has been suppressed, or at least vastly diminished . . . with the result that the interest centres solely and entirely in the individual, face to face with the universe. . . . It is no longer a violent, exceptional moment of life that passes before our eyes—it is life itself.[44]

The static drama that achieves its effects through "a solemn shadow" rather than naked action and by diminishing psychological as well as physical action is surely close, both in intention and form, to the "little ritual" that Yeats conceived for his ideal theatre. Maeterlinck's view in general was one that Yeats could obviously welcome and find of value in his own efforts to establish an ideal theatre in objective reality. His deep accord with Maeterlinck's view found affirmation in frequent echoes of his theory in Yeats's prose. Particularly noteworthy is the instance in which Yeats's echoing passage also projects his clearest definition of tragedy. Maeterlinck had asserted in an essay included in *The Treasure of the Humble*, reviewed by Yeats in 1897,[45] that "Racine's characters have no knowledge of themselves beyond the words by which they express themselves, and not one of these words can pierce the dykes that keep back the sea."[46] Yeats, thirteen years later, was to say: "Tragedy must always be a drowning and breaking of the dykes that separate man from man."[47] The repeated image of the dyke restraining profound passion looks less like a coincidence than a conscious or unconscious memory of the earlier passage; an assumption rendered more solid by the fact that in another essay in *The Treasure of the Humble* Maeterlinck claimed that a "new indescribable power dominates this somnambulistic drama."[48] In his essay on tragedy, Yeats had also claimed that "tragic art, passionate art, the drowner of dykes, the confounder of understanding, moves us by setting us to reverie, by alluring us almost to the intensity of trance."[49] The state of somnambulance and that of trance may differ in other contexts, but the probability is that in this instance and, given the other more obvious relationships already cited, Yeats's term is significantly close in meaning to Maeterlinck's.

There seems little doubt that Maeterlinck's thought affirmed and deepened Yeats's conviction that his own theories were correct. Thus, the likelihood is that Maeterlinck exercised a genuine influence over Yeats's dramatic conception; but, it must be added, an influence made difficult to prove because of the broad similarity of the two approaches even before Yeats could have learned much from Maeterlinck.[50]

However, if Yeats could accept Maeterlinck's theory at this time with something like complete approval, he had important reservations concerning the latter's plays. Writing in April of 1895 to Olivia Shakespeare, he criticized Maeterlinck's drama for "touching the nerves alone," a fault which seemed to him "to come from the lack of revery." [51] He was to criticize some of Maeterlinck's early plays for the same reason in a review of *Aglavaine and Sélysette* in the *Bookman.* Where he had unreserved praise for *The Treasure of the Humble,*[52] he found reason to doubt Maeterlinck's consistent ability to realize in his plays the insights of his critical theories. About *Aglavaine and Sélysette,* Yeats said: "The first act and part of the second act are a little absurd, because Meleander and Aglavaine explain when they should desire and regret . . . and because the art, which should be of a cold wisdom, has shared in their delusions and become a little sentimental." [53] Although noting beauty in the play, Yeats found a lack of purity, a heterogeneousness that robbed it of "that ceaseless revery about life which we call wisdom." [54] Apparently none of the plays of Maeterlinck impressed him as much as, say, Villiers de l'Isle-Adam's *Axël.* Yeats was, as Tindall suggests, more interested in the Maeterlinck dramas as part of the movement against the externality of contemporary realism and "was fascinated with Maeterlinck's repeated symbols of mysterious intruders, lighthouses, and wells in the woods." [55] Paradoxically one finds in the kind of praise that he had for Maeterlinck the very reason for Yeats's serious reservations about Maeterlinck's ultimate value as a dramatist. Yeats asserted in his essay, "The Autumn of the Body" (1898), that "Maeterlinck has plucked away" the desire found in Villiers' work

for that hour when all things shall pass away like a cloud, and a pride like that of the Magi following their star over many mountains . . . [and he has] set before us faint souls, naked and pathetic shadows already half vapour and sighing to one another upon the border of the last abyss.[56]

It is apparent from the outcome of the action in "Rosa Alchemica" that Yeats felt passivity and weakness could not bring man to heroic commitment and to spiritual vision. Yeats, both in temperament and theory, was bound to reject "faint souls, naked and pathetic shadows" for his own work. Walter E. Houghton points out that "every influence of his early life drew Yeats to the heroic idea," and that, for Yeats, "the positive virtues of courage, love, physical strength, decisive action, and above all, abounding energy . . . form the higher law of heroic morality." [57] Houghton's generalization applies even to the nineties, when Yeats was still strongly under the influence of a dreamy Pre-Raphaelitism.

In contrast to the passive, pathetically timid hero of the "Rosa Alchemica," the other important hero in the stories of *The Secret Rose* is Proud Costello, a man of gigantic strength and courage, a tragic hero because he is one of those typical Yeatsian figures who suffer "immortal passions in mortal hearts." It is the energy and passion of Costello, his intense thirst for, and his pure pride in, his ideal that make him heroic. Thus, it seems that Yeats felt more sympathy with Villiers' proud, vigorous characters than with Maeterlinck's subdued and pale ones. Yeats's fundamental objection to Maeterlinck, then, was that, though his critical insights were profound and his drama had a kind of ghostly beauty, he lacked the tragic sense—the ability to create heroic figures committed to a tragic passion. Maeterlinck's work partook of a passivity that was alien to Yeats's purposes, and, just as Yeats could not accept the Paterian hero, so he was forced to reject the hero of Maeterlinck.

If Maeterlinck's theories helped Yeats to define better his own theoretical attitude toward the drama, Villiers' *Axël* provided Yeats with a model of that drama. A brief examination of the play reveals why Yeats found in it much to admire and emulate.[58] The handsome, brilliant Count Axël, the youthful protagonist of the play, has withdrawn from the world to his castle in pursuit of some final spiritual truth and has put himself under the discipleship of a great master of the occult. During the course of the action, Axël duels with and kills a relative, Commander Kaspar, who represents worldliness, externality, and hedonism. Axël also comes upon a beautiful woman, Sara, who has discovered a secret treasure hidden in the Count's castle by his father. Sara wounds the young man, but they soon fall passionately in love, finding one another kindred spirits—both are proud and beautiful and given to the occult. With the immense treasure at their feet, they talk of their love, Sara planning exotic adventures in all the bizarre and romantic places of the world. Axël, however, rejects these plans, because the intensity of their love is such that worldly pleasures, no matter how exquisite, would be anticlimactic to their pure and intense passion of the present moment. He believes that even one night's physical pleasure would lead to the end of love, and he persuades her that the highest consummation of their relationship would be for both to commit suicide immediately; the play concludes with their deaths.

Axël is a veritable treasury of ingredients that would find immediate response in Yeats: the handsome, courageous, and intellectual hero who rejects the world for a more noble spiritual reality; his heroic commitment to his choice; his apprenticeship to a great occult teacher; his superb scorn for the successful and worldly Commander, a scorn capped by his triumph over Kaspar on the latter's own grounds, swordsmanship; and a beautiful woman who submits to the noble ideal out of love for the hero. Especially would Yeats, who had claimed that "the only two powers that trouble the deeps are religion and love," [59] find in the remarkable relationship of Axël and Sara a tragic resolution that combined both religion and love in a merging of philosophy and life pitched to intense and pure passion. Indeed, Axël and Sara go beyond the romantic *Liebestod* of lovers who choose death because they are entirely fulfilled and can only through death avoid falling into the bathos that must inevitably follow the climactic passion that is the highest human experience. As adepts of a faith that assures spiritual immortality after proper discipline, Villiers' lovers transcend death and can expect something like their earthly love transformed into the imperishable and divine. Obviously, this relationship was irresistible to Yeats, who believed that human triumph arose out of mortal defeat, because death was "but the beginning of wisdom power and beauty." [60]

Yeats saw a performance of *Axël* in Paris in 1894 and was deeply moved, even though his knowledge of French was poor. His review of the play made it clear that, as he was to say in *The Autobiography*, "here at last was the Sacred Book" [61] for which he had longed. In this review he summarized the point that he felt *Axël* was meant to convey: "The infinite is alone worth attaining, and the infinite is the possession of the dead. Such appears to be the moral." [62] The heroic renunciation of Axël and Sara, the total commitment to their ideal, became his model—as Joseph Hone asserts, the "guide and beacon in his theory and practice of a dramatic art where symbol replaces character, events are allegories and words keep more than half their secrets to themselves." [63] That renunciation was to some degree the theme of *The Secret Rose,* his book of stories published in 1897. One of the book's epigraphs is Yeats's favorite line from the play, Axël's haughty comment: "As for living, our servants will do that for us."

Not only the lovers' renunciation but also Axël's unequivocal and heterodox devotion to the occult stirred Yeats to admiration. Pater had pointed the way to a view that regarded subjective experience as unique. But Pater had valued the uniqueness for its own sake and, indeed, had seen no way to share with others the personal validity of a private experience. The symbolism preached by Symons and Maeterlinck and embodied by Villiers pushed beyond the private vision. For, though Axël rejects the world and its objective reality, he still engages in a discipline—that of the occult—which would merge his private reality, his unique personality, with a universal spirit. Being true to one's private vision, Yeats insisted, leads, especially for the magician or artist, to unity with a universal power. For intense emotion is a manifestation of divinity, and emotion is the root of individual personality stripped of circumstantial and accidental qualities, or, as Maeterlinck had asserted, personality purified of physical and psychological elements. Thus, Yeats stated that the self "is the foundation of our knowledge," [64] and, since it is through subjective knowledge that the artist comes to truth, the dramatist must embody the core of subjectivity, the passions. Axël's pure and ardent quest, then, reinforced Yeats's own view already clearly stated in an essay written in 1895:

Passions are angels of God, and . . . to embody them "uncurbed in their eternal glory," even in their labour for the ending of man's peace and prosperity, is more than to comment, however wisely, upon the tendencies of our time. . . . Art is a revelation, and not a criticism." [65]

There is no question that Yeats discovered profound support in Villiers' play. In it he found the kind of tragic dramatic hero he himself wished to create; and also in it he recognized as an unqualified assumption that the personal vision achieved validity through an occult connection with universal and spiritual reality. Furthermore, despite the fact that Villiers' play was too cluttered and too lengthy for its structure to be imitated,[66] Tindall is correct when he finds a clear debt to *Axël* in *The Shadowy Waters*.[67] That play, indeed, in its first version, is very much the result of Pater's aestheticism, Symons' symbolist theories, and Yeats's own readings in French literature, especially of Maeterlinck and Villiers. But these influences were not sim-

ply poured into a dramatic mold. Yeats brought them together
and transformed them into something very much his own. That
something is the theory that served as a standard for his dramatic
intentions in *The Shadowy Waters* and requires a brief examination before the play itself is discussed.

For Yeats, the symbolic artist was one who discovered "immortal moods in mortal desires." [68] The imaginative use of symbols was the method by which the artist bridged the gap between
the immortal and mortal; for, as Yeats wrote to George Russell
in the spring of 1900, the "imaginative deals with spiritual
things, symbolized by natural things—with gods and not with
matter." [69] The artistic achievement of the imagination was wisdom through the purification of "all passion into lyrical and
meditative ecstacies." [70] The "lyrical and meditative" ecstasy
was embodied in a literary form, symbolic in nature; that is, a
pattern of sounds, colors, and shapes whose harmonious relationship evokes the emotion, the spiritual reality, to be revealed
by the artist. He, like the magician, selected from the natural
world only those elements that call up the universal powers beyond the natural:

All Art that is not mere story-telling, or mere portraiture, is symbolic, and has the purpose of those symbolic talismans which
medieval magicians made with complex colours and forms, and bade
their patients ponder over daily, and guard with holy secrecy; for
it entangles, in complex colours and forms, a part of the Divine
Essence.[71]

For the tragic dramatist this reasoning had significant implications. The proper subject matter of drama had to be a
heroic involvement, since nothing less than heroic involvement
would be consonant with the intense passion that is necessary to
evoke spiritual reality.

Symbolic art, then, demands a return to the heroic age and

has made painters and poets and musicians go to old legends for
their subjects, for legends are the magical beryls in which we see

life, not as it is, but as the heroic part of us, the part which desires always dreams and emotions greater than any in the world, and loves beauty and does not hate sorrow, hopes in secret that it may become.[72]

Moreover, for Yeats in particular, Ireland's heroic age, the mythical age of superhuman figures and their deeds, seemed the fittest era for his attempts to evoke a greater than natural reality. Not only were the figures of Irish mythology remote and noble enough to suit heroic action and passions, but their greatness in the past seemed close to the supernatural reality that he wished to reveal on the stage. In this connection he asserted in 1903 that "the great virtues, the great joys, the great privations, come in the myths, and, as it were, take mankind between their naked arms, and without putting off their divinity." [73] Though this comment was written after the completion of *The Shadowy Waters,* he had earlier used such Irish figures as Oisin, Costello, Hanrahan, Cuchulain, and Fergus in his work.

Plots for such subject matter, however, must not require prolonged action full of violence and variety of situation. The fragile and brief mood of the "lyrical and meditative" ecstasy could not survive if action went beyond the brevity and unity that Pater suggested when proffering his view of the ideal drama modeled on the lyric poem or music.

Character, to be consistent with the world of action in such a drama, must not be based upon physical or psychological verisimilitude; indeed, as Maeterlinck indicated, a certain suppression of physical and psychological characteristics was advisable as a means of reducing the circumstantial differences among men and of reaching something of their essence. Yeats phrased this theory of character as follows:

A person . . . that is a part of a story . . . evokes but so much emotion as the story . . . can permit without loosening the bonds that make it a story . . . but if you liberate a person . . . from the bonds of motives and their actions, causes and their effects, and from all bonds but the bonds of your love, it will change under your eyes, and become a symbol of an infinite emotion, a perfected emotion, a part of the Divine Essence.[74]

Acting, to suit the aesthetic whole, must achieve "grave and decorative gestures" and be set in "grave and decorative scenery." Poetry must be the language of the play; verse, spoken with sensitivity and feeling, must fill the mind's eye with what the actual background only suggests by means of an impressionistic tree or wood; and costumes must not have an "irrelevant magnificence." [75]

THE SHADOWY WATERS

This was Yeats's theoretical position as he worked on *The Shadowy Waters* between 1894 and 1900, the years during which he was most deeply involved with the aesthetic and symbolist movements.[76] It was published, Parkinson notes, not in 1902 as Yeats was to claim years later, but in 1900. It was revised for a 1905 performance, and "Yeats continued tinkering with the play" after 1906.[77]

Writing to Fiona Macleod in January of 1897, Yeats stated that *The Shadowy Waters* was "magical and mystical beyond anything" he had as yet done, that "it goes slowly," and that he "wished to make it a kind of grave ecstasy." [78] Ellmann asserts that the reason the writing went slowly was because Yeats had difficulty in "knowing what he meant." [79] The fact that he had been working on the play since his youth may have had something to do with the laboriousness involved in its composition, since the play probably went through the same transitions as his own thought. He had apparently almost finished it in 1894.[80] But some special urge seemed to drive him to work on it in the following years until its actual publication in 1900. It was during these fruitful years (1894–1900), with the work and thought of sympathetic minds before him, that he was finally able to consolidate much of what heretofore had been random insights and unorganized impressions; only after such a consolidation was the play finally able to take the shape he desired. It was characteristic that his ability to formulate his thoughts clearly during this period related directly to his ability to complete his creative work. It is evident from the following that *The Shadowy Waters* was a work of enormous conscious effort and elaborate thought. Yeats declared in a letter to Mrs. Clement Shorter written in June of 1899:

I am working at my *Shadowy Waters* and it is getting on far better than when I left it aside a couple of years ago. Since then I have worked at Irish mythology and filled a great many pages of notes with a certain arrangement of it for my own purposes; and now I find I have a rich background for whatever I want to do and endless symbols to my hands. I am trying to get into this play a kind of grave ecstasy.[81]

To George Russell in August of the same year, he confided more specifically the underlying thought guiding his writing of the play. "I may be getting the whole story of the relation of man and woman in symbol—all that makes the subject of *The Shadowy Waters*" (*Letters,* p. 324). In December, 1899, just before finishing the play, Yeats boasted to Lady Gregory: "I am about twenty or thirty lines from the end. The thing grows wilder and finer as it goes on I think. I have thought out the staging carefully and will get a strange grey dreamlike effect" (p. 331). Such comments point to a long struggle, consciously undertaken, to shape a great mass of material gathered from his studies of mythology and the occult into a dramatic whole that would effectively symbolize spiritual reality. Moreover, Yeats's remarks suggest that the theoretical views he held at this time were consistently in his mind as guides to his selection and arrangement of this material. His repeated references to the "grave ecstasy" or "dreamlike effect" that he expected to achieve summed up the aims of all the aesthetic and symbolist strictures that he had made his own. *The Shadowy Waters* is to a great degree demonstrably the outcome of Yeats's intellectual development from 1894 to 1899.

The actual subject and plot are his own but show marked

resemblances to Shelley's *Revolt of Islam* and Villiers' *Axël*. Yeats's hero, like those of Shelley and Villiers, quests for some mystical revelation, meets a soul mate, and continues his quest with her. A major difference between Yeats's story and those of Shelley and Villiers is that, whereas the heroes of the latter two find their triumph in death, the hero of *The Shadowy Waters* drifts with his love into ambiguous mistiness. Yeats's own summary of the play is worth quoting in full:

Once upon a time, when herons built their nests in old men's beards, Forgael, a Sea-King of ancient Ireland, was promised by certain human-headed birds love of a supernatural intensity. These birds were the souls of the dead, and he followed them over seas towards the sunset, where their final rest is. By means of a magic harp, he could call them about him when he would and listen to their speech. His friend Aibric, and the sailors of his ship, thought him mad, or that this mysterious happiness could come after death only, and that he and they were being lured to destruction. Presently they captured a ship, and found a beautiful woman upon it, and Forgael subdued her and his own rebellious sailors by the sound of his harp. The sailors fled upon the other ship, and Forgael and the woman drifted on alone following the birds, awaiting death and what comes after, or some mysterious transformation of the flesh, and embodiment of every lover's dream.[82]

The plot, as Yeats described it, obviously embodied an actual, if symbolic, journey that was more like the journey of Shelley's hero than Axël's quest through study. Clearly, Yeats's choice of subject and action was determined by his belief that he could draw upon the heroic age to symbolize what he sought to reveal. Axël's more modern experience, no matter how attractive to Yeats, was not sufficiently remote and mythical to be a model. Also the plot of Yeats's play, unlike that of *Axël*, compassed the kind of action that Yeats felt would best evoke the mood he wanted. Yeats's plot was marked by a slow, almost dreamy movement, nearly all of the physical action taking place beyond the vision of the audience. Indeed, much of the action of the play is performed by characters in a state of trance. The slow, trance-like quality brings the play closer to those of Maeterlinck than to *Axël,* which for all its mysticism has many of the characteristics of realistic literature and bears a full complement of the circumstantial reality that Yeats sought to avoid in his drama. Further, unlike *Axël's* lengthy plot, that of *The Shadowy Waters* satisfied Pater's requirement that a play should have a unity resembling that of a lyric. There is only one major action, the meeting of the hero, Forgael, and the heroine, Dectora; that meeting is appropriately encompassed in one act. The emphasis upon one action characterized the plots of most of Yeats's earlier drama, but never until *The Shadowy Waters* had he worked with such conscious elaboration to invest his action with the significances of his now more expanded and organized vision. Parkinson asserts of *The Shadowy Waters:*

> To readers of Yeats's early verse the terms of the action are familiar: Forgael yearns for the impossible and gives up temporal life and its rewards for some experience of the unpeopled world beyond the sun. The immortals have pressed upon him, he commands magical power, and he longs for that mingling of the natural and supernatural which was one of Yeats' abiding preoccupations. Once more Yeats' poetic hero, singled out and perhaps victimized by the gods, fares over waters in search of happiness.
>
> If the play is in many respects typical of Yeats' early verse, it also embraces all the elements necessary, in Yeats' definition, to tragic drama. Straining against the obstacle presented by the merely worldly aspirations of his sailors and the "beautiful woman," Forgael might well attain the moment of passionate intensity that would make him stand as a hero worthy of Yeats' affirmation. And the material seems to allow for continual conflict culminating in the final scene.[83]

The action is plainly—in the Yeatsian manner but with new complexity and control—a symbolic journey of the tragic hero questing for the immortal.

If the plot is symbolic, so are the characters. Yeats himself suggested possible interpretations. First, in a letter to George Russell he had claimed that the hero and heroine symbolized the "whole story of the relation of man and woman," although it is obvious that he did not intend to create mere psychological archetypes. On the contrary, it was his aim to divest character of particularizing psychological traits so that he might get at the universal man and woman. Thus Forgael and Dectora are to be interpreted in their most abstract sense as "the polarity which we call sex, while it allows of the creation of an emotional unity." [84] Second, the action as an allegory of the human pilgrimage requires yet another, not quite so abstract, reading of character, suggested, as Ellman believes, by Yeats himself:

Forgael seeks death; Dectora has always sought life; and in some way the uniting of her vivid force with his abyss-seeking desire for the waters of Death makes a perfect humanity. Of course, in another sense, these two are simply man and woman, the reason and the will, as Swedenborg puts it.[85]

Then, in an unpublished prologue to the play, also quoted by Ellman, a third explanation is given: "These two are Aengus and Edaine. They are spirits and whenever I am in love it is not I that am in love but Aengus who is always looking for Edaine through somebody's eyes." [86]

Each of Yeats's interpretations deepens the significance of character. The first is the metaphysical interpretation of character and sex as symbols for the ontological polarity of all life at the moment of its working toward unity; the second is the allegorical interpretation of character and sex as symbols for the faculties of human nature cooperating for the soul's salvation; the third is the mystical or anagogical interpretation of character and sex as symbols for man's sanctification through divine union. And, of course, there is the unspoken, because so obvious, literal interpretation of character and sex as symbols for individual human aspiration and striving toward some ideal.[87] Combined, the interpretations might be summed up as follows: hero and heroine are meant to symbolize any pair of discords that can come to spiritual harmony through love.

In various degrees opposed to this pair are the sailors, chief among whom is Aibric, a man divided by a deep loyalty to Forgael and by a growing conviction that Forgael's aim is disastrously impossible. Other sailors represent common aspirations and complete attachment to the natural order of being.

The time and setting, consonant with such action and dramatis personae, have a clearly symbolic character. Time is kept indefinite, although set vaguely in the age of kings and heroes. A few major elements dominate the scene. There is, of course, the sea, to Forgael "the waters of Death," and to the life-loving Dectora perhaps "the signature of the fruitfulness of the body and of the fruitfulness of dreams." [88] Yeats had further found that "some Neo-Platonist" had described "the sea as a symbol of the drifting indefinite bitterness of life, and I believe there is like symbolism intended in many Irish voyages to the islands of enchantment" (*Reeds,* p. 90). The sea has also had in traditional literature many other meanings, among them change (its tides), mystery (its depth), and infinity (its breadth). The boat is a symbol both of man's isolated consciousness adrift on the sea of life and of his heroic quest for something beyond that mysterious sea. Upon the boat's sails are three rows of hounds, one of dark hounds, one of red hounds, and one of white hounds with red ears. Ellmann conjectures that these represent "thesis, antithesis, and reconciliation." [89] Mist conceals the sea, and moonlight shining through the mist is the only brightness. The mist is traditionally associated with strangeness, and the moonlight symbolizes for Yeats the "female" and the "emotional" [90] among other things. The "female" elements that, joined to the male, will make a perfect union are as yet not on the scene, they are only hinted at by the mist-shrouded moon; the "emotional," in its most intense and spiritualized sense, is what the action should rise to. In Yeats's view the mist-

shrouded moon is a more effective way of symbolizing emotion
than is a sharply delineated moon. For the symbolic dramatist
is one "who wraps the vision in lights and shadows, in iridescent
or glowing colour, until form be half lost in pattern." [91]

Other symbols, such as the lily on Forgael's breast and the
rose on Dectora's, are found both in the setting itself and in
the speeches of the actors. Perhaps the most important of these
symbols is the harp with which Forgael can entrance others;
this magic instrument has been given to him by a fool in a wood.
As Ellmann asserts: "This is not *a* fool but *the* fool, 'the fool
of the Rath, the fairy fool of modern Irish folklore, from whose
touch no man recovers—the divine fool.'" Ellmann also notes
that Yeats associated the fool with the Irish god of lovers,
Aengus, the fool being perhaps "some lower manifestation of
him. Hence the appearance of the fool along with the symbol
of perfect love in the union of Aengus and Edain." [92]

The tale of Aengus and Edain is frequently alluded to in
the play. Its relevance here is that their perfect union was broken
by a spell cast on Edain that turned her into a fly; Aengus

> made a harp with druid apple wood
> That she among her winds might know he wept;
> And from that hour he has watched over none
> But faithful lovers.[93]

In order to restore the perfect union of his love, Aengus must
embody his love in mortals and must see through mortal eyes
(*Waters,* p. 19). Forgael's possession of Aengus' harp suggests
that Forgael was to be used as a vehicle for a divine passion.
Such a suggestion is strengthened by Forgael's obsessive be-
havior; for the fact is that, though the harp is associated with the
perfect union of lovers, its recipient (anyone who has contact
with the fool) is driven mad. From a human standpoint Forgael
may indeed be as mad as his sailors imagine. This problem will,
however, be discussed more appropriately in connection with
the larger one of Yeats's dramatic intention and his success in
achieving his goal.

The harp not only relates to supernatural being; it is also a tremendous force, able to give its player power over men's wills. As Ellmann asserts, the harp is "the poetic imagination, vauntingly described in the play as 'mightier than the sun and moon,/Or than the shivering casting net of the stars.' " Ellmann further notes that Forgael plays two songs on his harp, one that stirs men to "dreams of love, while his second rouses dreams of a love beyond mortal love." [94] Thus, this instrument is at once a tool of power to its mortal bearer and an autonomous and supernatural power, flaring up by itself at significant moments in the action. It is, in sum, symbol of the divinely powerful poetic imagination (given by a god), an imagination capable of creating visions of natural and supernatural beauty that completely enchant its hearers. It is with this harp that Dectora is finally brought to reject life for Forgael's vision of perfect love.

Like all other elements of the play, the dialogue is rich with symbolism. The slow-moving verse is a culmination of all Yeats's Pre-Raphaelite tendencies. Shadowy, dreamy diction, langorous and stylized images studded with occult references constitute the normal language of the play:

> He watches over none but faithful lovers.
> Edaine came out of Midher's hill, and lay
> Beside young Aengus in his tower of glass,
> Where time is drowned in odour-laden winds
> And druid moons, and murmuring of boughs,
> And sleepy boughs, and boughs where apples made
> Of opal and ruby and pale chrysolite
> Awake unsleeping fires.   (*Waters*, p. 44)

Far more than in either *The Countess Cathleen* or *The Land of Heart's Desire,* the verse of *The Shadowy Waters* is given to the lyricism that Yeats believed to be the speech of trance and of tragic passion. Kevin's language, enriched by a treasure of occult words and phrases has taken complete command; and, true to Pater's definition, the play has become a lyrical unity, each voice speaking as one voice—remote, elevated, dreamily suggestive of depth within depth—until style, as represented by the whole dialogue, is a symbol for the mood that Yeats believed belonged to spiritual reality.

The play taken as a whole is surely a tribute to Yeats's indefatigable effort to bring the symbolic method to dramatic fruition, and yet one must agree with its critics that the effort was at best a qualified failure.[95] The multiplicity of symbols, from precious gems representing pure, intense, and eternal emotion to birds with human heads symbolizing the souls of dead lovers, though remarkably integrated in a philosophic sense, are not controlled dramatically; that is, many of the symbols, because of their obscurity or their ornamental value, do not function to advance or deepen the intention of the play.

The faults of the play go beyond the occasional failure to make symbols function dramatically. For instance, the plot is seriously weakened because it gives no sense of movement. Even Maeterlinck's "static" drama has some cadence, some pattern that arouses in the audience an interest in the life on the stage, and gives it a feeling that a genuine issue must be resolved; otherwise why would a dramatist bother with a form that presupposes some sort of conflict, some sort of variety in its parts? "A monotonous texture," Parkinson asserts of the play's style, "forbids dramatic variety. Without a variety of tone and idiom it is impossible to present various personalities and points of view." [96] Action can have the same monotony, and *The Shadowy Waters* suffers from this lack of variety and conflict.

The characters, as Parkinson suggests, do not offer sufficient variety of type; they all tend to speak with one voice, from the noble Forgael to the common sailors. Perhaps Aibric's stiffly formal lines are the closest thing to common speech:

> Forgael, seek out content, where other men
> Have found delight, in the resounding oars,
> In day out-living battle, on the breast
> Of some mild woman, or in children's ways.   (*Waters*, p. 20)

The tone of this argument could hardly be expected to persuade anyone of anything. As in the most intense lyric everything is subordinated to one demanding feeling or idea, so in *The Shadowy Waters* Yeats does not "admit the importance of anything but Forgael's aspirations." [97] Forgael's language and his ideals dominate the play and leave no room for any genuine challenge to his will. The play is in this sense lyrical, but at the expense of its dramatic possibilities. Like the sailors, Dectora speaks the language of Forgael and, after a few strokes of Aengus' harp, becomes, like them, a mere adjunct to his will. Those who are on the side of life in *The Shadowy Waters,* the sailors with their simple common-sense desires and Dectora with nobler ones, offer no meaningful contrast or conflict to Forgael and his death wish: he has both the irrefutable argument of mystical conviction and the absolute power to bend others to this conviction. Despite all the levels of meaning (*outside of the play*) to be found for the central characters, they tend to flatten out into one Pre-Raphaelite voice, suggesting, but not clearly meaning, more than is apparent.

Parkinson has found the fundamental failure of the play to be a stylistic one: Yeats, he believes, does not make poetry dramatic:

His characters spoke the language of his early poetry; their dialogues drifted into separate monologues, and their addresses to one another deviated into rhapsody and ecstasy. More damaging still was the vocabulary of the verse—the Pre-Raphaelite diction infused with occult and Irish symbols esoteric and personal in their bearing.[98]

Dectora's

> I had hoped to come, as dreams foretold,
> Where Gods are brooding in a mountainous place
> That murmurs with holy woods. (*Waters,* pp. 32–33)

cannot be stylistically distinguished from Forgael's

> The fool foretold me I would find this love
> Among those streams, or on their cloudy edge.   (p. 19)

Here, as in earlier plays, Yeats is found to be under the influence of a style that, far from expressing dramatic tension, leads to an elegiac or rhapsodic tone that, sustained through a whole play, strains the attention beyond what even a short play can afford. Inappropriateness of style, of course, accents the other failings of the play: the undramatic plot, the lack of variety and of opposition in character, and the presence of overly obscure and ornamental symbols.

Underlying all of these weaknesses and flaws is an uncertainty that characterized both Yeats's dramatic intention and infused the actual form of *The Shadowy Waters* itself. Yeats plainly was unsure about his theme, and the play as a consequence reflects his doubt. The very number of explanations Yeats gave for the meaning of the play suggests uncertainty. The obvious theme was, as critics are perfectly aware, the quest of the mortal for the immortal—in this particular instance, as in *Axël,* the attempt of human love to transform itself into spiritual love through a pure, intense union. This union required, as it did in *Axël,* death or some experience like death. Villiers, perhaps less complex than Yeats, showed with no equivocation that his lovers die; Axël and Sara knew where they were going as they knew where they had been. The same cannot be said for Yeats's lovers. They had, according to Yeats, the option of "awaiting death and what comes after, or some mysterious transformation of the flesh, an embodiment of every lover's dream." Or their experience, as Yeats asserted in another place, could be a "mystical interpretation of the resurrection of the body." Ellmann finds these "alternative possible expectations at the end . . . characteristic of Yeats's unwillingness to commit his poetry to locating the perfect state definitely in death or in life." [99]

Yeats's equivocation suggests a deeper doubt than that found by Ellmann. This doubt concerned the character of the supernatural into whose hands the lovers have given themselves. At this point it is well to recall the basic theme of Yeats's earliest plays: for example, in *The Seeker* the hero, who is totally committed to a supernatural vision, only ruins himself by this commitment, and his quest ends when he finds the bearded witch, Infamy. *The Seeker* embodies the theme of the "war of immortal upon mortal life" that "has been the moving thought of much Irish poetry."

The issue of this war is sometimes double-edged. Naschina in *The Island of Statues* gains an immortality that costs her her shadow (her soul?) and somberly isolates her from all mortal friends. As in these earliest plays, the quest for the immortal and the calamitous results of the quest seem to be the fundamental theme at work in *The Shadowy Waters*. Such a theme reflects Yeats's own complex doubt about the mystery of the supernatural, which he felt, despite his occasional Blakean optimism, was hostile to man's purposes. Moreover, this theme expressed Yeats's tragic view more characteristically than the surface theme of Forgael's easy victory over the opposition of the natural world and its representatives.

This interpretation of *The Shadowy Waters* as the result both of Yeats's uncertainty of intention and of his attitude toward the supernatural clarifies otherwise ambiguous elements in the action of the play. The first lines (surely, by their position, of special importance) bring attention immediately to the magic harp, its source, and the trouble that the instrument has caused:

> His face was never gladdened since he came
> Out of that island where the fool of the wood
> Played on his harp.   (*Waters,* p. 13)

The fool, as has been noted, is the fairy fool, who can be associated with the Irish love god, Aengus, and who possesses a touch fatal to sanity or mortal life. In this connection, it should be noted that, in 1901, Yeats stated: "What else can death be but the beginning of wisdom and power and beauty? and foolishness may be a kind of death." [100] In the light of such a claim, Forgael's acceptance of the harp made him a fool and guaranteed his own insanity or death; but through his foolishness he actually achieved a higher reality. However, there is the commonsense view (only relatively speaking, for in this play, the commonsense sailors fear the supernatural, but do not disbelieve it) that contact with the fool has made Forgael mad in the ordinary meaning of that word and that he is being driven in his madness on a fool's journey: "The fool foretold me I would find this love/ Among those streams, or on their cloudy edge" (*Waters,* p. 19). Strength is given this interpretation by the fact that, according to Yeats, the gods must have mortal help before they can accomplish their own ends: Aengus cannot be reunited with Edaine until he can bring human lovers together, in this instance Forgael and Dectora.[101]

   This contact of the hero with the fool is not the only hint that a maddened Forgael is perhaps being led to destruction for purposes known only to the gods. There is also the sinister and persistent note of warning from those who oppose Forgael's will: "gods/ Make galleys out of wind" (*Waters,* p. 23) to deceive men, and "The gods weave nets, and take us in their nets,/ And none knows wherefore" (p. 48); and the harp may have been a gift given out "of mere wantonness to lure a sail/ Among the waters that no pilot knows" (p. 20), and "The gods hate happiness, and weave their nets/ Out of their hatred" (p. 54). This warning note is buried under a constant flow of what might be termed Forgael's rhetoric of certitude. He seems, in his fanatic assurance, a fated man whom the audience might expect to go to his doom in the manner of heroes like Oedipus and Macbeth. Their *hubris* intensified by ambiguous oracles from the gods (the fool here), these heroes are ultimately punished by a calamity arising out of a misconception of oracular messages. Indeed, something like this proud, reckless, and fated commitment to disaster seems to be the latent pattern of tragedy in *The Shadowy Waters*. The conditions for such a tragic pattern are all in the play, and it would surely have been typical for Yeats to have pursued to its end the logic of this tragic pattern as he had done in his earliest plays. And yet the climactic resolution, the hero's doom, is missing from the play. Yeats's uncertainty of intention would not, it appears, admit of a resolution in which the dramatist would have to take a definite stand, even though such a resolution were a mystical one like Sophocles' in *Oedipus at Colonus*. Because Forgael has no true opposition, the tragic pattern is not allowed to take clear shape and complete itself. There is (to use Francis Fergusson's terminology) "purpose," but only the faintest "passion" (or "suffering") since real conflict is absent; and, for the same reason, there is no "perception" whatsoever, only a sailing off into a sea of ambiguity upon which Yeats floated meanings that are not functional to the play.

Had Yeats strengthened the opposition to Forgael and made the dire warnings about the will of the gods more than the plaintive resistance of the easily overwhelmed opponents to Forgael's will, the play might have become a tragedy in the sense that the earliest plays had been, only deeper and more satisfying. As *The Shadowy Waters* stands in the first version, it is a long lyrical poem, the drama in it adumbrated by a style ill-suited to a tragic action that should issue in choice, in suffering, and in perception. Yeats still mistook lovely dimness for heroic remoteness. It is one thing to present a sublime action, heightened beyond the immediacy of everyday life; it is quite another to embellish with exotic symbols and ornaments an action that is merely remote through its incredibility. When he better understood the requirement of the actual stage, Yeats quickly enough tried to mend his fundamental confusion of embellishment with function.

Yet, even though it is burdened with nonfunctional symbolic paraphernalia, and remains, through all its thematic equivocations, explicable without elaborate metaphysical explanations, *The Shadowy Waters* deserves the praise that Ellmann accords it:

On two counts, however, the nobility of its ideal and the virtuosity of its experimentation, the play must be defended. It embodies the central theme of all Yeats's early work, which is, to modify his language, the hunger to build everything anew. By casting all things into symbols he gave them a meaning and presence which they otherwise usually lacked. It represents, too, the farthest range of symbolism in dramatic poetry in English until the twentieth century.[102]

Its "nobility" and "virtuosity" contribute to the importance of the play, not only as an achievement in itself, but also as a foreshadowing of later drama. Besides, the play's shortcomings forcefully demonstrated to Yeats the sorry implications his beloved lyricism had for dramatic form. He now learned that lyricism lent itself to an ornamental rather than a dramatic conception of the symbol. The ostensible aim of the play, to embody the spiritual or superhuman reality, was impossible to realize. Symbols, instead of illuminating this reality, were arbitrarily made to represent exotic states and, by and large, embroidered onto the allegorical action. These symbols tended only to mystify, because they worked to obscure the action that they should ideally have rendered significant. Everything that is known or can be known—for all the exposition in and out of the play —is that just at the moment of choice, at the beginning of tragedy, the protagonists sail off into a mist the symbolical possibilities of which are apparently multiple, contradictory, and unresolvable.

In many respects *The Shadowy Waters* resembles the earliest of Yeats's plays. Its theme, its characterization, its poetic style all hark back to those first plays. Even the particular kind of failure of *The Shadowy Waters* is to be found in the early plays. Yeats had not yet learned to embody dramatically the spiritual order of reality. Even though he had left behind the ill-suited orthodoxy of *The Countess Cathleen* and come remarkably close to his own ideals of the period, he had certainly not written a tragedy in which the war of natural and supernatural orders was the real source of conflict. He had progressed no further than to portraying an incompleted action resulting from "immortal passions in mortal hearts." As a definition of tragic man, this was not enough; for tragic man must live in a world where tragedy is possible, where the immortal passions lead to some heroic commitment, to frustration, and to some issue like perception or fulfillment of destiny. It is true that such a world was implied in Yeats's other writings and in the domestic environment of *The Land of Heart's Desire.* But this world was not as yet grasped seriously by Yeats as the possible context of tragic man. The Paterian hero cannot, even if infused with the aggressive energy of Axël, attain tragic stature until he is forced to feel his mortal limits and to experience the great passions that arise out of a conflict with these limits. Ironically enough in the light of Yeats's conviction that drama must be purified of the circumstantial, what prevented a persuasive vision of spiritual reality in *The Shadowy Waters* was an absence of the sense of mortal limits and possibilities. In the "natural" world of the play the supernatural remained vague. For the supernatural order of experience could only define itself by a torturing conflict with the limited natural order; this was the conflict of "immortal passions in mortal hearts" and produced tragedy. Without the natural world, the supernatural one, as represented by Yeats in *The Shadowy Waters,* appears through an inflated rhetoric and through obscure symbols tacked on to the ambiguous allegory that constitutes the action.

It remained for Yeats to discover these flaws and their reasons in the next period of his development. *The Shadowy Waters* sums up Yeats's early period as a dramatist and thinker. Even as he was concluding his writing of this play, he was launching into a career that would bring him both to a fuller understanding of the limits of *The Shadowy Waters* and to a program for correcting them. This period would bring him into a vital contact with a living theatre, with kindred spirits, and with figures who could contribute to his knowledge as a playwright. Beginning in 1898, this period would ultimately lead to the Abbey Theatre and to some of his own most distinguished plays.

Tragicomedy, 1900–1908

Much has been said about the profound change that marked Yeats's creative work after the completion of *The Shadowy Waters*.[1] In the eight years following this play, Yeats moved toward the realism that earlier he so deplored and, paradoxically, he began to dramatize the spiritual by a careful delineation of the natural order. Yet this apparently radical change of direction can be overstressed; some critics have more recently noted that, while the change was real, the earlier and later works show a deep continuity.[2] Furthermore, whatever change took place was certainly the result of shifting emphasis, not of a clean break with the past. For the change was primarily the outcome of Yeats's practical experience with an actual stage on which he could work out undeveloped possibilities in his nineties thought. Indeed, Arthur Mizener goes so far as to assert that "the greatness of the later poetry is a kind of greatness inherent in the '90's attitude."[3] This is all to say that, while Yeats's tragic drama after the completion of *The Shadowy Waters* must be treated as resulting from a new phase in his thought and creative practice, the new phase itself must be expected to show strong evidences of thematic and stylistic qualities found in his earlier work. And, in fact, such is the case.

YEATS'S THOUGHT IN TRANSITION, 1900–1903

The change in Yeats's creative work is heralded by critical second thoughts that were promoted by contact with a real theatre beginning in 1899. An active participation in the making of a theatre carried Yeats deeply and continually into questions of what actually makes drama dramatic and how reality is brought effectively onto a stage.[4] "Reality" for Yeats was still conceived of in terms of the occult, of Blake's cosmography, and of the doctrines of aestheticism, just as tragedy was still seen as the result of the war of orders. But a dissatisfaction with the Pre-Raphaelite style, as perfected in *The Shadowy Waters,* began to evidence itself, however vaguely, even as early as 1888, long before he had finished the play. In a letter to Katharine Tynan, dated December of that year, he had asserted as a side comment to a criticism of some of her verse:

The want of your poetry is, I think, the want also of my own. We both of us need to substitute more and more the landscapes of nature for the landscapes of art. I myself have another and kindred need—to substitute the feelings and longings of nature for those of art.[5]

This precocious realization, though it does not appear to have much affected his dramatic practice, indicated an awareness that in a decade would grow to an applicable perception. Yeats's distinction between art and nature, if hardly a momentous discovery, suggests that he then viewed his Pre-Raphaelite attitudes and style as somehow leading away from a natural expression of natural feeling. When applied to the drama, Yeats's distinction would mean that *The Shadowy Waters* belonged in both feeling and landscape to the world of art even before his full acceptance of aestheticism. Yeats dimly perceived this world of nature that, at the turn of the century, had begun to assert itself, chiefly because on an actual stage the natural world is the one seen. Earlier experiments in presenting tragic conflict, the war of supernatural and natural, had failed. He began to see that perhaps he had made a fundamental blunder in his insistence upon a drama that ignored human limitations, that he had not embodied the supernatural effectively because he had so far failed to render a convincing natural world. His change of mind is clearly evidenced by a new dramatic criticism growing out of his theatrical experience and related matters. The new criticism, though it by no means indicated any sudden discontinuity with his earlier views, shows an uncharacteristic concern with the natural order of experience.

This concern is seen most clearly in the brief essay "Emotion of Multitude" (1903), in which Yeats criticized the "clear and logical construction" [6] of the French drama that he saw as the model for modern drama. His criticism was based upon the conviction that French drama lacked "emotion of multitude," a necessary quality present in all great literature. The absence of this emotion meant that drama became the rhetorical expression of the will "trying to do the work of the imagination" (*Essays*, p. 266). Since the imagination was the divinely given capacity to link the natural with the spiritual, a drama of the will meant to Yeats a drama in which an essential element of reality was excluded for the sake of a cold, if forceful, logic of structure. In contrast, dramas which exhibited the "emotion of multitude"—Greek drama, the plays of Shakespeare, Ibsen, and Maeterlinck—were informed by an imagination that created a rich basis for heroic action by linking isolated noble passions to a broader human feeling; this feeling resonated and spread individual tragic experience throughout the human world. Thus the chorus of the Greeks, Shakespeare's subplot, and the symbols of Maeterlinck and of Ibsen were all ways for linking the "little limited life of the fable [with] the rich, far-wandering, many-imaged life of the half-seen world beyond it" (pp. 266–67).

Yeats, using his familiar symbols of sun and moon, asserted that both the isolated, individual, heroic action (sun) and the "vague, many-imaged things" (moon) were necessary to the drama (p. 267). He could well have regarded his sailors in *The Shadowy Waters* as providing the "emotion of multitude"; certainly the Fool and Blind Man in *On Baile's Strand*, the first version of which he had finished in 1902, derived their existence from this conception, probably modeled on the fool in *King Lear*. Yeats concluded that the showing of "more ordinary men and women" was one way to provide convincing grounds for elevated heroic action and to give that action a richer significance. What the "emotion of multitude" certainly signified was a concession to Shakespearean heterogeneity and, as Parkinson notes, to tragi-comedy,[7] which Yeats had heretofore so unequivocally rejected.[8] In the group of plays written after *The Shadowy Waters*, Yeats consistently tried to compensate for the absence of the natural world in the early works by augmenting heroic action with a comic (or unheroic) echo, as by the subplot in *On Baile's Strand* or by the gradual growth of the heroic action out of natural life in *Where There is Nothing.*

If the "emotion of multitude" would bring the natural world into Yeats's plays, it also would bring with it a new prob-lem; for any move toward the natural was qualified by Yeats's steady intention to achieve a "poetical drama, which tries to keep at a distance from daily life that it may keep its emotion untroubled." [9] The problem for Yeats at this period was how to "keep at a distance from daily life" and at the same time use "daily life" to give the isolated heroic action roots in the natural order. His solution in general was to conceive of his ideal theatre as the means of showing that the heroic spirit rises out of a world inhabited by the common folk, who experience life deeply. The plot of the "simple fable" would constitute the tragic action; the "emotion of multitude" would provide the naturalizing soil that gives to tragic action a natural breadth, expressed, for

Yeats, not by the middle class that was the model for the social drama but by the "people," by whom he meant the Irish peasantry. In 1902, when he asserted that "we must found good literature on a living speech" (*Controversies,* p. 29), he meant the rich idiom of the folk, not the colorless, shallow chitchat of tea table and drawing room.

Yeats, then, during these first years in the theatre, envisaged a unifying of the heroic and the folk, each to augment the other, the first to ennoble human life, the second to give it a rich and vivid solidity. The pure and isolated remoteness of *The Shadowy Waters* was no longer adequate to his vision of tragic action. The war of orders could be more profoundly embodied, he now believed, in a richer, more inclusive drama. Such a conception underlies this credo that he wrote for the "Irish Dramatic Movement" in 1902:

Our movement is a return to the people, like the Russian movement of the early seventies, and the drama of society would but magnify a condition of life which the countryman and the artisan could but copy to their hurt. The play that is to give them a quite natural pleasure should tell them either of their own life, or of that life of poetry where every man can see his own image, because there alone does human nature escape from arbitrary conditions. Plays about drawing-rooms are written for the middle-classes of great cities, for the classes who live in drawing-rooms; but if you would ennoble the man of the roads you must write about the roads, or about the people of romance, or about great historical people. (p. 32)

The "natural pleasure" and the "life of poetry," combined or complementing each other in one theatre, would give lyric intensity a broad, solid, and vital base from which the heroic action could convincingly rise to tragic resolution in the remote ecstasy that resulted from the war of supernatural with natural.

The structural and stylistic implications of the new position did not escape Yeats; in the same year that he wrote "Emotion of Multitude," he stated, in a comment on his own *The*

Hour Glass, that "whatever method one adopts, one must always be certain that the work of art, as a whole, is masculine and intellectual, in its sound as in its form" (p. 47). The reference to "form" is clear enough, indicating an awareness that a play must "move," must have a strong logic to carry it forward, even though that logic, not enough in itself as the well-made French play proved, must be augmented by the "emotion of multitude." The reference to "sound" is not so clear, but seems to mean style and the tone it produces. If, as seems likely, matters of style were what Yeats meant, then the Pre-Raphaelitism of verse in *The Shadowy Waters* is repudiated here, at least with respect to the drama. And, indeed, after Yeats had seen a performance of *The Shadowy Waters* in 1904, he "changed the play 'greatly,' cut out many 'needless symbols,' and made the ground work 'simple and intelligible.' " [10] In short, the new awareness of the value of the natural world decisively influenced Yeats's whole outlook, from his ideas about the basic structure of the drama itself to point-by-point stylistic considerations; this is no less important than larger considerations because Yeats's style arose directly out of, and was constantly refreshed by, a conscious philosophizing on the nature of human experience.

Yet it should not be forgotten that these fundamental alterations in view did not constitute a reversal so much as a profound modification of thought and practice. The view of tragedy and much of the attitude toward stagecraft found in *The Shadowy Waters* period, and before, are still to be found in this new phase. For instance, in the essay in which he had asserted that drama must be "masculine and intellectual," his comments about staging reveal a continuity of attitude: "It is necessary to simplify both the form and colour of scenery and costume." [11] Moreover, the new phase was itself transitional, directed to a yet more thoroughgoing change that would be marked later by profound revisions in the plays of this period.

In sum, the tragic view crystallizing around 1902–3 combined old and new elements. The hero's passionate quest for something beyond natural experience remained the central theme of Yeatsian tragedy, but now the landscape of that quest was to be made, through "emotion of multitude," more immediate and vital, and the action of the quest was to have the clear unity of a "masculine logic." Yet, as in the earlier period, the whole drama was to make a single impression—stage, properties, costume, acting, and speech all combining in one pattern of lyric unity. However, this intense lyric unity of effect must go beyond Pater's stylistic conception of a play as approximating the state of music, for a "masculine and intellectual" art and a fable broadened by the natural world meant a new stress on action and on common humanity. In the 1905 revision of *The Shadowy Waters,* Forgael's rather Rossettian crew became

sensual men with a common-sense view of life. . . . By making them the type of the ordinary man, by distinguishing their speech and interest from those of Aibric and Forgael, Yeats establishes the circumstances that make Forgael's dream appear less vague and false: for if the sailors have seen magical birds and gods, they may truly exist.[12]

It is precisely this "common-sense view of life" that provided, in Yeats's new view, the immediacy for the heroic action, otherwise impossibly remote; this immediacy brought the heroic action into the realm of human possibility without destroying lyrical intensity, that all-but-impossible moment of "immortal passions in mortal hearts."

It is in the light of this general critical view that the next important tragedies following *The Shadowy Waters* must be examined, for the view developed between the completion of *The Shadowy Waters* and the criticism of 1903 must be regarded as having shaped and having been shaped by Yeats's actual dramatic practice of these years.

Of the six plays that Yeats wrote in the earlier years of this new period, two tragedies, *Where There is Nothing* and *On*

Baile's Strand, represent profound attempts to go beyond the limits of *The Shadowy Waters.* Of the other four, *The Pot of Broth, Cathleen Ni Houlihan, The Hour Glass,* and *The King's Threshold,*[13] one is a comedy, and three, though in some sense serious, are not genuine ventures into the realm of the tragic, but, at best, dramatic statements only tangentially related to Yeats's tragic theme.

The least important of the four was *The Pot of Broth* (1903), a slight work written with Lady Gregory in an effort to venture wholly into the natural world of comedy.

Cathleen Ni Houlihan (1902), a patriotic play, was a noble statement of faith in Ireland, and in plot resembled *The Land of Heart's Desire:* a household involved in a wedding (in the later play, the wedding has yet to take place) is disrupted by a supernatural intrusion; instead of the Fairy Child, it is an old woman, representing the queenly spirit of Ireland come to this domestic sanctum to lure away the groom in the cause of Irish independence. Like *The Land of Heart's Desire,* the play's simple conflict precludes any deep exploration of the war of orders that, to Yeats, made for tragic action; however, unlike the earlier play, *Cathleen Ni Houlihan* exhibits a clarity of motive that strengthens the conflict and makes the play effective, if not profound, drama.

The Hour Glass (1903) was also taken up with an elementary conflict, this time between the blind pride of reason or abstracting intelligence, as embodied in the Wise Man, and the clear-eyed humility of intuition or direct understanding, as represented by the Fool. The Wise Man, having conquered with his superstition-demolishing and irrefutable logic the whole world (king, populace, pupils, and his own family), learns from an angel that he is about to die and that his soul is destined for Hell. His salvation, he is told, lies in finding someone who believes in the old "superstitions." All those whom he has converted are now of no help, and only the Fool remains, the humblest creature, too simple for the Wise Man to have been bothered trying to convert to reason; it is the Fool, of course, who saves him through an innocent belief in the supernatural. The play, in its original version, was, as were Yeats's earlier plays, close to allegory. The war of orders was so simplified that the plot resembled that of a morality play or that of a conventional religious drama like *The Countess Cathleen*. The play did not please Yeats, as his repeated tinkering with it suggests. His own later comment serves as an adequate judgment of the play:

I have for years struggled with something which is charming in the naive legend but a platitude on the stage. . . . I was faintly pleased when I converted a music-hall singer and kept him going to Mass for six weeks . . . but I was always ashamed when I saw any friend of my own in the theatre.[14]

The King's Threshold (1904), though Yeats at the time of writing thought it one of his best plays, is with *Cathleen Ni Houlihan* a simple statement of faith (in this instance, aesthetic faith). The work is based on a conflict between Yeats's exalted view of poetry and all opposing views, from those of the most crass Philistine to those of the poets who had less exalted views of their craft than Seancan, the heroic representative of the arch-poet in the Yeatsian cosmography. The problem of bringing the supernatural or spiritual order into the action does not arise in the play, and the absence of the problem as a central one excludes the play from among Yeats's tragedies having the war of orders for theme. Like *Cathleen Ni Houlihan, The King's Threshold* was an argument for an attitude rather than a dramatic embodiment of one; the conflict was between two intellectual positions and did not lead to revelation through heroic transcendence, and, therefore, did not involve a war of orders. In the simplicity of its moral issue, *The King's Threshold* resembled an English morality play like *The Castle of Perseverance* more than a Greek play (despite Yeats's intention),[15] since the plot was based upon the same pattern as the morality play; that is, the protagonist is confronted with a series of tempters whose aim is to lure him from adherence to his duty. Yeats later conceded that the play was part of a program: the Irish National Theatre's "fight for the recognition of pure art in a community of which one half is buried in the practical affairs of life, and the other half in politics and a propagandist patriotism." [16]

Ellman rightly finds connections in this play, and the others of this period, with *The Shadowy Waters,* particularly in basic pattern, even though the plays represent a notable stylistic advance.[17] Certainly the new plays, with the exception of *The Pot of Broth,* grew out of *The Shadowy Waters,* each developing, like the earlier play, a simple conflict through symbol, to the point, indeed, of being allegories of the Yeatsian outlook. And certainly, also, each showed an advance in style, a sheering off of the excesses of Pre-Raphaelitism and a toughening arrived at by the experience of writing for the stage, whose basic requirement was an undallying logic. The absence of such a logic permitted action to drift in the manner of the 1900 version of *The Shadowy Waters,* whose later revisions were radical attempts to introduce a more "manful energy," a more "cheerful acceptance of whatever arises out of the logic of events," and a more "clean outline, instead of those outlines of lyric poetry that are blurred with desire and vague regret." [18]

WHERE THERE IS NOTHING (1903)

The two fully engaged efforts at tragicomedy, *Where There is Nothing* (1903) and *On Baile's Strand* (1903), were, for this transitional phase, Yeats's most serious attempts to realize in actual drama his theory of tragedy. Both plays were intended to embody the tragic duality of and hostility between spiritual and natural. In both plays, moreover, the aim was to embrace the "emotion of multitude," to broaden, that is, the base of the heroic and naturalize it with an earthy, peasant sense of the world in all its richness and variety. This aim represented above all a concession to the comic or low world associated in Yeats's mind with the natural order. In a letter to Lady Gregory dated December 4, 1902, Yeats revealed his serious concern with the comic in the writing of *Where There is Nothing,* for he asserted: "I think that some comedy . . . will help the balance of the play." [19] Concern for "balance" was not merely a question of mechanics of structure, but part of a more general concern for giving due weight to a side of experience that Yeats, in his own mind, had before regarded as alien to his aims and had, therefore, neglected.

Other apparently alien qualities also enter the play, chiefly a powerful new influence on his thought, the writings of Friedrich Nietzsche, whom Yeats had begun to read in 1902. In a letter to Lady Gregory in September of that year, Yeats revealed how important the German philosopher seemed to him: "Nietzsche completes Blake and has the same roots—I have not read anything with so much excitement since I got to love Morris' stories which have the same curious astringent joy." [20]

This juxtaposition of Blake and Nietzsche was hardly fortuitous, especially if it is recalled that Blake's dualistic conception of spirit and nature helped define Yeats's view of the war of orders. Nietzsche's influence is first seen in connection with Yeats's growing concern for masculinity and tough logic, that "astringent joy" which he now aimed at in his thought and work. In a letter written on May 15, 1903, Yeats remarked to John Quinn:

I have always felt that the soul has two movements primarily: one to transcend forms, and the other to create forms. Nietzsche, to whom you have been the first to introduce me, calls these the Dionysiac and the Apollonic, respectively. I think I have to some extent got weary of that wild God Dionysus, and I am hoping that the Far-Darter will come in his place. (*Letters,* p. 403)

A more important influence, and one which provided the explanation of how exactly Nietzsche "completes" Blake, is Nietzsche's Dionysian "mystery doctrine of tragedy . . . the fundamental knowledge of the oneness of everything existent, the conception of individuation as the prime cause of evil, and of art as the joyous hope that the bonds of individuation may be broken in augury of a restored oneness." [21] Such a definition of tragedy might with no great effort be seen as implicit in the Blakean cosmology, which Yeats, after some modifications, had already adopted in the nineties. In Blake's conception, a universe evilly shattered into rebellious individualities is also restored to oneness by art, that is, by the divine imagination working through individuals for a universal harmony. Nietzsche indeed improved on Blake by inferring from this conception of the cosmos the Dionysian definition of tragedy, a definition which deeply influenced *Where There is Nothing* and *On Baile's Strand.* So, too, did another of Nietzsche's definitions of tragedy, the Apollonian, which he perceived as the suffering of some individual through "pride and excess." Indeed, ideal tragedy combined the two kinds of tragic experience. Yeats's heroes in the two plays participate in Apollonian tragedy since their excesses lead to self-destruction, even though their ecstatic passion unites them to the superhuman "fundamental oneness" of the Dionysian tragic experience. This double effect of the two types of tragic experience probably lay behind Yeats's conception of "emotion of multitude": in the complete tragedy "emotion of multitude" is the Dionysian element and individual heroic action the Apollonian element. There is little doubt that Yeats aimed to synthesize both kinds of tragic experience in his own tragedies. Nietzsche's definitions, seeming to extend Blake's thought into the field of drama, made explicit for Yeats what was only confusedly apparent to him before.

Besides providing philosophical support and a comprehensive definition of tragedy, Nietzsche's lucidity surely would have clarified and reinforced other areas of Yeats's thought. For instance, the German philosopher's belief that music was at the heart of tragedy must have seemed like an overwhelming echo of Pater's view of music as the ideal condition of art. Further, Yeats's growing conviction that the hero at his high moments was not a man of action, but a man given over to trancelike reverie, may have been an outgrowth of Nietzsche's assertion that the Greek drama aimed not at action but at pathos. Finally, Nietzsche's great devotion to myth would have heartened Yeats's own belief in the central importance of myth as the perennial source of inspiration to the creative artist.

If Nietzsche, along with Blake, was a telling influence on *Where There is Nothing,* Yeats's own reading as an official in the Irish National Theatre had its effect also. The modernity of setting in the play may well have been the result of an unconscious influence of Ibsen; and, as with many of Ibsen's plays, the structure of *Where There is Nothing* developed out of a rebellion against the middle-class drawing room and its values. Though Yeats repeatedly expressed his opposition to realist drama, his own plays at this period deal with the realist theme of rebellion against the constrictions of a stifling environment and the often self-destructive consequences of such rebellion.

The plot of *Where There is Nothing* quickly shows the play to be anything but Ibsenesque despite the modernity of setting and structure. Paul Ruttledge, the hero, breaks out of a comfortable, gentlemanly existence in order to find an adequate object for a passion satisfied only by supernatural reality and, in breaking out, finds himself in violent conflict with the social order. His next step is a Blakean war to restore the Golden Age of total harmony (or, in Nietzsche's terms, a Dionysian oneness) by the Nietzschean methods of transcendence through destruction of law, society, and church. Ellmann cites Yeats's use of Nietzschean laughter as a means for this destruction.[22] The plot is the working out of this apocalyptic attempt to destroy the normal order of things.

In the first act, Paul Ruttledge, a sensitive misfit in upper-middle-class society, rejects his family and friends for the freedom of the life of wandering tinkers. The rejection is not a psychological declaration of freedom (like that of Nora in *A Doll's House*) from rigid social restraint, but a philosophical declaration of freedom from all restraints based upon reason as an instrument for ordering human experience. Paul says to a defender of modern progress: "I am among those who think that sin and death came into the world the day Newton eat [*sic*] the apple." [23] Act I, then, is an attempt to delineate the hero's motivation by setting him in a situation that he must transform in order to achieve his proper goal. The family (his brother and sister-in-law) and his boringly conventional friends, well-to-do, gentlemanly upholders of the social order, represent life narrowed by "reason" [24] and base goals; their lives lack freedom, passion, and, most significantly, a sense of the Dionysian reality lying beyond the walls of a well-kept garden. The tinkers possess that "lawless" freedom which Paul dreams of as the road to Dionysian reality. In the eyes of his practical antagonists Paul seems mad to have joined the tinkers, but his madness is the beginning of a new life, escape from the tame barnyard existence of his old environment which he has, up until now, only mocked by clipping bushes to look like his practical friends, transformed by his imagination into fowls.

The scene of Act II is the open country of the tinkers' camp. Paul's introduction to the tinkers' life is interrupted by the entrance of a friend, Father Jerome, who attempts to bring him back to his senses. Paul replies that he has been driven to this apparently reckless action by his vision that eternity is a war and that the music of paradise is the clashing of immortal swords in joyous battle. He can only seek the (Nietzschean) wild beast of laughter and realize his vision by casting off the institutional restraints of his old life. Father Jerome, scandalized, is jeered at by the tinkers and forced to withdraw.[25]

In Act III, Paul pushes his pursuit of the wild beast a further step, celebrating his unorthodox marriage to a tinker girl,

Sabina Silver, by purchasing liquor for everybody in the village near his estate.[26] A universal drunkenness is the only way, he believes, to reach the ecstasy of divine existence (*Nothing*, p. 54). In the midst of the wild scene that follows, Paul's indignant friends enter with his brother. They are outraged by the general disorder and the consequent suspension of work caused by Paul's several-day-old celebration, and they demand that Paul stop undermining all of the values which they hold dear: respect for sobriety, orderliness, conventional morality. Appalled by the chaos around them, they summon the police, the last recourse of an imperilled social order. Paul's reply is a defence (drawn obviously from Blake) of drunkenness as a kind of beauty and wisdom come to by very excessiveness: "Some poet has written that exuberance is beauty, and that the roadway of excess leads to the palace of wisdom" (p. 62). Taunting his antagonists with the charge that their respect for propriety is essentially selfish, Paul, improvising a court, tests their claim to be Christians. The "trial" reveals their actual lack of Christianity: the Colonel in service to his country contradicts Jesus' demand that Christians turn the other cheek; Mr. Dowler's wealth makes is impossible for him to pass through the needle's eye; Mr. Green, the representative of man-made law, encourages others to break Christ's commands when he orders the police to use force. The arrival of the police ends the game, and the tinkers and Paul depart, the latter with a final accusation that his brother has begotten fools.

In Act IV, the time is a few years after the events of Act III. The tinkers, in a brief first scene, regretfully leave Paul at the door of a monastery because he is too ill to travel. In the second scene, five years have passed since Paul's separation from the company of tinkers, and he has become a friar. The scene opens in a crypt under the monastery church in which some friars are dancing slowly around Paul, who is evidently in a trance. Two friars, discussing the strange scene, reveal that the dance is the result of Paul's instruction that the brothers should perform this ritual if they ever found him in a state such as the one that occurred exactly a year before; after that trance he had given a great sermon. It is learned also that Paul is fantastically devout in his fasting; and, though at first a favorite of the Superior, he has now fallen under the latter's suspicion because of eccentric practices such as asking other friars to perform a hardly orthodox meditation involving the pursuit of some joyful thought to its end. Paul, according to one of the friars, "calls that getting above law and number, and [the meditator] becomes king and priest in one's own house" (pp. 80–81), another echo of Blakean dicta. To the horror of the speakers, the dancing friars begin singing the twenty-third Psalm.[27] The Superior, entering suddenly, commands a stop to the unorthodox ritual and insists that Paul (who is now waking) not only abstain from preaching but also render his submission to his Superior.

Father Jerome, Paul's old friend, promises to reason with the hero, who is now awake and tries to recollect his trance dream, but he only succeeds in recalling snatches of it. He remembers being first bitten and clawed by birds and beasts (perhaps reminiscent of the creatures that he had clipped out of bushes to represent the souls of the practical men). Then he recalls white angels riding white unicorns in a place of light. The unicorns had trampled the ground, their riders crying out that Brother Paul should go and preach. One clawed him and looked at him with great heavy eyes. Jerome, deeply troubled, urges Paul to make his submission and live within the rules of the order. It is here that Paul states succinctly and unequivocally the central Yeatsian theme that so far underlay all his earlier tragedies: "I have learned that one needs a religion so wholly supernatural, that is so opposed to the order of nature that the world can never capture it." [28]

Jerome departs, having given up, and Paul begins his sermon on the text, "He ascended into heaven." Paul's sermon, the intellectual climax of the play, reviews first the genesis of life and sin. Newly created life, still half-blind with the "drunken-ness of Eternity," wandered a long time, living by the impulse of the heart. Temptation came from animal spirits that loved "things better than life." Men and women, who had lived "according to the joyful Will of God in mother wit and natural kindness," now began to value safety more than blessedness; they made the Law, which was the first sin, and death was the result. The Law must be put out just as a candle is. (Each time Paul speaks of putting out a candle figuratively, he extinguishes one of the five candles.) Paul continues his unorthodox interpretation of genesis; the people now preferred comfort to bless-edness; they built big towns, big houses, and acquired money. The town must be snuffed out as one snuffs out a candle. The people, ignoring the fact that all things were holy, have nar-rowed holiness to an institution, the Church. It too must be snuffed out. The Superior, entering and hearing the last of the sermon, is horrified by Paul, who exultantly continues with the assertion that Christian duty is not reformation but revelation, that divine drunkenness is good. Men must, he continues, be-come blind, deaf, and dumb, give up hope, memory, and thought, put out the light of sun and moon and even the world itself. Now, all the candles extinguished so that he stands in darkness, Paul concludes, insisting that law and number must go, for "where there is nothing, there is God" (pp. 93–98).

Unmoved by the Superior's wrath, he defends his sermon as having been derived from Jesus Christ (or, he might have quali-fied, Blake's image of Him), who "made a terrible joy, and sent it to overturn governments, and all settled order" (pp. 98–99). Although Paul warns of the terrible trial in store for them, some of the friars wish to follow him, so inspired are they by his words. The Superior sends Paul away with the few friars who are not afraid of his apparent heresy and its consequences for their souls.

Act V takes place in the isolated precincts of a ruined eccle-

siastical building. Here, Paul's discouraged followers are discussing the growing difficulty of their position. With the
orthodox clergy preaching against them, they are barely able to
beg enough to live on. Moreover, their own effects on the community are mixed; domestic animals tend to die in the vicinity
of their preaching. Beginning to feel sorry for themselves and
mildly indignant with Paul's neglect of worldly affairs in his
search for spiritual realization, his followers have the idea that
they could weave and sell baskets to make at least enough money
for survival. Paul, entering with Charlie Ward, a friend of his
days with the tinkers, listens to the plan for basket weaving,
based on the argument that people do not respect beggars and
no longer come to hear Paul preach, a fact Paul readily admits.
But in a Socratic dialogue, he leads his followers to the point
at which it becomes plain that their desire for a basket-weaving
trade would carry them straight into the social organization that
Paul wishes to destroy and which, no matter how noble and
altruistic its motives, will lead back again to corrupting acquisi-
tiveness and moral restraint. Paul rejects their plan and insists
that he is the very teacher who offers his followers nothing and
who refuses to dip into nature's old bag of illusions. Brother
Aloysius suggests that Paul should organize the tinkers and
beggars into a great army and, in that manner, gain the power
to realize his desires; Paul, interpreting Aloysius' suggestion in
own way, envisages a great force to destroy institutions. When
Aloysius suggests that the troops must be organized, Paul angrily
reminds him that the desire for organization is the fatal impulse
that he is trying to correct. Seeing now that all the armies are
useless in the war of spirit on the natural order, Paul declares
that it "is inside our minds that it [the world] must be destroyed." At this moment Brother Bartley rushes in to announce
the approach of an angry mob which is coming to avenge itself
for what it supposes to be the ill effects of Paul's mission. All
the brothers urge an immediate withdrawal, but Paul decides to

stay, a decision which prompts Aloysius to say that Paul wants the "crown" of martyrdom (p. 124). Paul, left alone, asserts that he has entered into the second freedom, "the irresponsibility of the saints" (p. 125). The mob enters, fells Paul, and rushes off after the others in the group, who, returning, think Paul is dead and leave again. Charlie Ward and Sabina Silver now enter and hear Paul's final words, the result seemingly of a delirium in which he raves about the "wine barrel of God" and cries again that "Where there is nothing, there is God." A few members of the crowd return and find Sabina Silver keening for the dead man, and they remove their hats in respect.

Because of its rambling plot, its monolithic characterization, and its undistinguished prose dialogue, Yeats's critics have tended to ignore *Where There is Nothing,* or, like Ellmann, to dismiss it as a "bad, clumsy" play that yet yields autobiographical significance as a kind of wish fulfillment for its author.[29] Ellmann says that it "is an attempt to write a realistic drama about a mystic." [30] Certainly it is true that the play does not fit easily into the Yeats canon—a difficulty not eased any by the fact that in writing *Where There is Nothing* Yeats had two collaborators, Lady Gregory and Douglas Hyde, and all worked in great haste.[31] Like *The Words Upon the Window-Pane* (1934), the play seems to be a concession to the realistic theatre which Yeats fought so bitterly throughout his career. Moreover, *Where There is Nothing* is clumsy, the events having little of the dramatic in their development, a fact which makes the plot seem to be arbitrary or to hinge on an abstruse thesis to be asserted and explained rather than a vision to be embodied. The characterization, like the plot, appears arbitrary; characters tend not to give a sense of independent life, but rather to stand for or personify a point of view. A more serious weakness in characterization is the fact that Paul Ruttledge's motivation is seldom convincing, especially his initial decision to leave with the tinkers. Yeats establishes no adequate sense of the stifling boredom of his hero's middle-class surroundings or of the special value in the tinkers' life. Equally enfeebling is the flatness of the play's style, which gives no means of differentiation among characters except for the rather conventional "low" dialect of the tinkers and the ideas which the speakers utter. The dialogue is usually bland, rarely rising to the power and believableness of Paul's candle sermon. However, in the general condemnation of the obvious faults of the play, its deeper faults and what merit it has tend to be ignored.

Two related faults of the play connect *Where There is Nothing* with the earlier tragedies in which the hero is in the center of the war of orders. First, the play gives no dependable clues as to how Yeats felt about Paul's quest; for while there is no question, as Ellmann suggests, that Paul is Yeats set free of all doubt and trepidation,[32] Yeats's judgment on that quest is made equivocal by the conclusion of the play. The audience is free to assume either that Paul was indeed a saintly martyr for his unorthodox belief or that he was, in the strictest sense, mad. His cruel neglect of his followers and the frank pride in his martyrdom do not suggest the humanity and humility of a saint so much as the *hubris* of the pagan hero who defies the ignoble and timid world of more ordinary men and whose death, except as heroic model, has no significance beyond itself. Though the Paul of the second act preaches—perhaps caustically—the gentle Jesus to the Colonel, the Paul of all the other acts preaches, until his last moments, the doctrine of salvation through violence. The apparent contradiction suggests Yeats's unwillingness or inability to decide, at least in public, what his hero finally was. Sympathy is with Paul much of the time, but his vision is so remote and strange to those not initiated into its mysterious value that his martyrdom appears to be the result of *hubris*.[33] Perhaps it was a blunder on Yeats's part, the same blunder found in the treatment of *The Countess Cathleen*, to apply the terms of orthodoxy to an unorthodox situation. For,

if Paul's conduct is not really that of a Christian saint, by applying Christian terms to Paul's experience Yeats invites confusion
by the inexplicable incongruity of term and fact. If Paul, too
arrogant in his heterodoxy, is no saint when measured against
Christian saints, is he a saint in some other sense, some pagan
or occult sense? The play's conclusion does not answer this question. Paul is, in fact, reminiscent of the hero of the early play
The Seeker, that knight whose reward for the mystic quest was
Infamy, and reminiscent also of Forgael who is at once heroic
and mad, victim of the divine fool whose touch renders man
insane.

This typical ambiguity in Yeats's judgment on his tragic
heroes leads directly to the second weakness: the play's blurred
treatment of the relationship of natural and supernatural orders.
Throughout the action, Paul, to the point occasionally of shrill-
ness, asserts the preeminence of the supernatural order and the
need for men to destroy the world to make possible that order
and, through it, their own salvation. But if Paul is in some sense
mad, this fact renders his utterances, if not meaningless, lacking
in the authority of a genuine visionary or prophet. Yeats's tendency to be ambiguous about the supernatural and its place in the
natural order is, as I have said before, a typical weakness in many
of his plays. So long as these plays can be explained as harmless
fantasy (*The Land of Heart's Desire*) or as orthodox moralities
(*The Countess Cathleen* and *The Hour Glass*) or be justified
with a realist rationale (*Where There is Nothing,* if Paul is
taken to be mad) that can as easily justify Ibsen's plays, Yeats
had not yet succeeded in adequately embodying his vision of
the war of orders. It is true that we can give Yeats the benefit of
the doubt and see this play, like *The Shadowy Waters,* as a revelation of the mysterious effect of supernatural power on mortals,
of the destructive and maddening consequences of men glimps-
ing the face of the divine. This revelation, in fact, is probably
(as it was in *The Seeker* and in *The Shadowy Waters*) a sub-

merged theme in *Where There is Nothing.* Yet the exaltation that would make the theme tragic in Yeats's view is missing. The play ends somewhat pathetically with Paul's final apocalyptic utterances ironically qualified by coming from a man possibly demented and having achieved his "heroic" elevation at the hands of a mob.

The conclusion of the play is also rendered less effective by the general clumsiness of its construction. This clumsiness, in part, was surely due to the manner and the haste in which the play was written. But *Where There is Nothing* was a conscious experiment, so Yeats wrote to A. B. Walkley in June of 1903, to see "how loose" he

could make construction without losing the actable quality. Perhaps I have lost it, but when I tried at the outset to construct more tightly I found Paul losing his freedom and spontaneity. Other people's souls began to lay their burden upon him. I thought I would try if a play would keep its unity upon the stage with no other device than one always dominant person about whom the world was always drifting away.[34]

This is a courageous, if unrealized, purpose. Still, the play has a vitality and openness not found in *The Shadowy Waters,* even though *Where There is Nothing* fails to live up to either traditional or Yeatsian dramatic standards. In his introduction to a later revision of the play, Yeats himself perceived the fatal ambiguity in Paul's character, the real possibility, because of the lack of convincing motivation, of mistaking Paul's vision for pride and madness:

The chief person of the earlier Play [*Where There is Nothing*] was very dominating, and I have grown to look upon this as a fault, though it increases the dramatic effect in a superficial way. We cannot sympathise with the man who sets his anger at once lightly and confidently to overthrow the order of the world, for such a man will seem to us alike insane and arrogant. But our hearts can go with him, as I think, if he speak with some humility, so far as his daily self carry him, out of a cloudy light of vision.[35]

Perhaps the basic fault of the play which underlies all its other faults and indicates the uncertainty of Yeats's ability as yet to carry theory into practice is that, in an effort to give the natural its due, Yeats gave it too much place and overwhelmed the possibility of the appearance of the supernatural as a convincing element in the action. The modernity of the play, the low pitch of the dialogue, the relaxed sprawl of the plot—all these imply a realist convention that makes the supernatural explicable only in terms of psychological phenomena. In short, Yeats had gone to the other extreme from *The Shadowy Waters*. If in the latter play he had rendered the supernatural implausible because of the absence of the natural order, he had still to put the two into a relationship that would prove dramatically satisfying.

ON BAILE'S STRAND (1903)

The second important attempt at tragicomedy during these years was *On Baile's Strand,* even more than *Where There is Nothing* a revelation of Yeats's development and special problems as a tragic dramatist. Begun in 1901,[36] and published in 1903, *On Baile's Strand* spanned the first phase of the period following *The Shadowy Waters* and shows both strong links with the earlier drama and the imprint of the new critical approach. Yeats, conscious of the play's special qualities, wrote to Lady Gregory in January of 1903, "I was never so full of new thoughts for verse, though all thoughts quite unlike the old ones. My work has got far more masculine. It has more salt in it." [37] Unlike *Where There is Nothing, On Baile's Strand* required drawn-out, laborious effort:

The first shape of it came to me in a dream, but it changed much in the making, foreshadowing, it may be, a change that may bring a less dream-burdened will into my verses. I never re-wrote anything so many times.[38]

The implication here is that the dream came to him much earlier and had to be reshaped in terms of the thought of the new phase. The dream, in fact, may have been the source of his early nineties narrative poem, "Cuchulain's Fight With the Sea." [39] The characteristics of that poem mark it as Pre-Raphaelite. The heroic events do not concern the poet nearly so much as the lyric moments arising out of events. The central action receives a scant few lines, the characterization is sketchy; the aura of mysterious beauty surrounding Cuchulain's battle with the sea is what Yeats attempted to suggest. But to be made into a drama the subject required more of plot and much more of character. Yeats had come to realize in his experience with stage production that the dramatic form depended for life on vital action and vivid characterization. The latter especially preoccupied him at this time. Yet his concern for character, particularly the character of the hero, went far beyond stage mechanics, because the hero, as the very center of the war of orders, demanded the fullest attention.

He had begun to devote much attention to the nature of the hero around the turn of the century, as evidenced chiefly in his discussions of Shakespeare and of Irish mythology. Out of these discussions came the clearest conceptions of the hero that he had yet achieved. I have noted already that Yeats tended to rely for his view of Shakespeare on the opinions of Walter Pater, especially those found in Pater's essay "Shakespeare's English Kings," from which Yeats borrowed for his own essay on Shakespeare's drama, "At Stratford-on-Avon" (1901). Yeats was particularly attentive to Pater's remarks concerning Shakespeare's Richard II and Henry IV and V. Pater finds in Richard II a charm and beauty that, because it cannot survive the vulgar rigors of kingship, is far more touching and sympathetic than the "showy heroism" and popularity of Henry V.[40] Yeats, in his own essay, amplified this view. He imputed to Shakespeare a deep sympathy for Richard and an understanding of the tragic discrepancy between a sensitive, imaginative, lovable personality and an office that demanded "qualities that were doubtless common among his scullions." Shakespeare, Yeats believed, saw in Richard

the defeat that awaits all, whether they be Artist or Saint, who find themselves where men ask of them a rough energy and have nothing to give but some contemplative virtue, whether lyrical phantasy, or sweetness of temper, or dreamy dignity, or love of God, or love of His creatures.[41]

Poets of Shakespeare's day, according to Yeats, could still watch the fading of the idealistic Middle Ages and the "procession of the world with that untroubled sympathy for men as they are, as apart from all they do and seem, which is the substance of tragic irony" (*Essays*, p. 130). It is clear that he was describing his own heroes here: men driven by ideals and destroyed in a conflict with a world in which such ideals had no place. Yeats, no doubt thinking of his own personae, which he conceived in terms of radical oppositions, envisaged in Shakespeare's tragedy a simple conflict of types, of imaginative man with practical man. "Shakespeare's Myth," Yeats conjectured, "describes a wise man who was blind from very wisdom, and an empty man who thrust him from his place, and saw all that could be seen from very emptiness" (p. 131). This view of the conflict of opposites actually goes far beyond what had been suggested by Pater, who saw in Richard's fate only the melancholy triumph of crass reality over the imaginative man. Not found in Pater either is Yeats's idea that the lyrical temper in the hero was not merely a pathetic grace but connected him with a reality beyond the natural order of things. For Yeats the combat between the lyrical temper and the active practical one should not lead simply to the regrettable defeat of the helpless, if imaginatively superior, man. Rather, the exaltation of tragedy should emerge from a struggle in which the imaginative hero may be defeated, but somehow transcends his defeat.

That Yeats found passivity an inadequate vehicle for heroism set severe limits on how far he could follow Pater's views,

even though he would rely heavily on Pater's interpretation of
Shakespeare's Richard II. The discovery of Nietzsche, along
with a new inclination toward masculine structure and style,
had merely reinforced Yeats's earlier belief that heroism meant,
as it did to Shelley (much imitated in Yeats's early work) some
idealistic action made tragic by inevitable but ennobling failure.

In *Where There is Nothing* Yeats had already attempted to
present active heroism, though in a modern setting; but he
found the heroes in Celtic mythology modeled closer to his own
taste. He discovered in figures from Irish heroic sagas a heroism
that went beyond the pathetic experience of aesthetic sensitivity,
of a Paterian fineness of personality. In his preface to Lady
Gregory's translations of Irish heroic sagas, the major source for
Yeats's new tragedy, he defined both the nature of the active
hero and his true place in the war of orders.[42] Discussing "the
sap of divinity that makes Cuchulain mysterious to men, and
beloved of women," [43] he put heroism in both its historical and
philosophical contexts:

As life becomes more orderly, more deliberate, the supernatural
world sinks farther away. Although the gods come to Cuchulain,
and although he is the son of one of the greatest of them, their
country and his are far apart, and they come to him as god to mortal.
(Agate, p. 17)

Gods are indeed more wise and beautiful than men; but men, when
they are great men, are stronger than they [gods] are, for men are,
as it were, the foaming tide-line of their sea.   (p. 26)

If in the time of Finn natural and supernatural were "but one
life flowing everywhere" (p. 26), in the time of Cuchulain, himself an offspring of supernatural life, heroic man was more and
more confined by the natural order and subordinated to those
who ruled that order. Thus a "tragic irony," as in the instance
of *Richard II* or *Hamlet,* arises out of the ruinous incongruity
between heroic nature, still alive to the glory of supernatural
reality, and some confining and debasing office that heroism,
now confined to natural limits, must endure.

In this same preface, whose ideas so clearly inform the world of *On Baile's Strand,* also appeared Yeats's conception of the two kinds of reality necessary for a full dramatic embodiment, that "marriage of the sun and moon in the arts I take most pleasure in." The partners of this marriage were explained by Yeats in the following manner:

To lunar influence belong all thoughts and emotions that were created by the community, by the common people, by nobody knows who, and to the sun all that came from the high disciplined or individual kingly mind. (p. 27)

The marriage Yeats envisaged, then, is between the wide, rich, earthly experience of folk imagination and the noble, intense, and remote imagination of the isolated hero.[44]

On Baile's Strand owes much of its conception to these attempts to define heroism and its role in the war of orders. Yeats put everything he knew and felt into the play and aimed, as he had not in *Where There is Nothing,* at heroic tragedy. In the first version of *On Baile's Strand* the weakness and strength of his effort show not only the degree of skill that he had acquired by practical stage experience but, just as important, how and to what degree the theories of the new phase affected his dramatic practice.

The plot of *On Baile's Strand,* like that of most of Yeats's earlier plays, hinges on one incident: the meeting of Cuchulain and his unknown challenger. The play opens in a "great hall by the sea close to Dundalgan." [45] The hall is empty except for Barach, a fool, and Fintain, a blind man, whose elaborate exposition of the action to follow establishes the character and relationships of the main figures: Conchubar,[46] the High King; Cuchulain, a lesser king; and a young warrior, a stranger, called in the play the Young Man, who Fintain knows is actually Cuchulain's son by Aoife, a warlike Scottish queen whom Cuchulain had defeated in battle years before. Aoife, seeking revenge against the hero, has raised the son of this bitter union for the sole purpose of having him kill his father whom he does not know. After this information is given to the audience by the two low characters, Cuchulain enters, followed by some extravagantly attired young kings who praise him exuberantly. The dialogue is excitedly lyrical, and Cuchulain, reveling in his followers' admiration, reveals the qualities that Yeats had attributed to Richard II: youthful playfulness, spontaneity, and irresponsible fancy, with, however, more fierceness and hardness than is found in his English counterpart. When Conchubar enters a prosaic contrast to what has gone before is introduced; his talk is of trade and practical matters. From this point on until the young warrior enters, the two men's attitudes are counterpointed: Cuchulain mocking the practical, cautious, and comfort-seeking values of Conchubar; the latter defending himself, his concern for domestic order, and the wealth and power needed to maintain it.

Conchubar's purpose in calling the council of kings is to make plans for rebuilding Emain, the capital of the realm, burned in the wars that were necessary to make "what's noble nobler" (*Strand,* p. 89), that is, to make a rich and splendid kingdom to pass on to his heirs. And although Conchubar wants to make his town a vital source of heroism, of "the hard will,/ The unquenchable hope, the friendliness of the sword" (pp. 90–91), it is plain that his aim is for the domestication of heroism so that it can be used in the service of his own practical purpose. But Cuchulain ridicules everything practical and domestic, even the gentleness of women obedient to the wills of their husbands; his own preference for women who are wild and fierce ironically echoes Fintain's story of Cuchulain and Aoife and foreshadows the entrance of his own unrecognized son. The Young Man's sudden entrance and bold challenge to Cuchulain bring the opposition between Conchubar and Cuchulain to its climax. The heroic demeanor of the Young Man and his resemblance to Aoife inspire an immediate sympathy in Cuchulain, who is strangely prompted to talk about himself and his own heritage:

I am their [the gods] plough, their harrow, their very strength,
For he that's in the sun begot this body
Upon a mortal woman, and I have heard tell
It seemed as if he had outrun the moon,
That he must always follow through waste heaven,
He loved so happily.   (p. 96)

On the basis of his instinctive fondness, Cuchulain decides to
befriend the youth, foreseeing a close companionship spent in
hunting and listening to the harp. Conchubar and his council
immediately see the friendship as a threat to established order,
but the menace of Cuchulain's sword keeps the youth from
harm. Cuchulain and the Young Man exchange rich gifts. But
Cuchulain is finally persuaded by Conchubar and the old kings
that witchcraft has caused him to befriend this enemy to the
kingdom, and the angry hero demands that the Young Man go
outdoors to Baile's Strand, there to meet in single combat. The
Fool and the Blind Man reenter the now emptied room. Barach
accuses Fintain of tricking him out of his dinner and threatens
to tell Cuchulain, who returns after killing the Young Man and,
in the course of listening to their quarrel, learns to his horror
the true identity of the youth he has just slain. Ranting and
furious, he hacks at the empty chair of Conchubar, then races
out to kill the High King. From that point on, Barach describes
Cuchulain's action to Fintain, who learns that Cuchulain has
run past Conchubar and on to the sea where he now hews the
waves with his sword.[47] The play ends with Fintain, hearing that
everyone is watching the fantastic battle, urging Barach to
"Come this way, come quickly; the ovens will be full; we will
put our hands into the ovens" (*Strand*, p. 117).

Structurally, the play is simple, its plot built on the intensifying opposition between Cuchulain and Conchubar and between all that they represent. The tragic action arises out of the
submission of Cuchulain's to Conchubar's will. The immediate
and ironic result of submitting is that Cuchulain kills the only

person who could attach his heroism to domestic affection. The hero's absolute isolation is symbolized in a fight, not with other humans from whom he is now wholly cut off, but with the sea, an impersonal power commensurate with his superhuman rage and grief. To this great action, fool and blind man play counterpoint, their own opposition serving as an ironic, almost burlesque, commentary on the main theme.

Characterization, in this first version, is typically Yeatsian, each of the dramatis personae representing some simple and explicit outlook. Cuchulain, his youthful kings, and Aoife's young champion are the spokesmen for the reckless, wild, and exuberant spirit of heroism, now a little diminished in its historical subordination to the values that Conchubar and his old kings represent. Conchubar and his followers (with the exception of Daire, a sort of drunken and disruptive Cuchulain *manqué,* represent a ruthlessly practical power seeking to perpetuate itself by subduing all dangerous energy. Cuchulain, however, is more complex than any of Yeats's earlier heroes, embodying both of the qualities that Yeats at this time believed were to be discovered in heroism: the ineffectual, if extravagant, lyricism that he found in Pater's interpretation of Richard II; and the cold, hawklike energy that Yeats found in the heroes of Irish mythology. Cuchulain's dialogue with his followers and his contempt for and boredom with Conchubar's "plans" echo the sentiments appropriate to the King Richard of Pater's criticism. When Conchubar asks Cuchulain what manner of men his followers are that the "odour from their garments when they stir/ Is like the wind out of an apple garden," Cuchulain replies, "My swordsmen and harp players and fine dancers,/ My bosom friends" (p. 84). Yet Cuchulain also has the characteristics, appearing later in the action, of a bird of prey to whom killing is natural. Other characters are simpler than the hero. The Young Man is a slighter version of Cuchulain. Conchubar, Cuchulain's opposite, is, like the old kings, the epitome of sobriety, prudence, and cunning directed to organizing and preserving his rule over men. All of these figures in the main action belong to the high, remote, and heroic "life of the will," even Conchubar, who, though obviously the antagonist, is stronger and more able than ordinary men.

If the characters of the main action are the articulations of the heroic will, of solar energy, the characters who open and close the action belong to lunar energy, the "emotion of multitude" which Yeats found in the subplot of *King Lear*. Fool and Blind Man, figures out of the folk tradition, bring heroic action, through their own choric immediacy, within the scope of human credibility. Beyond this function, this naturalizing of a remote, supernaturally endowed heroism, the two also serve as the low counterparts of Cuchulain and Conchubar, engaged like the heroes in a perpetual war of values: the Fool is childlike, living mostly in a fanciful world where the supernatural is a vivid, immediate reality; the Blind Man is cunning and worldly-wise. The relationship between the two is like that between Cuchulain and Conchubar: the Blind Man needs the Fool's eyes for survival; but, while insisting that the simple Fool needs him, the Blind Man continuously tricks the Fool out of his share of what the two can steal or catch.[48] The High King needs Cuchulain's strength for conquests; but, while Conchubar argues that Cuchulain needs the practical wisdom to which the High King lays claim, the latter forces Cuchulain to kill his own son. The Blind Man's last words, summoning the Fool from witnessing the marvelous struggle of man and sea, amount almost to a travesty of Conchubar's command to Cuchulain to fight his son. Yeats himself summed up the similarity in a letter to Frank Fay, written in January of 1904:

He [Cuchulain] is the fool—wandering, passive, houseless and almost loveless. Concobhar is reason that is blind because it can only reason because it is cold. Are they not the cold moon and the hot sun?[49]

The setting of the play, unlike that of *Where There is Nothing*, is simple; it is unified by limiting the action to one place:

the stage is occupied by a simple replica of a primitive hall of heroes, a few chairs and benches, an ale vat, side doors, and a large door at the back through which the sea is visible.

The play's style shows clearly the effects of Yeats's new concern with "masculinity." The language of Fool and Blind Man is a prose tinged with dialect, but heightened by strong cadences and vivid images: "He has gold and silver dishes, and chessboards and candlesticks made of precious stones. Fool, have they taken the top from the ale vat?" (*Strand*, p. 72) More successful than the dialect of the tinkers in *Where There is Nothing* because not straining after verisimilitude, this speech represents an effort to achieve some of the best qualities of peasant expression, particularly its idiomatic vividness and richness. The blank verse spoken by the heroic characters is a mixture of the luxuriant early style and a new barer one. When Cuchulain and his followers speak in what Yeats thought was the vein of Richard II, they are exuberantly luxurious with image and allusion:

First Young King.	You have hurled that stone beyond our utmost mark Time after time, but yet you are not weary.
Second Young King.	He has slept on the bare ground of Fuad's Hill This week past, waiting for the bulls and the deer.
Cuchulain.	Well, why should I be weary?
First Young King.	It is certain His father was the god who wheels the sun, And not King Sualtam.
Third Young King	(*to a* Young King *who is beside him*). He came in the dawn, And folded Dectara in a sudden fire.
Fourth Young King.	And yet the mother's half might well grow weary, And it new come from labours over sea.

THIRD YOUNG KING.   He has been on islands walled about with
    silver,
    And fought with giants.   (p. 80)

When later Cuchulain becomes the cold bird of prey, his speech,
though still elevated, is harder, more taut:

CUCHULAIN.   That buckle should be tighter. Give me
    your shield.
    There is good level ground at Baile's
    Yew-tree,
    Some dozen yards from here, and it's
    but truth
    That I am sad to-day and this fight
    welcome.   (p. 95)

There is, perhaps, in both kinds of speech an echo of Shakespeare. Indeed, Ure asserts that in *On Baile's Strand* it "is evident . . . that Yeats' technique is Elizabethan or Jacobean." [50]
The "Elizabethan or Jacobean" technique is possibly responsible
for the relative liveliness of the blank verse when compared with
the verse of earlier plays; neither the stiff formality of the dialogue in *The Countess Cathleen* nor the overrich fluency of
that in *The Shadowy Waters* is as dramatically effective as
Daire's speech from *On Baile's Strand:*

> Where's Main Morgor and old Usnach's children,
> And that high-headed even-walking Queen,
> And many near as great that got their death
> Because you hated peace? I can remember
> The people crying out when Deidre passed
> And Maine Morgor had a cold gray eye.
> Well, well, I'll throw this heel-tap on the ground,
> For it may be they are thirsty.   (*Strand,* pp. 89–90)

In such a passage there is the impression of one person talking
to another, instead of, as in the earlier plays, one lyric mood
simply shading into another so that a single voice seemed to
serve for all characters.

    Yeats's treatment of symbols in *On Baile's Strand* is another index showing how far he had come from *The Shadowy Waters*. Though numerous, the symbols in *On Baile's Strand* seldom seem arbitrarily imposed on the action or dependent upon some knowledge extraneous to the play for understanding. Some vestiges of the earlier symbolic method appear; for instance, a fish-tailed woman carved on Conchubar's chair, a dog's head carved on Cuchulain's. It is necessary to go beyond the play to discover that the mermaid perhaps signifies the "drifting indefinite bitterness of life," that is, the sea which overwhelms Cuchulain at the end. Clearer and more functional is the symbolic use of birds, chiefly the aloof hawk, and, contrastingly, baser birds like the sparrow and magpie. Both Cuchulain and the Young Man identify themselves with the hawk (pp. 94–95). A chicken, appropriately, is the cause of contention between Fool and Blind Man; after the battle between Cuchulain and the Young Man, the Fool sticks some of the chicken's feathers in his hair.[51] And Cuchulain wipes his son's blood from his sword with feathers of the same bird. The bird symbol here dramatically unifies other elements in the play by foreshadowing the ironic reversal of Cuchulain's victory.

On Baile's Strand is Yeats's coherent effort to bring the supernatural into the world of the play with what might be called a natural symbol, that is, a symbol which seems to grow naturally out of the environment of the action rather than, as in *The Shadowy Waters* or *Where There is Nothing,* a symbol superimposed from outside that action. Symbolism, in fact, is as central to *On Baile's Strand* as to any of Yeats's earlier plays, but with this significant difference: the symbol takes its meaning from the world of the play, rather than from a system of meanings external to the play, a system required to explain both Forgael's adventure and Paul Ruttledge's vision.

The theme of *On Baile's Strand* is the characteristically Yeatsian one of the noble spirit whose passions calamitously overreach the limits of the natural order. Or, to define the theme in terms that Yeats had used in "At Stratford-on-Avon," the incongruity of what a man is and what role circumstance forces upon him leads to "tragic irony." The tragic irony takes the form in *On Baile's Strand* of a defeat in the circumstantial world, transcended by a sublime gesture that reveals a spirit, which, because capable of superhuman experience, is heroic. The gods have mysteriously "chosen" Cuchulain for exceptional suffering because of his special qualities: his excessive strength and pride, his Apollonian individuality; but, at the highest pitch of his agony, he achieves a Dionysian oneness (significantly described by the Fool, who represents the "emotion of multitude"). Yeats thus suggests the supernatural order in the strange, irrational actions of the hero in his moments of agony. This method of suggesting the supernatural resembles that used in *The Shadowy Waters*. Forgael's actions in the earlier play were meant to "prove" the effects of the supernatural on the natural. However, instead of relying on a heavy overlay of suggestively mysterious symbols to support the impression that the hero was supernaturally possessed, Yeats employed "emotion of multitude"; for the Fool, Cuchulain's double in the subplot, lives close to the supernatural, to those haunting witches who seem to him a "natural" part of his world. Yeats's aim was to have the Fool's contact with the supernatural echo and reinforce Cuchulain's. In this way, the "emotion of multitude" (the world beyond "the limited life of the fable") becomes symbolic of the anima mundi or superhuman oneness which the hero finally achieves through his suffering. In this way Cuchulain is, as Yeats asserted, "the fool," and his fight with the sea a divine foolishness.

Parkinson defines the hero's last gesture

as a symbol of a universal mood; his single-minded devotion to his guiding passion results in an act of sublime simplicity, expressive of his lack of concern for the limitations of life, ruinous to his temporal existence, evocative of terror and admiration. Such figures as Deirdre and Cuchulain grant us a revelation of human possibility.[52]

This statement clearly delineates the intention informing *On Baile's Strand,* the highest achievement among the group of plays so far discussed. The question remains: did Yeats in the first version of the play achieve his purpose any more satisfactorily than in *Where There is Nothing,* an admitted failure in his own eyes?

Certainly of all Yeats's tragic dramas up to 1903, the first version of *On Baile's Strand* came nearest to fulfilling his own standards. Surface flaws there are: the plotting is marred by the rather long-winded and mechanical introductory exposition by Fool and Blind Man. Occasionally, revealing comments on the nature of character are clumsily handled—for instance, Cuchulain's on the Fool and the Blind Man:

> They always flock together; the blind man
> Has need of the fool's eyesight and strong body,
> While the poor fool has need of the other's wit,
> And night and day is up to his ears in mischief
> That the blind man imagines.   (*Strand,* p. 81)

These remarks are improbable and obtrusive; a passionate hero could hardly be expected to give so much attention to low characters. Plotting is further weakened because the conflict leading to the climactic duel is put off by the prolonged conversation of Cuchulain and his followers. This conversation does not advance the theme, and it reduces the effectiveness of Conchubar's entrance by blurring the real opposition between Cuchulain and the High King. The conflict central to the play is weakened for a dearly bought exposition of one side of Cuchulain's nature. Yet the plot is perhaps weakest at the sudden reversal of Cuchulain's attitude toward the Young Man. That Conchubar and the old kings could so easily convince Cuchulain he had been bewitched is not wholly credible.

The weaknesses of plot result in a confusion of thematic emphasis. A long discussion between Cuchulain and his followers concerning different types of love is meant as dramatic irony looking forward to Cuchulain's failure to recognize his son. But the discussion seems excessively long for this function and has nothing to do with the central opposition of Cuchulain and Conchubar, for Cuchulain's passion for fierce, undomesticated women suggests that Conchubar, as his opposite, must cherish the domestic virtues of gentle nature and passive love. But Conchubar hardly represents such virtues in this version of the play; thus, Cuchulain's preference for heroic love over domestic love is not clearly brought into effective relationship with the play's main theme, which hinges upon the opposition of Cuchulain and Conchubar. The same must be said of the conflict between father and son; though a matter central to the play, this conflict is not clearly connected to the central theme. Had Yeats (as he would do in the later version) set Cuchulain's relationship to his son in contrast to Conchubar's relationship to his children, the conflict of Cuchulain and the Young Man would have enhanced and clarified the theme.

However, the most significant weakness of this version, one which, in fact, is responsible for many of the others, is a failure in characterization. Yeats's usual tendency to personify some attitude or quality is present in *On Baile's Strand* and leads to an oversimplification of the moral issues of the play and an overstressing of the polar opposition between characters representing good and evil: Fool and Blind Man, Cuchulain and Conchubar, the young kings and the old kings—each of these oppositions heavily underscored by the fact that one member is entirely sympathetic, the other entirely unsympathetic. While Cuchulain, unlike Forgael, has real opposition that ultimately defeats his purposes, the opposition is given so little attractiveness and depth of conviction that it functions solely to explicate its own too obviously disagreeable point of view. The antagonist has neither the intelligent competence of Claudius in *Hamlet* nor the passionate conviction of Creon in *Antigone.* This lack of conviction in Cuchulain's antagonists makes for actions that are not clearly or convincingly motivated.

Beyond this weakness, and perhaps even more basic, is the

deeply split personality of the hero, who suffers from his inventor's divided view of what constitutes heroism: the Cuchulain of the earlier part of the play is the offspring of Pater's interpretation of Richard II—reckless, generous, extravagant, charming, and ineffectual; the Cuchulain of the later part is more like Shakespeare's Coriolanus—arbitrary, cold, and fierce, somehow older, and a man not of words but of action. The change does not represent merely a shift of mood possible to one character, but a radical alteration which has no apparent reason beyond the playwright's confusion as to who his hero in fact is. A letter to Frank Fay, dated January of 1904, shows that Yeats was indeed confused about Cuchulain's identity:

About Cuchullain . . . I have . . . to make the refusal of the son's affection tragic by suggesting in Cuchullain's character a shadow of something a little proud, barren and restless, as if out of sheer strength of heart or from accident he had put affection away. He lives among young men but has himself outlived the illusion of youth. . . . Probably his very strength of character made him put off illusions and dreams . . . and made him become quite early in life a deliberate lover, a man of pleasure who can never really surrender himself. He is a little hard, and leaves the people about him a little repelled—perhaps this young man's affection is what he had most need of. Without this thought the play had not had any deep tragedy. I write of him with difficulty, for when one creates a character one does it out of instinct and may be wrong when one analyzes the instinct afterwards. It is as though the character embodied itself. The less one reasons the more living the character. I felt for instance that his boasting was necessary, and yet I did not reason it out. The touch of something hard, repellent yet alluring, self assertive yet self immolating, is not all but it must be there. He is the fool—wandering, passive, houseless and almost loveless.[53]

The portrait fits the second Cuchulain, not the first who has not put by "illusions and dreams" as his language during his brief friendship with the Young Man reveals. At such moments, he hardly seems the "very strength" of the gods.

Yeats's style at these moments rises to an irrelevant exuberance out of keeping with the general tone of the play. Cuchulain-Richard II and his young followers seem to have no dramatic function; their vagrant and charming fancy is out of place in the heroic world and gives the impression merely of confusing irrelevance that has no genuine kinship with the Elizabethan variety and complexity of character that Yeats may have been striving for.

Cuchulain's leaping from capricious wilfulness to high seriousness reveals a defect not only in stylistic appropriateness but also in coherence of character. There is no inclusive personality into which Cuchulain's two voices intelligibly fit: the almost captious voice that urges those around it to ignore the High King for the sake of continuing a boyish conversation:

> Come nearer yet;
> Though he is ringing that old silver rod
> We'll have our own talk out. They cannot hear us.
>
> (*Strand,* p. 88)

and the solemn voice asserting what deeds could be done by two such as Cuchulain and a hypothetical son:

> He would avenge me
> When I have withstood for the last time the men
> Whose fathers, brothers, sons, and friends I have killed
> Upholding Ullad; when the four provinces
> Have gathered with the ravens over them.
> But I'd need no avenger. You and I
> Would scatter them like water from a dish.   (p. 102)

These weaknesses suggest one other, and, so far as Yeats was concerned, a calamitous one: the treatment of the supernatural as a force in the play. As the offspring of the sun-god, Cuchulain has a direct relationship with divine reality, although, as Yeats had asserted, in Cuchulain's age the gods were more remote from men than they had been in an earlier age. There are, in the play, besides this implicit connection of mortal and immortal, many references to the supernatural, particularly by the Fool and Cuchulain. The Fool's great preoccupation is with witches and their power over men:

It's a woman from among the Riders of the Sidhe. It's Boann herself from the river. . . . Nobody knows how lecherous these goddesses are. I see her in every kind of shape but oftener than not she's in the wind. . . .   (p. 70)

And Cuchulain refers to the supernatural cloak that he received from the sea god, Manannan, whose wife, Fand, had once been Cuchulain's lover.[54] Despite these references, there is nowhere in the play evidence of the supernatural actually affecting the action; all motives throughout the action are accountable in terms of naturalistic psychology. Even the hero's fight with the sea does not necessitate an interpretation involving, in the Yeatsian sense, the supernatural order. Cuchulain's gesture can be seen as the result of a great passion out of control and, as such, is surely explicable without reference to a superhuman order of experience.

It might be argued on good grounds that Yeats's use of the supernatural was, in the strictest sense, always psychological. That is, in an attempt to push beyond what he regarded as the narrow mechanistic 19th-century interpretation of human motivation, Yeats introduced the supernatural in his work, much as Euripides, according to E. M. W. Tillyard, had used the gods to project greater-than-human motives.[55] But the evidence suggests otherwise: Yeats in *On Baile's Strand,* as with all his tragedies, aimed for the state of transcendence that defies mortal limits and glimpses, amid personal ruin, the higher reality or Dionysian oneness. He hoped to embody in Cuchulain's action a sense of supernatural presence both as the inscrutable motive force of a hero's fate and the culminating vision of heroic suffering. The evidence of page upon page of theory—ontological and dramatic—points to such an aim in *On Baile's Strand.*

However, as the play stood in its first version, the supernatural was neither the symbol for an extraordinary psychological state nor an objective reality in its own right. *On Baile's*

Strand suffered, as markedly as the earlier tragedies, from an uncontrolled ambiguity that can be traced to a characteristic ambiguity of motive in Yeats himself. His conception of naturalizing the heroic experience by the "emotion of multitude" was a brave attempt to give the war of orders a convincing context, but in execution so far it proved a shaky solution to his problem. Beyond the serious weaknesses of the plot and the failure to create convincing characterization and consistent style, the very presence of Fool and Blind Man appears arbitrary, often clumsily contrived; this fault cuts the ground from under the heroic fable.

The general lack of coherence—in plot, in character, and in style—is the result of Yeats's failure to embody as drama the tragic theme of the war of orders. Even though he claimed that the first version of *On Baile's Strand* was the best play that he had written,[56] it did not long satisfy his conditions for great tragedy, a fact which becomes clear in his criticism between the time the play was finished and its next important revision.

SHELLEY AND DICKENS IN THE ONE BODY: YEATS'S THEORY OF TRAGICOMEDY, 1903–1908

The new criticism does not so much represent the emphatic change in thought seen at the turn of the century as a working out of certain lines of the theory that Yeats developed from 1900 through 1903. Set forth chiefly in writings for the Irish dramatic movement and in random essays collected under the title of *Discoveries* (1906),[57] this new criticism reveals the reasoning behind Yeats's revisions of *Where There is Nothing* and *On Baile's Strand* and in his writing of *Deirdre*.

Plays and Controversies begins with essays from *Samhain*, an occasional publication started in 1901, the third year of the Irish dramatic movement, and includes essays on the drama written during the next eighteen years. The volume constitutes a significant record of Yeats's developing thought, both theoretical and practical, for this span of time. Most noteworthy is that, after the first two years of *Samhain,* Yeats's contributions dwell more and more on the human personality as a vigorous and creative natural energy, as the full expression of some vital excess. Pater's image of the ineffectual, passive hero seems inappropriate to this new concern, though Yeats can still praise such an image in "First Principles" (1904).[58] But, generally in a different mood now, Yeats more often defined personality as a self-contained, joyful wholeness of the individual:

> Every argument carries us backwards to some religious conception, and in the end the creative energy of men depends upon their believing that they have, within themselves, something immortal and imperishable, and that all else is but as an image in a looking-glass. So long as that belief is not a formal thing, a man will create out of a joyful energy, seeking little for any external test of an impulse that may be sacred and looking for no foundation outside like itself.   (*Controversies*, pp. 99–100)

It is well to recall, however, that his growing concern with personality was by no means unprecedented. In his essay "The Queen and the Fool" (1901), he had asserted that the "foundation of all our knowledge" is the self.[59] Moreover, when it is remembered that emotions or "moods" were, for Yeats, expressions of the divine, it is logical that passionate selfhood would be central to the Yeatsian conception of tragedy. Yet, passionate selfhood can mean two very different things: on the one hand, the dreamy, remote, and ecstatic self-absorption of Forgael or the Richard II seen through Pater's eyes; on the other, the vigorous, self-delighting energy of Cuchulain or of Yeats's favorites at this time among Shakespearean characters—Antony, Cleopatra, and Coriolanus—whose "high pride" is brought to intense passion "by opposition with some other passion, or it may be with the law, that is the expression of the whole whether of Church or Nation or external nature." [60]

Yeats obviously now preferred the latter kind of passionate selfhood. The new figures that occupy his thought, both characters from literature and actual men, represented the active personality in the process of making some noble gesture as a unique expression of selfhood:

There are two kinds of poetry, and they are commingled in all the greatest works. When the tide of life sinks low there are pictures, as in "The Ode to a Grecian Urn" and in Virgil at the plucking of the Golden Bough. The pictures make us sorrowful. We share the poet's separation from what he describes. It is life in the mirror, and our desire for it is as the desire of the lost soul for God; but when Lucifer stands among his friends, when Villon sings his dead ladies to so gallant a rhythm, when Timon makes his epitaph, we feel no sorrow, for life herself has made one of her eternal gestures, has called up into our hearts her energy that is eternal delight. In Ireland, where the tide of life is rising, we turn, not to picture-making, but to the imagination of personality—to drama, gesture.

(*Controversies,* p. 115)

In short, an attitude which up to now had marked all of Yeats's work, both theoretical and practical, was rejected in favor of its opposite. The lyrical mood clothed in shadowy and exotic style, "life in the mirror," that he identified with his early masters, particularly Rossetti and Pater, was put away. Now he sought a wholehearted passion, "drama, gesture," springing from the immediacy of peasant life and from the heroic selfhood of the personality. But if passion was the source of noble, generous, overflowing action that ultimately transcended human limits, the transcending personality must be understood as achieving the tragic experience, the spiritual completeness, only by being rooted in and springing out of the natural world that imposes limits on men.

This new version of the heroic personality was also the subject of many of the essays in *Discoveries,* in which Yeats abandoned much of the theory that informed *The Shadowy Waters* and which, five years before, he had regarded as sacred. He now asserted:

Walter Pater says music is the type of all the Arts, but somebody else, I forget now who, that oratory is their type. You will side with the one or the other according to the nature of your energy, and I

in my present mood am all for the man who, with an average audience before him, uses all means of persuasion—stories, laughter,
tears, and but so much music as he can discover on the wings of
words. I would even avoid the conversation of the lovers of music,
who would draw us into the impersonal land of sound and colour,
and I would have no one write with a sonata in his memory.[61]

Seeing a guitar player suggested this to him:

A movement not of music only but of life came to its perfection. I
was delighted and I did not know why until I thought, "That is the
way my people, the people I see in the mind's eye, play music, and
I like it because it is all personal, as personal as Villon's poetry."
The little instrument is quite light, and the player can move freely
and express a joy that is not of the fingers and the mind only but
of the whole being; and all the while her movements call up into
the mind, so erect and natural she is, whatever is most beautiful in
her daily life.   (*Essays,* p. 333)

Such observations marked a conscious rejection of his earlier
views and were incipient in the criticism between 1900 and
1903; but here they are uttered with unequivocal assurance. In
"Holy Places," the last essay in *Discoveries,* Yeats put his early
view of art into historical relationship with the new view, finding a grievous separation between the literature of dream and
the literature of personality. A lamentable phenomenon in modern life was, he observed, the split of the subtle art of high
culture from the imagination of the common people. In ancient
times and in the middle ages, artists and folk were at one, were
like "a Shelley and a Dickens in the one body" (p. 367). Yeats
admitted that the divorce of soul and body, of Shelley and Dickens, presented a desperate choice for the modern artist. But
about Yeats's choice there seemed little doubt. His complete
identification earlier with the Shelley half of the unhappy schism
now dwindled to a profound sympathy; he had come to accept
Dickens with the hope that somehow the split might be mended,
the essential opposites remarried. Out of this remarriage Yeats
hoped to produce a whole art, one in which he could achieve

that "Unity of Being" so often spoken of by him as the ideal state of the creative work, the individual, or of the nation.[62] An explanation of how the art of higher culture escapes Dickensian daily life prompted him to set against such an escape an affirmation of the value of daily life:

One of the means of loftiness, of marmorean stillness, has been the choice of strange and far-away places, for the scenery of art, but this choice has grown bitter to me, and there are moments when I cannot believe in the reality of imaginations that are not inset with the minute life of long familiar things and symbols and places.[63]

Yeats felt that if an art could be achieved in which the dreaming imagination was countersunk in daily reality, he might fuse soul and body, spirit and nature. In such an art

a man should find his Holy Land where he first crept upon the floor, and that familiar woods and rivers should fade into symbol with so gradual a change that he may never discover, no, not even in ecstasy itself, that he is beyond space, and that time alone keeps him from Primum Mobile, Supernal Eden, Yellow Rose over all.

(*Essays*, p. 368)

In some degree, *Where There is Nothing* and *On Baile's Strand* had been efforts to find this fusion; in both plays vigorous action, physical and verbal, precipitated the tragic resolution. And, at least in *Where There is Nothing,* the action worked slowly toward the climax, naturally moving from the everyday world to the world of vision, from the known to the unknown. Yet neither of these tragedies, based upon confused purposes, had begun to achieve the ideal fusion of spiritual and natural. Indeed, until about 1904 Yeats had not clearly seen the need of such a fusion. From this time on his theorizing is devoted to defining its components, their relationship, and his own purposes with respect to bringing the components together in the drama. His criticism and plays between 1900 and 1903 had been the products of a partially understood conception which after 1904 took clearer shape, clear enough, at any rate, so that he could in *Discoveries* take a strong position for a more extensive use of the natural world in his art.

ON BAILE'S STRAND REVISED (1907)

In the light of this theoretical clarification, he set about making major revisions that revealed his conscious effort to put theory into practice. The results were genuinely new versions of *The Shadowy Waters* (1906), *On Baile's Strand* (1907), and *Where There is Nothing* (1908), as well as a new play, *Deirdre* (1907). The purposiveness of his revising at this time is revealed in a letter to Florence Farr written about the middle of 1905, in which he discussed his new version of *The Shadowy Waters:*

I am making Forgael's part perfectly clear and straightforward. The play is now upon one single idea—which is in these new lines—

> 'When the world ends
> The mind is made unchanging for it finds
> Miracle, ecstasy, the impossible joy,
> The flagstone under all, the fire of fires,
> The root of the world.'

There are no symbols except Aengus and Aedane and the birds—and I have into the bargain heightened all the moments of dramatic crisis—sharpened every knife edge.

He conceded, however, that because the play was rooted in an older life, it could not, except for its high moments, be made right:

The play as it was came into existence after years of strained emotion, of living upon tip-toe, and is only right in its highest moments —the logic and circumstances are all wrong.[64]

The logic of structure, reflecting the Apollonian masculinity that a few years before he had discovered as necessary to his work, could never enter a play that was built on the static "mood" or the "intellectual essence" and pitched like *The Shadowy Waters* to an unremitting, dreamlike ecstasy. Yeats was only able to tighten the structure, define the characters more sharply, and purge the style of excessive dreaminess and needlessly obscure symbol. Moreover, it was difficult to give the natural world of Dickens its due in a play so wholly devoted to remote symbol and dream, although Yeats did toughen the speech of the sailors. Yet the revisions could only be, at best, imposed from the outside on a work inherently belonging to a mode of expression to which he no longer subscribed.

With *On Baile's Strand* Yeats had a structure already built on the logic that was missing in the earlier play; for even the first version of *On Baile's Strand* was a product of his partial rejection of the aesthetic upon which *The Shadowy Waters* was based. The failure of the first version of the play was, in some measure, the result of Yeats's divided attitude between 1900 and 1903. Watching performances and mixing in the business of actual stage production, he had seen during this transitional period that the aesthetic of the static "mood" was wanting as a means of achieving tragic drama, and that action in the natural world was essential for a wholeness of dramatic expression. But up to 1903 he still clung to elements of the old view; that this view, which had so much in it of Pater's thought, caused him much uneasiness was evident in 1902 by his delight in Nietzsche and his growing concern for masculine logical dramatic structure. By 1906, in *Discoveries,* the break with Pater's conception of ideal drama as a state of music seemed complete. The extensive revision of the plot and character in *On Baile's Strand* reveals how much that break implied for Yeats's creative work, particularly his tragedies.

Yeats wrote to A. H. Bullen in November of 1905 that the whole first half of the play was new (*Letters,* p. 465), the half, significantly enough, which mainly exhibited Cuchulain as spiritual kin of Pater's Richard II. Of all the revision in the play, changing the first half was most critical; the quality of what follows was thus radically altered and a new play resulted.

Yeats's reworking of the plot alone is a revelation of the clarity
of purpose with which he returned to the play. Now, the long
exposition of Fool and Blind Man is reduced and made dramatically functional by taking the form of a mock play within
the serious play. The Blind Man, mounting Conchubar's throne
and demanding that the Fool give him allegiance, terrorizes his
witch-haunted and hungry companion. The pair, through travesty, foreshadow and comment on the conflict arising from
Conchubar's demand that Cuchulain swear an oath of allegiance
to him. In his role as the mock Conchubar, the Blind Man,
using the very reasoning that the High King will use on Cuchulain, argues that since the mock hero lacks intelligence, riches,
and heirs he is a useless creature and ought to submit to those
who do possess these things:

What are your wits compared with mine, and what are your riches
compared with mine? And what sons have you to pay your debts and
to put a stone over you when you die? Take the oath, I tell you.
Take a strong oath.[65]

Spoken by a blind man, these words take on telling irony, sharpened by the fact that the speaker, dropping his role as High
King, portentously suggests that, at least in the matter of heirs,
Conchubar may be wrong. However, the plot is not "given
away" in this initial exposition as it was in that of the first
version, for the Blind Man only hints that the Young Man newly
landed and threatening the kingdom is Cuchulain's son. In
short, the major theme is subtly but clearly established in this
initial dialogue: the opposition of Cuchulain and Conchubar
and the implications of that opposition—primarily, the inevitable isolation of the heroic man whose fate is to go without love
or kin precisely because he is heroic. Moreover, as they had
failed to do in the first version, Fool and Blind Man provide
a framework for the coming action and suggest credible causes
or motives for what seemed fortuitous earlier: Conchubar's visit
to Cuchulain, the sudden entrance of the Young Man, the other-

wise obtrusive preoccupation with love and offspring. In their own right, moreover, Fool and Blind Man have become closer to the "emotion of multitude" that naturalizes the high action.

The entrances of the principals are now far more effectively direct: Cuchulain comes on stage with Conchubar, angrily denouncing the oath that the High King wishes to impose upon him. As G. B. Saul notes, the oath of allegiance provides a genuine basis for the conflict between the two.[66] In the background the Young Man's menacing presence, more or less fortuitous in the first version, functions to provide Conchubar with a concrete example of the importance of making Cuchulain take the oath. Moreover, by bringing Conchubar in immediately no time is wasted with a long, dramatically irrelevant conversation between Cuchulain and his followers or for the equally irrelevant discussion between Conchubar and the old kings about the rebuilding of Emain. Now, the passions arise out of a clear issue: Cuchulain's desire to remain free of all confining bonds that would domesticate his wild nature and Conchubar's opposing desire that Cuchulain's otherwise dangerous heroic energy should be harnessed to the task of consolidating the social order that the High King wishes to pass on to his children:

> I am High King, my son shall be High King.
> And you for all the wildness of your blood,
> And though your father came out of the sun,
> Are but a little king and weigh but light
> In anything that touches government,
> If put into the balance with my children.
>
> (*Strand,* 1907, pp. 273–74)

After Cuchulain submits to the oath, the conflict of wills is powerfully heightened by the entrance of the Young Man and the immediate friendship of Cuchulain and the intruder, until Conchubar, refusing to let the Young Man's challenge go ignored, threatens to fight the Young Man himself. Conchubar's action precipitates the final stages of the drama.

The central dramatic ironies of *On Baile's Strand,* which before were blurred, are clarified through the logic of the new plotting. Now Conchubar's concern for his offspring is the occasion for Cuchulain's destroying his own; now the moment it compromises with the social order Cuchulain's wild and lonely heroism destroys its only hope of continuity beyond itself in the natural world. Finally, these two ironies unite to make the tragic irony of the play: that the hero's very uniqueness, his excessive "heady" strength and vitality, cut him off from the life of which he is the most noble representation. Frustrated by the social order of mediocre men and too great for normal human relationships, Cuchulain reacts by destroying the only possibility of perpetuating heroism: he kills the unrecognized son to whom he has passed his unique strength. Being still a man, he is maddened by both the agony of what he has done and his complete awareness of his now ironically demonstrated matchlessness (the other side of which is absolute and sterile isolation). But also being himself a hero and the son of a god, he must find release for his agony in an act that seems to pass beyond the range of ordinary human comprehension—thus his battle with the sea, the emblem of the "bitterness of life." The sea will defeat him, but it will also allow him the scope for the superhuman energy impossible in Conchubar's world that perpetuates itself by diminishing man to a servant of some narrowly abstract or selfish or mundane purpose.

As a result of the new plotting character is significantly strengthened, and the confused complexities of the first version are replaced by clarity and simplicity. Yeats's tendency to simplify toward a sound clarity is indicated by his relegating the young kings and the old kings to a position outside the hall. In line with the overall simplifying, Fool and Blind Man lose their proper names, becoming, appropriately for their function as the anonymous "emotion of multitude," generalized. Daire, the drunken Old King, is properly excised, having had no particular significance in the first version. The reactions of minor characters effectively function to enforce the central theme. Cuchulain's followers, for instance, side with Conchubar in urging Cuchulain to take the oath, and in doing so they toughen the opposition to Cuchulain's will. This portentous isolating of Cuchulain's reckless and stubborn will gives Conchubar's desire to strengthen his kingdom the validity of genuine and sympathetic motivation. Cuchulain, given his new stubbornly concentrated temper, seems more dangerous. His boyish charm and exuberance mostly gone, his is the grim, aloof figure that Yeats envisaged in his letter to Fay. Conchubar's position, in the face of a not altogether sympathetic disruptive force, takes on a new persuasiveness, even though it represents an essentially ruthless and selfish will ready to sacrifice beauty, creativity, honor, and integrity to achieve its end of dynastic self-preservation.

The clearer definition of character also unifies what was disparate in the earlier Cuchulain. His obtrusive preoccupation with the kinds of love possible to men and women is now brought directly to bear on the main theme. His description of Aoife to Conchubar makes it clear that only some heroic woman's answering fierceness would have meaning for him; heroic lust or life, just like heroic fighting instinct, is only roused by the most difficult challenge. Gentleness, softness—any of the romantic or parental feelings—have no place in Cuchulain's relationships. He knows only generosity for and a sense of fairness toward what he admires; for the rest, indifference or the cold, implacable will. For this reason, his relationship with his son is made all the more poignant, for there is that side in Cuchulain which cannot be developed or expressed because his is the lonely fate of the hero. In the new play, Cuchulain's isolated character is effectively defined: a nature almost godlike in its superiority to the ties of kin and society, but vulnerable to these ties because *not* completely godlike. After killing the son whom he cannot "recognize," his final battle with the sea logically resolves the seemingly unresolvable. Cuchulain finds in his superhuman madness all human opposition too small for his roused passion and attacks the sea whose infiniteness is commensurate with his heroic energy, which, as the Blind Man had said, was foolish, poor, and isolated—its very uselessness, in the natural world, paradoxically lifting it into the mystery of superhuman experience.

The style of the revision is more austere. Yeats aimed throughout the play at a more forceful speech to accord with the tightened logic of the new plotting. The argument between Cuchulain and Conchubar is the genuine dialogue of men who have their powerful and considered reasons. The irrelevant exuberance of the earlier play is almost gone, Yeats having excised such passages as Cuchulain's address to one of his followers:

> If I'd that ball
> That's in your hair and the big stone again,
> I'd keep them tossing, though the one is heavy
> And the other light in the hand. A trick I learnt
> When I was learning arms in Aoife's country.[67]

Nor is the language of the play burdened with symbol; the distracting and dramatically inconsequential carvings on the chairs are not mentioned. The bird imagery, without losing its significance, is better integrated into the fabric of conversation.

The language of Fool and Blind Man is reworked to function more in terms of the main theme of the play. Small but crucial touches have increased the dramatic value of their dialogue, as a comparison of the versions show. In the important last exchange, the first version reads:

FINTAIN.   What is he doing now?

BARACH.   Oh! he is fighting the waves.

FINTAIN.   He sees King Conchubar's crown on every one of them.

BARACH.   There, he has struck at a big one. He has struck the crown off it, he made the foam fly. There again another big one.   (*Shouting without.*)

FINTAIN. Where are the Kings? What are the Kings doing?

BARACH. They are shouting and running down to the shore, and the people are running out of the houses, they are all running.

FINTAIN. You say they are running out of the houses, there will be nobody left in the houses. Listen, fool.

BARACH. There, he is down! He is up again! He is going out into the deep water.

FINTAIN. Come here, fool; come here, I say.

BARACH *(coming towards him but looking backward towards the door)*. What is it?

FINTAIN. There will be nobody in the houses. Come this way, come quickly; the ovens will be full; we will put our hands into the ovens.

(They go out.) (Strand, pp. 116–17)

The second version is the same up to where the fool describes Cuchulain going into the water:

FOOL. There, he is down. He is up again. He is going out into the deep water. There is a big wave. It has gone over him. I cannot see him now. He has killed kings and giants, but the waves have mastered him, the waves have mastered him.

BLIND MAN. Come here, Fool!

FOOL. The waves have mastered him!

BLIND MAN. Come here, I say.

FOOL *(coming towards him, but looking backwards towards the door)*. What is it?

BLIND MAN. There will be nobody in the houses. Come this way; come quickly. The ovens will be full. We will put our hands into the ovens. *(They go out.)*
CURTAIN [68]

In the second version, the need for the Blind Man to summon the Fool twice makes all the difference: it calls attention to the Fool's complete absorption in the event that he is describing to the audience. The relationship between Blind Man and Fool at this moment is that of Conchubar and Cuchulain, but seen as in a distorting mirror that reveals the debasing effect of Conchubar's "victory" over heroism; the triumph of the High

King's prudence over the hero's recklessness becomes the triumph of thievish cunning over simpleness.

One innovation in the revised play—the presence of three
women musicians—deserves separate attention. This choric-like
addition, representing a new dramatic technique in Yeats's plays,
may have been suggested by his reading in Greek drama and by
his concern for augmenting the "emotion of multitude" provided by Fool and Blind Man. Conchubar, in the new version,
summons three women to sing a spell for warding off evil spirits
from the fire over which the oath is to be sworn. The spell is
against the same witches earlier spoken of with dread by the
Fool and later recalled by Conchubar's explanation that Cuchulain's friendship with the Young Man was the result of witchcraft. Yeats saw these witches, actually Celtic goddesses, as representing the supernatural forces, the mysterious, attractive powers that enter the life of the hero and inspire him both to greatness and ruin. As far back as the *The Seeker,* Yeats conceived
of the hero as mysteriously impelled to pursue these obscure
spirits, who, out of love or hate, change like the wind with which
they are frequently identified. They are, in fact, the anima
mundi bursting into the anima hominis, the impersonal superhuman whirling over the domestic "threshold and hearthstone."
The musicians sing of these inhuman passions become palpable
beings:

> The women, none can kiss and thrive,
> For they are but whirling wind,
> Out of memory and mind.
> They would make a prince decay
> With light images of clay,
> Planted in the running wave,
> Or, for many shapes they have,
> They would change them into hounds,
> Until he died of his wounds,
> Though the change were but a whim;
> Or they'd hurl a spell at him
> That he follow with desire

Bodies that can never tire;
Or grow kind, for they annoint
All their bodies, joint by joint,
With a miracle-working juice
That is made out of the grease
Of the ungoverned unicorn.
But the man is twice forlorn,
Emptied, ruined, wracked, and lost,
That they follow, for at most
They will give him kiss for kiss;
While they murmur, "After this
Hatred may be sweet to the taste." (pp. 287–88)

It is, in fact, these powers, female in their attractiveness and shape-changing, that Cuchulain, as a Yeatsian hero, has always pursued, through love which turns to hate and through strength to conquer which turns to self-injury. The end of his quest is the severing of his connection with all human life and a grief which finds only the sea its fit object. Like heroic love, heroic hatred is beyond human objects and touched with witchcraft. The musicians' description of these superhuman and destructive passions of love and hate provides some ground for the excessiveness of Cuchulain's final fury, which without some explanation might seem obscure. The musicians' song makes credible acts that in their frenzy transcend the range of normal human feeling and perception. The essential function of the musicians, then, is to supply a clear statement of what motivates Cuchulain as a figure in the war of orders. This choric voice is the most impressive device that Yeats had yet been able to find for clarifying, within the framework of the play, the rationale underlying that all-important war.

Even though this second version of *On Baile's Strand* was the finest tragic drama that he had yet achieved, Yeats was aware of weaknesses in the play as it stood. "It is now," he said in 1906, "as right as I can make it with my present experience, but it must always be a little over-complicated when played by itself." [69] His remedy was a projected cycle of plays which would make sense of some of the complications of *On Baile's Strand* (though he is not clear as to what these are).[70] There is, however, a more significant overcomplication. The chorus of musicians, which comes closest to solving the always central problem in Yeats's tragedies—the relationship between natural and super-natural—has little part in the action and seems imposed on the dramatic structure from the outside; the musicians' sole func-tion, like that of Fool and Blind Man in the first version, is to explicate. Unlike the chorus of *Oedipus Rex,* which, through its reactions to events, brings those events within the range of human comprehension, Yeats's musicians fill a pause in the action with a perfunctory definition relating the supernatural women to the hero. But the explication, as it stands, is undra-matic and mechanical. Still the choric use of musicians was a foreshadowing of a far more effective use of this device in later plays and, therefore, must be treated as an important advance in Yeats's dramatic technique; certainly the chorus is the best solution so far to the problem of handling the presentation of the war of orders on the stage. But the improved *On Baile's Strand,* while a solid achievement, still falls into the category of plays whose action is explicable in terms of naturalistic psychology, and, as such, represents no final solution to the for-mal problems of embodying Yeats's tragic vision.

DEIRDRE (1906)

Deirdre was yet another attempt at such an embodiment. Completed in 1906 and somewhat revised in 1908, its subject is also a heroic fable, in this instance the last events in the life of Deirdre, one of the most famous heroines of Irish mythology. Yeats had been working on the play since at least 1904, when he mentioned it in connection with a chorus, somewhat in the Greek manner, to be included.[71] Writing to Katharine Tynan late in 1906 or early in 1907, he asserted that it was a great play.[72] Although it hardly lived up to this claim, it proved to be of great moment in his search for a satisfactory dramatic embodiment of the war of orders.

Deirdre, concerned with the final hours of its heroine's life, is a short play whose plot, like that of *On Baile's Strand,* isolates a catastrophic moment in the life of a great figure. The play opens in the one room of a roughhewn guesthouse in a wood; the room is furnished simply, and on a small table are a chessboard and chessmen, a wine flagon, and a loaf of bread. The back part of the room is curtained off; unlit torches line one wall, and against the other stands a brazier with a fire. The setting is completed by a door right, one left, and windows through which trees can be seen. As the action begins, day is turning to evening. Two women with musical instruments crouch by the brazier, and a third enters to tell them what she has heard about this place to which they are evidently strangers. There follows an explication (much in the manner of the first version of *On Baile's Strand*) of the events leading to, and the figures involved in, the coming action. The story told by the musician who enters is that twelve years before the action begins King Conchubar found a beautiful child, Deirdre, being nursed by an old witch, and, though her parents were unknown (there is a suggestion that she may be the offspring of supernatural beings), Conchubar decided to raise her. When she grew older she was so beautiful that Conchubar desired her for his wife, but just before the wedding, Naisi, a young hero and follower of Conchubar, ran off with her. As the musician seems on the verge of revealing that something ominous and connected with this tale is about to happen, Fergus, an old friend to Conchubar, enters and explains that he has been instrumental in the forthcoming reconciliation between the High King and the lovers, who have been wandering as fugitives for six years; Fergus has persuaded Conchubar to forgive and take back the couple who are now about to return. Bustling about to put things in order in the guesthouse (Conchubar is not yet ready to receive them at the palace), Fergus becomes irritated when the musicians doubt the sincerity of Conchubar's forgiveness; what troubles them is the sinister presence of dark-faced men who are seen from time to time passing by the windows. But, at the urging of Fergus, the musicians sing a song to welcome the fugitives; the song concerns the Irish goddess Edain, who is crying inexplicable tears; her mortal lover explains that, since love is always an overflowing excess, "born out of immoderate thought," [73] lovers who cannot laugh must cry. Passion can never be confined, but must express itself either in wild delight or in deep grief.

Too distracted by their own thoughts to hear the song, Deirdre and Naisi enter, and, from their entrance onward, the bright sky progressively darkens, and the room, except when lit briefly by the torches, is dark so that the effect is "either dark amid light or light amid the darkness." The "lighting and the character of the scenery, the straight trees, and the spaces of sky and mountain between them suggest isolation and silence (*Deirdre,* p. 425). The scene is made more ominous for the lovers by the presence of the chessboard, which calls up associations of the story of another hero and his "sea-mew" wife who had played chess years ago on the very board while waiting for death. Furthermore, Conchubar has sent no welcoming messenger. Fergus, however, insists that Conchubar will keep faith and, looking for reasons to be optimistic, points to the flagon and loaf, only to have Naisi find the flagon empty except for cobwebs and the bread moldy. Fergus and Naisi, to reassure themselves, go out to look for messengers, leaving Deirdre to talk to the musicians who, now revealing their grim suspicions, tell her of the bridal bed that Conchubar is preparing with a love charm sewn in its curtains. Deirdre, deeply frightened, calls Naisi back and begs him to leave with her again. But he and Fergus reassure her, Naisi putting his faith in the integrity of a king's word. Unconvinced and desperate, she threatens to destroy her beauty so as

never again to cause dissension and suffering between men.
Made more and more uneasy by Deirdre's doubts and Conchubar's strange silence, Naisi at length decides to confront Conchubar himself. However, a messenger from Conchubar forestalls
this rash move. But the relief that his entrance arouses is short-
lived, for the messenger calls Naisi a traitor and he is the only
one not included in Conchubar's invitation to the palace. Naisi
follows the insolent messenger out in an attempt to get him to
take a challenge to Conchubar, while Fergus, foreseeing calamity, goes for help. Naisi returns quickly, having observed the
dark-faced men surrounding the house. He has the calm of one
who has accepted the worst implications of what he has wit-
nessed and insists that he and Deirdre play chess in imitation
of the long-dead hero and his beloved who had sat at the board
with a noble indifference to their fate. To the demand of
Deirdre for some more positive action, Naisi replies:

> You are in my charge.
> We will wait here and when they come upon us,
> I'll hold them from the doors, and when that's over,
> Give you a cleanly death with this gray edge.　　　(p. 450)

Deirdre argues that she, unlike the "sea-mew" woman, has
hot mortal blood and cannot emulate so calm a pattern. She
then proudly assumes her tragic role, asserting that love is
enough to have made a difficult, lonely life worth living. The
torches are lit, and Deirdre asks the musicians for "no sad
music." They repeat the theme of their earlier song that love
is immoderate and cannot be contained in mortal bounds, and
add a new idea (one already made familiar by the song of the
chorus in the second version of *On Baile's Strand*): that immoderate or heroic love is a longing for immortality that must
destroy mortal life:

> Love is an immoderate thing
> And can never be content,

Till it dip an ageing wing
Where some laughing element
Leaps, and Time's old lanthorn dims.
What's the merit in love play,
In the tumult of the limbs,
That dies out before 'tis day:
Heart on heart, or mouth on mouth,
All that mingling of our breath
When love longing is but drought
For the things come after death?   (p. 454)

Deirdre, however, is too restless and passionate to keep to the game of chess and begs Naisi to kiss her for she knows "nothing but this body" (p. 456).

Conchubar abruptly appears at the door, but remains only an instant; an exultant Naisi runs after him. Left alone, Deirdre takes a knife from one of the musicians and declares her readiness to accept the consequences of her "immoderate" love. Conchubar now enters with the dark-faced men, and Naisi is dragged in, trapped in a net after his headlong pursuit. He is offered his life if Deirdre will come to Conchubar freely; Deirdre, after trying vainly to obtain Conchubar's forgiveness for Naisi and herself, offers herself, but Naisi refuses this compromise. Kneeling to Conchubar in despair, Deirdre takes upon herself the blame for running away with Naisi; but, unseen by Deirdre, Conchubar has sent her lover into the curtained section of the room to be killed. When Deirdre perceives what has happened, she feigns a calm indifference, a fickle willingness to come to Conchubar, if only she might be permitted the chance of performing the last duties for her dead lover. When Conchubar suspects her purposes, she replies scornfully, predicting that her life with him will be wretched. Although he suspects that she may possess a knife, Conchubar is moved by Deirdre's offer to be searched, and he lets her go behind the curtain.

The musicians make a final lament, punctuated by shouting outside the room as Fergus enters with support for the lovers, only to be told by Conchubar that he is too late. Conchubar then flings the curtain back, and it is indeed too late, for Deirdre has killed herself beside Naisi. Conchubar, in a rage of frustration, accuses everyone of betraying him, while outside Fergus' followers are shouting for revenge. At the last, Conchubar recovers himself and his last words defend his actions:

> I have no need of weapons.
> Howl if you will but I, being king, did right
> In choosing her most fitting to be queen
> And letting no boy lover come between. (p. 480)

The plotting of *Deirdre*, like that of the second version of *On Baile's Strand*, defines the play's theme with economy and a logic that drives hard toward the climax. The conflicts, sharp and clear, leave small doubt about motive and, therefore, about the probability of the action. The efficiency of plot is a sure sign of Yeats's mastery of the practical problems of staging.

The characterization in the play is typically simple, though Deirdre is the most complex figure that Yeats had up to this time created. Fergus is throughout only a trusting and generous man who cannot believe bad about anyone until it is too late. Conchubar, whose love has turned through frustration and jealously to a desire for vengeance, is an utterly selfish old man, willing to expend enormous energy and make dishonorable compromises to gain his object. The lovers are exemplifications of a heroic integrity to their own "immoderate" passion. Deirdre is the center of the action because it is she, not Naisi, who has the heroic choice between some self-willed gesture that will preserve her heroic integrity or a debasing submission to another's will. And she is a more complicated figure than Naisi, her passions less able to fit the pattern of heroic calm which Naisi reaches the moment he has realized the hopelessness of their plight. All Deirdre knows is the body, as she says, the human need and desire, whereas Naisi has the warrior's heroic code to reinforce his natural capacity to take things as they are. Somewhat like the Cuchulain of the 1903 version of *On Baile's Strand*, but for dramatically valid reasons, Deirdre is divided against herself, and her last gesture is a triumph over that division, as well as a victory for purely impersonal nobility over the personal selfishness of Conchubar.

Deirdre shares another, more significant characteristic with Cuchulain; she is, like him, the personality who is intended to carry the burden of the war of orders. Her mysterious (possibly supernatural) birth, her being nursed by a witch (possibly a witch in the same sense as in *On Baile's Strand*, that is, a goddess), her destined agony that reaches its climax in a superhuman gesture of sacrifice—all these mark her as a Yeatsian tragic figure: one who rises out of a painfully limiting temporal order to an order beyond ordinary human experience. She is an Apollonian heroine who must suffer from the excess and pride of her superior nature.

The Dionysian framework or "emotion of multitude" that deepens and reinforces her tragic experience was to be provided by the chorus. The musicians of *Deirdre*, though extremely sketchy as characters, do represent a distinct improvement over those in *On Baile's Strand*. They provide the initial exposition, participate in the action, and define the tragic nature of excessive, heroic love as a pursuit of death or of an experience beyond the human. In *Deirdre*, as in *On Baile's Strand*, Yeats attempts to give the heroic fable its natural grounds and a suggestion of something beyond the natural with these wandering musicians. In their first function, they are wandering entertainers who have seen much of life, both peasant and courtly life; in their second function, they are storytellers, poets, whose imaginations participate in a mysterious, superhuman realm of being. They are intended, in short, to serve the function of Blind Man, Fool, and musicians in *On Baile's Strand*.

The scene is kept simple, and it functions dramatically in the action: chessboard, flagon, and bread become credible symbols for the betrayal. The isolation suggested by the setting, as well as the contrasts of light and dark, effectively echoes a human world in which all relationships have been betrayed or destroyed: Fergus' friendship with Conchubar, Naisi's love for Deirdre, and Conchubar's final loss of Deirdre.

Along with the general simplicity of structure, character, and setting, the most notable attribute of the play's style is a sustained bareness of diction, image, and figure. The poetry, though it abounds in natural images that take into account the personal daily self, generally avoids extravagance of expression, even in the choric songs. Two of Deirdre's speeches fairly reveal the range of expression:

> Wanderers like you,
> Who have their wit alone to keep their lives,
> Speak nothing that is bitter to the ear
> At random. If they hint of it at all,
> Their eyes and ears have gathered it so lately
> That it is crying out in them for speech.   (pp. 435–36)

> Oh, do not touch me. Let me go to him—— (*Pause.*)
> King Conchubar is right. My husband's dead.
> A single woman is of no account,
> Lacking array of servants, linen cupboards.
> The bacon hanging—and King Conchubar's house
> All ready too—I'll to King Conchubar's house.
> It is but wisdom to do willingly
> What has to be.   (p. 471)

The blank verse, though bare, is appropriate to the qualities of the characters, who, as they had begun to do in *On Baile's Strand,* speak in their own voices. And the verse bears its burden of symbol unobtrusively. The musicians carry much of the symbolism in the song about Edain, but in a manner perfectly explicable by the context of the play itself. There is no obvious concern in *Deirdre* for the exotic mysteries of occult ritual and symbol.

There is, in fact, a kind of chill bareness in the whole play, out of which the final passion must work itself. And, although the theme of the play is an assertion of the joyous and destructive isolation of all "immoderate," excessive passion, the action seems far from the exuberant Villon-like product of a life founded on daily activities praised in *Discoveries*. Yet neither is *Deirdre* a richly jeweled product of the aesthetic that went into the making of *The Shadowy Waters*. It seems, in fact, to suggest a third kind of drama altogether and its quality evidently troubled Yeats, for he was not satisfied even after revising:

I rewrote from the entrance of Deirdre to her questioning of the musicians, but felt, though despairing setting it right, that it was still mere bones, mere dramatic logic. The principal difficulty with the form of dramatic structure I have adopted is that, unlike the loose Elizabethan form, it continually forces one by its rigour of logic away from one's capacities, experiences and desires, until, if we have not patience to wait for the mood, or to rewrite again and again till it comes, there is rhetoric and logic and dry circumstance where there should be life.[74]

The number of faults in the play surely justify his doubts. In this first version there are serious lapses in plotting and characterization. For instance, the return of Deirdre and Naisi into Conchubar's power could be questioned as to adequacy of motivation; so, too, could Conchubar's permitting Deirdre a last visit to Naisi's body although he suspects her of possessing a knife. Moreover, the chorus, as with the Fool and the Blind Man in the first version of *On Baile's Strand*, sometimes is present only to serve up necessary exposition in a flat-footed and mechanical way. Too, the bareness of style, especially in these expositional parts, sometimes falls to the drabness of metered prose as in the opening words of the first musician:

I have a story right, my wanderers,
That has so mixed with fable in our songs
That all seemed fabulous. We are come by chance
Into King Conchubar's country, and this house

Is an old guesthouse built for travellers
From the seashore to Conchubar's royal house
And there are certain hills among these woods,
And there Queen Deirdre grew.   (*Deirdre,* p. 412)

This might well have been put in prose without loss of effect.

Finally, Yeats's ever-present problem of how to introduce
the supernatural into the tragic drama is not solved in *Deirdre.*
References to the supernatural in the play are peripheral and
ambiguous. While it is fairly certain that Cuchulain is a demi-
god, Deirdre's mysterious birth only *may* have been the result
of supernatural love; the musicians sing, as their counterparts
sang in *On Baile's Strand* (1906), that passionate love is a longing for a life beyond life. But the supernatural in no way overtly
influences the action as it did, say, in *The Shadowy Waters.* As in
Where There is Nothing and *On Baile's Strand,* the spiritual
order, if anything, seems to be the motive force of character or
the intense heroic desire itself, released by opposition from the
natural order. The "immortal passions" of love and hate are
signs of a transcendent reality in the "mortal hearts" of heroes.

This new tendency to internalize the supernatural, though
by no means the result of Yeats's clearly defined aim, is enormously significant, particularly if it is remembered that in the
nineties he had believed human feeling or "mood" to be man's
share in spiritual reality, in the anima mundi. Though after
1900 he strove for a drama of action in an objective world, *On
Baile's Strand* and *Deirdre* seem a return to the older subjec-
tivism, but embodied in a new way. Yeats had, in fact, hit upon
an effective method for presenting the supernatural. By making
it the motive force of character he could solve the problem of
its credibility in the theatre. He had yet to see this possibility
inhering in his own plays. In 1908 he had not—and knew he
had not—achieved a satisfactory dramatic form. In *Deirdre,* as
in *Where There is Nothing* and *On Baile's Strand,* Yeats still
gave his audiences the option of regarding any reference to the

supernatural as merely a convention to explain the psychology of character living beyond the normal pitch of life. Nor did the constant and improving revisions of *Deirdre* give any reason for modifying this judgment.[75]

THE UNICORN FROM THE STARS
AS A CONFESSION OF FAILURE (1908)

The fact is that the ideal marriage of body and spirit had not been consummated in any of the plays. For while Yeats's criticism was praising the natural world of Dickens, his dramatic practice was inevitably leading to a portrayal of the spiritual world of Shelley, but a Shelley now hardened because stripped of dreaminess and vague abstraction. Yeats's awareness of this disparity between his criticism and practice is seen in remarks made in 1909 as he looked back on his dramatic career:

I could not get away, no matter how closely I watched the country life, from images and dreams which had all too royal blood, for they were descended like the thought of every poet from all the conquering dreams of Europe, and I wished to make that high life mix into some rough contemporary life without ceasing to be itself, as so many old books and plays have mixed it and so few modern. . . . I feel indeed that my best share in it [*The Unicorn from the Stars*] is that idea, which I have been capable of expressing completely in criticism alone, of bringing together the rough life of the road and the frenzy that the poets have found in their ancient cellar,—a prophecy, as it were, of the time when it will be once again possible for a Dickens and a Shelley to be born in the one body.[76]

This statement constitutes a confession that the idea in which he believed as critic was not realizable for him as tragic dramatist. The major tragedies of the period between 1900 and 1908, with the exception of *Where There is Nothing*, are closer in spirit to *The Shadowy Waters* than to the richly complex and variegated Elizabethan drama, which Yeats thought had combined Dickens and Shelley in one body. *Where There is Nothing*, the only tragedy in which the Dickensian world is given its full due, was an admitted failure; and it is, ironically enough, to a radical revision of this play, now called *The Unicorn from the Stars,* that the self-criticism quoted above is attached.

The Unicorn from the Stars is actually more than a revision; it is a new play with some elements of the old one remaining. In another comment on its making, Yeats credited Lady Gregory with having provided Dickens' share and admitted his own inability to achieve even the smallest success in bringing common humanity into the ideal of the theatre:

I found myself . . . with an old difficulty, that my words flow freely alone when my people speak in verse, or in words that are like those we put into verse; and so after an attempt to work alone I gave my scheme to her [Lady Gregory]. The result is a play almost wholly hers in handiwork, which I can yet read, as I have just done after the stories of *The Secret Rose,* and recognize thoughts, a point of view, an artistic aim which seem a part of my world. Her greatest difficulty was that I had given her for chief character a man so plunged in trance that he could not be otherwise than all but still and silent, though perhaps with the stillness and the silence of a lamp; and the movement of the play as a whole, if we were to listen to hear him, had to be without hurry or violence. The strange characters, her handiwork, on whom he sheds his light, delight me. She has enabled me to carry out an old thought for which my own knowledge is insufficient and to commingle the ancient phantasies of poetry with the rough, vivid, ever-contemporaneous tumult of the road-side; to create for a moment a form that otherwise I could but dream of, though I do that always, an art that prophesies though with worn and failing voice of the day when Quixote and Sancho Panza long estranged may once again go out gaily into the bleak air. Ever since I began to write I have awaited with impatience a linking, all Europe over, of the hereditary knowledge of the country-side, now becoming known to us through the work of wanderers and men of learning, with our old lyricism so full of ancient frenzies and hereditary wisdom, a yoking of antiquities, a Marriage of Heaven and Hell.[77]

While he still found his "artistic aim" in *The Secret Rose* stories whose "one subject," it must be recalled, was "the war of spiritual with natural order," yet the world of Dickens, of Sancho

Panza, and of the "emotion of multitude" was admittedly beyond him.[78]

In the play, the theme of *Where There is Nothing* is retained; the plot, however, is recast and tightened, and the characters are changed, along with the scene and style. The title itself, as Yeats asserted in a letter to his sister Elizabeth in autumn of 1920, is symbolic; the unicorn "is a private symbol belonging to my mystical order. . . . It is the soul" (*Letters*, p. 662).[79] The symbol had been used in the earlier play with this meaning in mind. Set in a coachmaker's shop of the early 19th century, the action centers on Martin Hearne, who, like his prototype Paul Ruttledge in *Where There is Nothing*, is given to trances. Martin's great project is the building of a marvelous gilded coach with lion and unicorn for its emblem. The play opens with Thomas Hearne, sober, practical shop owner and uncle to Martin, arguing with a priest, Father John, as to the best method of reviving Martin from his latest trance. Much of the argument is expository and suggests the character of Martin as sensitive, bookish, and imaginative beyond the understanding of his uncles, the second of whom, Andrew, enters and reveals himself as somewhat irresponsible and flighty, but held in check by his brother, Thomas. Awakened and left alone with the sympathetic Father John, Martin describes his trance vision; in it unicorns trample vineyards amid laughter, and Martin is commanded to take some action, but he was awakened too soon to hear what specifically he is to do. After the priest leaves, there is an argument between Martin and Thomas over the work, the latter arguing that dreams should be forgotten for the realities of practical necessity. Andrew intervenes, sympathetic with Martin, but misunderstanding him as much as Thomas does. For Andrew is no visionary, but a hedonist who simply doesn't like to work. After this argument some tramps enter the shop to rob it; they are caught and one of them exclaims in surprise, "Destruction on us all!" [80] This cry Martin interprets as the command that he had not received clearly in his dream, and the act closes with Martin sending Andrew and one of the tramps out with money for food and drink in preparation for carrying out the command.

Act II is built on a series of misunderstandings concerning Martin's purposes. Father John truly recognizes them, as he has experienced Martin's vision himself and paid the penalty by being sent into obscurity by orthodox superiors. But Andrew, imagining that Martin's revolt is against authority for the sake of pleasurable self-indulgence, gets everyone drunk. The tramps, mistaking his lion and unicorn design for emblems of England and Ireland respectively, believe that Martin is actually an Irish rebel, Johnny Gibbons, come to lead a raid against the oppressors. Martin, living in his own imagination, prepares to destroy the world so that man can return to the fierce, free innocence of his unfallen state. Thomas, entering upon this wild preparation, is shocked and manhandled when he protests. As the first step to destruction, Martin sets his gilded coach afire, and the mission has begun, each member, however, bent to his own purpose.

The third act begins in a "wild, rocky place," with Martin "lying as if dead"; the tramps around him discuss the burning and looting of a great house in a raid that they have just completed under Martin's heroic leadership. Now, thinking that he is perhaps dead, they have summoned Father John, who has begun to doubt the source of Martin's command: "and how do I know what devil's message it may have been that brought him into that devil's work, destruction and drunkenness and burnings! That was not a message from heaven!" (*Unicorn*, p. 115) Martin stirs and wakens, revealing that he has been again in a state of trance and has discovered an error in his interpretation of the first vision. The command, he has learned, was to reveal, not to reform. The battle that must be fought, he knows now, is within the individual mind. The tramps accuse Martin of betraying them since they cannot begin to comprehend his talk of the "fiery moment" when the individual becomes "part of the host of heaven." Martin, swept up in the vision of the heavenly battle, wanders off. Thomas enters to warn them of the approach of constables who burst in as Martin returns, but are hushed by the others because it is so perfectly obvious that Martin is in some state that deserves reverence from ordinary men. It as at this point that Martin gives, in a somewhat less extravagant tone, Paul Ruttledge's candle sermon (using candles taken from the "great house" and lit by the tramps when they thought him dead). The gist of the sermon is that joy is attainable only when, after all human senses are snuffed out, heaven is attained, a heaven of delightful battle. "Where there is nothing," he concludes, "there is God" (p. 130). The tramps, deeply moved by Martin's words, refuse to give him up to the constables. In the fight that follows, Martin is shot and mutters, as he dies, of ascending Abeignos.[81] The tramps decide to give him a "great burying," and Father John, Thomas, and Andrew, all bemused by the strange turn of events, give their views on the action that has apparently taught nothing but that life is mysterious.

This plot obviously is far tighter than that of *Where There is Nothing*. Treatment of character does not differ substantially from the earlier play, except for the addition of Andrew. Martin and Father John, probably Yeat's creations, have their source in *Where There is Nothing*. Martin is Paul Ruttledge, but considerably less wild and imaginative, has Dickensian parts removed and given to Andrew and the tramps. Father John is a deeper version of Father Jerome from the earlier play, and provides a link between the unworldly hero and the worldly people who surround him but cannot understand him. The style is subdued, even that part belonging clearly to Yeats: Martin's speech, which is less lively and reckless than Paul's. So it is only setting and plot that have undergone radical reworking; the scene has been demodernized and the plot tightened, though by no means made into an inevitable logic of events from beginning to end.

Because so little is really changed in the play, its theme remains the war of spiritual on natural order; but now the intense and extravagant energy that the study of Nietzsche and Blake encouraged is less in evidence than it was in the first version; as a result, references to the supernatural order do not seem so sharply separated from the natural order of events.[82] Yet if *The Unicorn from the Stars,* in sacrificing the reckless energy of *Where There is Nothing,* becomes a more coherent play, it loses the exuberance of the first version. However, more is lost than exuberance, for the play is uninspired and lacking in the passion that informed the first version; *The Unicorn from the Stars* is, ironically, overwhelmed by a Dickens (Lady Gregory) who was, in this effort at least, dull. The play, no more than its first version, represented a solution to embodying the war of orders dramatically. Indeed, *The Unicorn from the Stars* is, in a deep sense, a confession of failure. For, even with the collaboration of one who might have provided a convincing natural order out of which spirit could rise to the tragic gesture, Yeats had not found a means to create a play which answered all his critical requirements for tragedy. In *On Baile's Strand* and, to a lesser degree, in *Deirdre,* he had come far closer to fulfilling his dramatic aims, and yet even these earlier dramas did not fully satisfy him.

Yeats's awareness of his failure as a tragic dramatist must have been made more acute by external circumstances that drove home how far he was from creating an ideal theatre. The implications of the famous riots in 1907 over *The Playboy of the Western World* and the seemingly irresistible triumph at this time of realistic drama in the Abbey Theatre appeared to point clearly to an audience rejection of both heroic and peasant drama; and it was symbolically appropriate that in 1911 he turned the Abbey's management over to Lennox Robinson, a realist dramatist.[83]

However, amid these disappointments and with an acute sense of not having found himself as a tragic dramatist, Yeats was gradually, but with his usual energy, working toward a new dramatic position. Already slightly hinted at in *On Baile's Strand* and more strongly in *Deirdre,* this new position—involving the internalizing of the supernatural as human motive [84] —was neither a return to the aestheticism of the nineties nor an extension of the barren quest for a form that would include Shelley and Dickens in one body. Both of these abandoned positions, however, would share in the third, and be brought into a new and more fruitful relationship to each other. As was typical of his methods, nothing was to be entirely cast off; old views and old ideas remained useful to Yeats because of the deep continuity in his career.

The Development of the Theatre's Antiself, 1908–1938

Though his search for a tragicomic form had proved futile, Yeats's effort was by no means wasted if only because that effort turned up an idea that in the next decade would develop into the solution to his dramatic problems. The idea involved a new and fruitful way of perceiving the relationship between the natural and supernatural and a method for an effective dramatization of that relationship. As early as in "Discoveries" (1906), he had asserted, in defense of the teller of earthy old wives' tales, that such a man

has felt something in the depth of his mind and he wants to make it as visible and powerful to our senses as possible. He will use the most extravagant words or illustrations if they suit his purpose. Or he will invent a wild parable, and the more his mind is on fire or the more creative it is, the less will he look at the outer world or value it for its own sake. It gives him metaphors and examples, and that is all. He is even a little scornful of it, for it seems to him while the fit is on that the fire has gone out of it and left it but white ashes. I

cannot explain it, but I am certain that every high thing was invented in this way, between sleeping and waking, as it were, and
that peering and peeping persons are but hawkers of stolen goods.[1]

This comment, although a slap at the realists, is more than that:
it hints at a new way of seeing the connection between the two
orders of reality. The key word is "metaphor," which is visual-
ized as the link between the depth of mind and the outer world.
Metaphor, in the sense that Yeats obviously meant it (a substitution of one thing for another), implied a different relationship
between natural and supernatural from both that of the aestheticism of the nineties and of the tragicomedy with which he was
presently experimenting. On the one hand, the approach derived from aestheticism excluded the temporal order or filtered
out of it all earthy circumstance until, as in *The Shadowy Waters,* the natural world was as remote and dreamy as any other
elaborately imagined fantasy. Within this fantastic "nature"
symbols were carefully positioned like elements of a code that,
understood intellectually by the initiate, gave the spiritual message to be conveyed by the drama. At best, the result was
precious theatre. On the other hand, the method of tragicomedy
put emphasis on the earthy world of nature, as if to compensate
for its absence in the early plays. The natural world, so Yeats
believed at least until about 1908, would be the ground out of
which supernaturally touched heroism might rise to tragic
stature without violating the sense of probability, for, in keeping human wholeness before the audience, the drama would not
seem to falsify either the claims of the natural or the spiritual.
However, in actual productions based on this view the natural
tended to absorb the spiritual, whose presence could easily
enough be explained away as symbolic of heightened states in
the psychology of characters.

Neither of these approaches satisfied Yeats. A third possibility, already hinted at as early as 1906, lay in the conception
of a vivid natural reality becoming a figurative substitute for

the spiritual reality in the mind's depths. This new possibility, if examined carefully, can be seen to be no more than an ingenious rehabilitation of the older views. Yeats's use of the term "metaphor" retained the nineties' idea of symbolic substitution for spiritual reality, except that metaphor, unlike the nineties' symbol, was not primarily a device to exclude all except occult understanding, but rather a vivid use of nature to express something not directly expressible. Moreover, metaphor, as Yeats used the term, did not pretend to be a way of conceding Dickens some sort of democratic right to a share in tragic drama, but rather implied the necessity of formalizing the natural world until it became the medium through which the audience might pass into a deeper world.

His discovery of a new dramatic possibility in the failure of old ones is another example of the profound continuity in Yeats's development as thinker and playwright. He had, from the outset of his career, believed that reality was subjective, was experienced most wholly by the individual in those intense states of consciousness that he had called "moods" or "intellectual essences"; "moods" for him were the true subject of the tragic dramatist. Yet experiments in both obscure symbolism and in tragicomedy had not produced a drama in which the "depth of his mind" could be effectively revealed on an actual stage. His next move was, typically, not a radical break with his past, but rather a return to it with a clearer sense of what his early views implied for dramatic form. Out of this return was to come the final form of his tragic theatre.

YEATS'S THOUGHT IN TRANSITION

After the setbacks of 1907–8 Yeats became more and more concerned with the relation of individual mind to tragic experience. In 1909 he was groping back to his earliest ideas about the self as the sole source of reality, yet without forgetting his present commitment to the Villon-like personality:

The soul knows its changes of state alone, and I think the motives of tragedy are not related to action but to changes of state. I feel this but do not see clearly, for I am hunting truth into its thicket and it is my business to keep close to the impressions of sense, to common daily life. Yet is not ecstasy some fulfilment of the soul in itself, some slow or sudden expansion of it like an overflowing well? Is not this what is meant by beauty? [2]

The essential question raised by this passage was how the "motives of tragedy" could be kept "close to the impressions of sense" without being "related to action." The question was at least partially answered in his well-known essay, "The Tragic Theatre" (1910); here, in addition to summarizing in the most general sense the elements of his tragic theory that remained unchanged throughout his career, he pushed beyond to a fresh insight into the relation of self to tragedy. Typically, he defined tragedy in Maeterlinckian terms:

Tragic art, passionate art, the drowner of dykes, the confounder of understanding, moves us by setting us to reverie, by alluring us almost to the intensity of trance. The persons upon the stage, let us say, greaten till they are humanity itself. We feel our minds expand convulsively or spread out slowly like some moon-brightened image-crowded sea.[3]

The process of transcendence aroused the tragic emotion, which was not the Aristotelian compound of pity and awe but the more Nietzschean ecstasy that Yeats in "Poetry and Tradition" (1907) had seen as a compound of melancholy and joy, shared by hero and audience, and growing out of the hero's defeat and his mocking defiance of the human condition that defeats him:

Shakespeare's persons, when the last darkness has gathered about them, speak out of an ecstasy that is one half the self-surrender of sorrow, and one half the last playing and mockery of the victorious sword, before the defeated world.[4]

The suffering of the hero is the result of his irremediable defeat; the joy is the result of his capacity to rise above defeat to a "reverie" in which individual suffering is contemplated under the aspect of spiritual reality, the anima mundi. This momentary identification with all humanity through spirit is tragic ecstasy, which audiences must not pity but participate in:

we too were carried [by Synge's "Deirdre of the Sorrows"] beyond time and persons to where passion, living through its thousand purgatorial years, as in the wink of an eye, becomes wisdom; and it was as though we too had touched and felt and seen a disembodied thing.[5]

The problem remained of how to present on an actual stage "the wink of an eye," that place and moment "which is the best that art—perhaps that life—can give" (*Essays*, pp. 295–96), and which Yeats had best defined earlier as "the mingling of contraries . . . perfection of personality, the perfection of its surrender, overflowing turbulent energy, and marmorean stillness . . . the trysting-place of mortal and immortal, time and eternity." [6] In "The Tragic Theatre" he suggested a new way to present this crucial moment on the stage:

If the real world is not altogether rejected, it is but touched here and there, and into the places we have left empty we summon rhythm, balance, pattern, images that remind us of vast passions, the vagueness of past times, all the chimeras that haunt the edge of trance; and if we are painters, we shall express personal emotion through ideal form, a symbolism handled by the generations, a mask from whose eyes the disembodied looks, a style that remembers many masters that it may escape contemporary suggestion; or we shall leave out some element of reality as in Byzantine painting, where there is no mass, nothing in relief; and so it is that in the supreme moment of tragic art there comes upon one that strange sensation as though the hair of one's head stood up.[7]

The conception of mask, while Yeats here applies it to painting, can be translated into literary terms by recalling the significance of metaphor used in the "Discoveries" passage on tragedy. Like metaphor, mask is a convention, a substitution of an artifice for the otherwise inexpressible, in this instance, the

"ideal form" of "personal emotion," "disembodied looks."
Realistic means of embodying nature, whether represented by
the middle-class drawing room or by the human face, cannot
express spirit or ideal form. Metaphor and mask are both
formalized patterns derived from nature; these patterns or conventions do not imitate reality, but rather, by intense abstraction, richly suggest it. The spirit can peer through conventionalized nature without becoming subject to the criterion of probability that determines appropriateness in realistic drama. Not
only does the metaphor-mask convention permit expression of
the otherwise improbable "disembodied looks" of an inner
reality; action is minimized by this convention, which depends
for its effects upon a rhythmic balance of lines, an intense pattern, rich with images that fan out in endless associations. In
conventional structure, action, as Yeats thought of it—a sort of
complicated busyness and involved plotting—could be diminished and, along with action, character, at least as understood
in the traditional sense:

in mainly tragic art one distinguishes devices to exclude or lessen
character, to diminish the power of that daily mood, to cheat or
blind its too clear perception.   (*Essays,* p. 300)

Character, belonging to the limited world of busy action, of
society, or of comedy in some ultimate sense, is incapable of
rising to tragic passion, a state open only to the fluid, free, self-
generating personality that cannot be measured by the standards
applied to social man.

The dramatic structure, then, must subordinate action and
character to the convention of metaphor-mask whose overt
artificiality gives personality the rich "stillness" needed to reveal
its depths, without the distractions of the comic variety and
busyness of the natural world. In short, the natural world, made
static, heightened by artful formalization, directly presents the
spiritual order. That is to say, metaphor or mask utters what it

is a substitute for and what is in no other way expressible to the senses.

At this point some sticky questions arise about a dramatic theory which apparently still assumed a war of orders as the basis of the tragic experience. Doesn't war imply conflict and conflict imply some kind of action? How, then, can a static form present the war of orders? The answer to these questions was implicit in the convention of the metaphor-mask. For this convention is simply the formal presentation of a conflict in the personality itself. It is here that Yeats's obscure remark that "the motives of tragedy are not related to action but to changes of state" becomes clearer. The war of the supernatural with the natural is not to be understood as a battle having its origins in the objective world, but rather as beginning in the hero's self. The dramatic form must, accordingly, reflect this war, which is literally invisible to the objective world. As I have said, in *On Baile's Strand* and, more noticeably in *Deirdre,* the center of tragic conflict shifted from objective to subjective, from the social to the internal. Now, having abandoned his effort at Dickensian objectivity, Yeats saw clearly that such an internalization must be complete. That he understood the direction which his drama had taken and that his theory must now also take is demonstrated by an addition to "The Tragic Theatre" appearing in 1911:

It was only by watching my own plays that I came to understand that this reverie, this twilight between sleep and waking, this bout of fencing, alike on the stage and in the mind, between man and phantom, this perilous path as on the edge of a sword, is the condition of tragic pleasure, and to understand why it is so rare and so brief.[8]

This revelation had been incipient in his own plays always, waiting, so to speak, on his readiness to see clearly its implication: that tragedy was a state of mind and had to be embodied as such on an actual stage.

Now, seeing mind and stage as interchangeable, he could also see how much of his effort of the last decade, though fruitful for his poetry, was misspent on a drama in which he arbitrarily attempted to relate supernatural to natural. If the best plays of this period, *On Baile's Strand* and *Deirdre*, were mainly attempts to deal with tragedy in the objective world of action and society, more telling plays might come if he reached into the mind for the very origin of the tragic emotion. In the depths of the mind occur those initial and most difficult spiritual tests that shape a man's later fate in the objective world. These tests, therefore, had moral priority over all other events, as well as an intensity matchless because consisting of pure passion not diluted by the complexity of or qualified by the limits of the natural world. An ideal tragic drama, then, would embody the war of orders, but a war that took place in a setting that had never before in western theatre been seen on an actual stage. After many years of casting right and left, Yeats was at last aware of what precisely he was trying to dramatize:

Now the art I long for is also a battle, but it takes place in the depths of the soul and one of the antagonists does not wear a shape known to the world or speak a mortal tongue. It is the struggle of the dream with the world—it is only possible when we transcend circumstances and ourself, and the greater the contest, the greater the art.[9]

Yet, though the discoveries of "The Tragic Theatre" carried forward the possibility of a new drama, they did so in a very general sense; details, both philosophical and dramatic, had to be further clarified and put into a usable relationship. This took some years, but when the clarification came it provided the rationale for the rest of Yeats's tragedies and so heralded the conclusion to a long pursuit of a theory and a dramatic form which would satisfy his own standards and create enduring plays. The theoretical conclusion is to be found chiefly in two key essays: "Per Amica Silentia Lunae" (1918), a philosophical statement, and "Certain Noble Plays of Japan" (1916), Yeats's program for an ideal theatre. The dramatic conclusion, in its initial stage, is to be found in *Four Plays for Dancers* (1921), a group of tragedies based upon the ontology developed in "Per Amica" and the dramaturgy outlined in "Certain Noble Plays."

Though "Per Amica" was not the first to be published among the works of this new phase, it may be thought of as having logical priority, since, in Yeats's development as playwright, drama grew out of and tested his philosophical outlook. In a letter to his father written in May of 1917, Yeats explained "Per Amica" as "a kind of prose backing to my poetry." [10] What marked "Per Amica" as novel among Yeats's writings up to this time was not its terminology or ideas—all found with relative frequency in his earlier work—but its overtly theoretical character. Though sharing with his other ontological speculations the tendency to blur assertion by an impressionistic style, "Per Amica" went beyond such earlier efforts because in it Yeats attempted to make systematic categories for the natural and supernatural orders of experience and for the relationships between them. Because of its relative clarity, this essay constitutes the best statement up to the publication of *A Vision* (1925) of the ontology that underlay Yeats's dramatic theory and practice.

In "Per Amica" reality is conceived of as twofold. There is, first, human reality, the anima hominis or the "terrestrial"; this consists of heterogeneous, transient, and incompleted phenomena which are accessible to common human perception and which in turn imply two further characteristics of this sphere: a unique power in its capacity for action and a unique weakness (or evil) in its disintegrative effect on human personality:

All power is from the terrestrial condition, for there all opposites meet and there only is the extreme of choice possible, full freedom. And there the heterogeneous is, and evil, for evil is the strain one upon another of opposites.[11]

There is, second, superhuman reality, the anima mundi or "condition of fire"; this consists of homogeneous, eternal, and completed beings, of timeless and spaceless spirit attainable by those who have endured the discipline of terrestrial divisiveness and have transcended the human sphere. The superhuman is characterized by ecstatic concord with itself and the universe: "in the condition of fire is all music and all rest" (*Essays,* p. 524).

There is a third state, the purgatorial "condition of air," which is the place of the dead in passage between the anima hominis and anima mundi.[12] In this passage the dead become like mirrors, reflecting a borrowed identity from either human or superhuman reality. Souls of the dead, taking memory of heterogeneity from the former or intensity of being from the latter, linger in this condition until they are reborn to human reality or attain superhuman reality. The dead of this state are also the source of the living's instinct; that is, the memory of the souls in "purgatory," in the "condition of air," influences the emotions of the living, to such an extent, in fact, that un-witting individuals in the human sphere are often driven to actions that defy their own interests.[13]

Of these three spheres of reality, the "condition of fire" is the highest, for in it being achieves the ideal state—completion, unity, and an ecstatic harmony, attendant upon its completion, with the universe. To rise from the "terrestrial" condition to the "condition of fire," however, is only possible through suf-fering and defeat. This process of transcendence, leading through agony to an ecstasy Yeats regarded as the most impor-tant experience human life can attain, is so difficult that only heroic figures seek it for their destiny.[14] Heroism is required because the process of transcendence demands exceptional ca-pacity—an inordinate love for the "terrestrial" sphere, but also the prodigious courage to rise, through conflict and defeat, above worldly rewards and punishments. Unlike the saint who comes to perfection by rejecting the world and its defeating conflicts, the hero achieves perfection (his vision of and identifica-tion with the "condition of fire") by embracing the life to which he is committed as man. Out of the world's opposition to his great will, that is, out of the opposition stirred by human limits in collision with a superhuman appetite for experience, arises the tragic war that defeats the hero, yet reveals to him the higher reality while he stands in the ruins of the lower.

In short, because the hero is a creature of the world, he is like other men committed to it, but, because he is a hero, he must strive against the world with his excessively passionate longing for perfection, for Unity of Being, and is necessarily defeated by his own and the world's limits. The very character of the world, of which he is a part, its perpetual divisiveness, makes Unity of Being impossible; thus anima hominis must frustrate any who seek Unity of Being in it. Yet those whose dream of perfection drives them to seek out an image of unity must exert their will against the world, and out of this conflict comes a vision of the true nature of the human sphere, a realization of heroic destiny, and, ultimately, if perhaps for only an instant, achievement of the superhuman Unity of Being. The hero is said then, according to Yeats, to have assumed his "mask," a symbol of unified being, of the personality stripped of all that is idiosyncratic or accidental and now living by choice its proper destiny—perfect and complete selfhood.

The process of conflict, defeat, superhuman vision, and Unity of Being is, for Yeats, tragic, both in the sense that it involves loss of the world with its pleasures and consolations and in the sense that the process transforms that loss into perception of and identification with a state of being incomparably more desirable and consoling than that of the anima hominis at its best. But the tragic process, Yeats believed, must arise out of a heroic choice to accomplish what is most difficult to men without being impossible. However, this choice is not only hard to make because of its forbidding nature; the very range and complication of circumstances make the hero's task of selecting what will lift him to his proper destiny virtually impossible. To help bring him to his heroic destiny, to bring him to his proper choice, there exists in man a daemon, a spirit opposite to his daily self in all respects and, therefore, representing all that the self lacks to be complete:

The Daemon, by using his mediatorial shades [spirits who in the purgatorial state constitute human instinct], brings man again and again to the place of choice, heightening temptation that the choice may be as final as possible, imposing his own lucidity upon events, leading his victim to whatever among works not impossible is the most difficult.   (*Essays*, p. 529)

This daemon provides the link between the "terrestrial" condition and the "condition of fire"; the daemon concept also describes the tragic process and delineates exactly the Yeatsian view of the relationship between natural and supernatural. The spirits, the "mediatorial shades," using men to purge themselves, arouse passions that can lead to suffering and transcendence; it is for this reason that a number of Yeats's last plays take place in "purgatory," the depths of the mind in which life and death, desire and dream, and human will and daemon meet for the conflict that always means suffering and sometimes can result in tragic ecstasy.

The conflict of man and daemon, being in the self, precedes other conflicts and is, therefore, the formative struggle of the hero; its outcome, the heroic choice that issues from it, shapes all future action and is the cause of later conflicts between the hero and the world. The internal nature of the primary daemonic struggle makes it a purely subjective event, taking place in the depths of the individual mind.

If the struggle in the depths of the individual mind, outlined in "Per Amica," is primary in the heroic destiny, certain implications become immediately obvious for the tragic dramatist who seeks to embody the tragedy of heroism. The depths of the mind are not susceptible to realistic presentation. Only an elaborately conventional method could "stage" subjective experience effectively; although the slowly developing conception of metaphor-mask certainly pointed one way to a subjective drama, it did so as yet in very general terms. The specific form that would satisfy all the conditions that Yeats set for an ideal drama was by no means within his grasp during the writing of "The Tragic Theatre." However, a paradigm for such a form did come several years later through a lucky contact and Yeats's own fine instinct for seizing upon what would prove useful to him. The contact was provided by Ezra Pound, who at this period was redacting and editing Ernest Fenollosa's work on the Japanese Nō.[15] The Nō took on such significance for Yeats that he wrote a long commentary on it, "Certain Noble Plays of Japan," [16] with the explicit aim of relating the Japanese form to his own purposes. And in the same year he began a series of plays growing out of his contact with the Nō.

The Nō that Yeats found in the Pound redaction of Fenollosa's work was a courtly form, depending for its effects on a subtle stylization that replaced action with recitation, mimicry, and gesture.[17] Reduced to its basic elements, the typical Nō structure consists of a dialogue followed by a dance, the former either interpreting the latter or preparing for it. The plays often open with the entrance of a traveler who recites a couplet appropriate to the events to come; the traveler, after introducing himself and naming his location, takes a metaphorical journey in a descriptive "Song of Travel." At journey's end (many times at some religious shrine) another character, the protagonist, enters, and a dialogue begins which slowly and painfully reveals the identity of the protagonist, often a ghost haunting the shrine. The first part of the play closes with the protagonist's dance and his entreaty that the traveler pray for his lost soul. After a comic interlude (which, though it frequently pokes fun at the serious play, is not considered part of the Nō structure), the rest of the drama concerns the protagonist's tormented reliving of his last hours on earth, and, if the traveler's prayers are answered, the gradual dimming of the protagonist.

The number of characters of the typical Nō seldom exceeds five, along with a seated chorus of eight to ten who chant to the protagonist's dance. The actors, their speech intermittently supported by the music of a flute and small drums, perform in traditionally fixed positions, their rich and elaborate costumes a contrast to the bare stage whose only permanent property is a pine tree painted on a backdrop; other properties, such as the masks worn by the leading characters, suggest rather than imitate the qualities of the objects that they represent. The speech of the actors is in formal prose, elevated to verse at moments of intense emotion; the language of both prose and verse is full of subtle puns and rich in traditional allusions to places, events, people, and well-known literature. The whole effect of the Nō is one of intense ritual; the intentionally extreme stylization of form puts the whole action at a distance from the audience, while the richness of language, gesture, and costume makes the remoteness vividly immediate.

Beyond these objective characteristics, so acceptable to the author of "The Tragic Theatre," Fenollosa and Pound interpreted the form in a manner that would surely have encouraged Yeats's conviction that the Nō was far less alien to him than was the drama of Shakespeare or Ibsen. Fenollosa was chiefly concerned with the spiritual profundity of Nō, asserting that in the Japanese form the deepest emotions could be

elevated to the plane of universality by the intensity and purity of treatment. Thus the drama became a storehouse of history, and a great moral force for the whole social order of the Samurai. . . . The most striking thing about these plays is their marvelously complete grasp of spiritual being.[18]

The reason for the "complete grasp of spiritual being" characteristic of the form is to be found in its capacity for dramatizing the supernatural:

In no other drama does the supernatural play so great, so intimate a part. The types of ghost are shown to us; we see great characters operating under the conditions of spirit-life.[19]

To Fenollosa the marvel of Nō is that its structure incorporated the whole being—natural and supernatural—with a concentration which is the form's "beauty and power." [20] To this evaluation must be added Pound's assertion that the Nō plays were "at their best . . . an image; that is to say, their unity lives in the image—they are built up about . . . a single moral conviction." [21]

The form itself, and the implications that Fenollosa and Pound discovered in it, seemed superbly suited to realize Yeats's ontological and dramatic theories. In its strict refusal to compromise with realism, its intense concentration of effect, and its frank inclusion of the supernatural, the Nō seemed to Yeats the answer to his long and so far unsuccessful search for an ideal theatre. At the very moment that he had largely clarified his earlier ontological confusions, a dramatic form was made available that, though alien to Western culture, seemed to imply the same philosophical assumptions upon which he had wished to build a drama.

In his commentary "Certain Noble Plays of Japan," Yeats literally translated the Nō into his own terms, bringing it into line with his theories until he had composed a clearly defined program for a new kind of tragic drama:

with the help of Japanese plays "translated by Ernest Fenollosa and finished by Ezra Pound," I have invented a form of drama, distinguished, indirect, and symbolic . . . an aristocratic form.[22]

The invention was to provide the ideal theatre for the spiritual struggle explicitly described in "Per Amica" as taking place within the self, or, as he asserted in "Certain Noble Plays," within "the deeps of the mind" (*Essays*, p. 277). The first step in creating an ideal theatre was for the dramatist to be aware that the Nō form, like the convention of metaphor-mask, was a means of expressing the otherwise inexpressible. Thus, the dramatist must use nature figuratively so that human perception might pass through the objective world into the subjective, there to witness the spiritual struggle:

Our unimaginative arts are content to set a piece of the world as we know it in a place by itself, to put their photographs as it were in a plush or a plain frame, but the arts which interest me, while seeming to separate from the world and us a group of figures, images, symbols, enable us to pass for a few moments into a deep of the mind that had hitherto been too subtle for our habitation. (p. 278)

Subject and plot must be extremely simple, the former drawing upon the folk legends or myths out of which arise universal emotions, the latter centering on the kind of meeting frequently found in such legends or myths—between traveler and supernatural figure. He found in his Japanese model that the

adventure itself is often the meeting with ghost, god, or goddess at some holy place or much-legended tomb; and god, goddess, or ghost reminds me at times of our own Irish legends and beliefs, which once, it may be, differed little from those of the Shinto worshipper.
(p. 287)

The plot must not develop rapidly, but with a slow and intense rhythm culminating in a dance. Remarking this quality in the Japanese form, Yeats wrote:

At the climax instead of the disordered passion of nature there is a dance, a series of positions and movements which may represent a battle, or a marriage, or the pain of a ghost in the Buddhist purgatory. . . . The interest is not in the human form but in the rhythm to which it moves, and the triumph of their art is to express the rhythm in its intensity.   (p. 285)

The stage must put the action amid the audience so that the strangeness of the fabulous plot will seem closer to human experience. Yeats described his experience watching a Japanese dancer perform:

In the studio and in the drawing-room alone, where the lighting was the light we are most accustomed to, did I see him as the tragic image that has stirred my imagination. There, where no studied lighting, no stage-picture made an artificial world, he was able, as he rose from the floor, where he had been sitting crossed-legged, or as he threw out an arm, to recede from us into some more powerful life. (p. 277)

Yeats, here revealing an independence of his model, would go beyond what Japanese tradition permitted, he would take the play off the specially built stage and into more intimate surroundings. The purpose of this move, as his comment suggests, is to leave as much as possible to the imagination, freeing it from the distracting limitations of realistic verisimilitude. For the same reason, setting and properties must be kept to the minimum, their function being to suggest locale or objects in the most general sense.

Perhaps the most important property of Nō for Yeats was the mask, a device to which he attached philosophical importance beyond its dramatic function:

A mask never seems but a dirty face, and no matter how close you go is yet a work of art; nor shall we lose by stilling the movement of the features, for deep feeling is expressed by a movement of the whole body. In poetical painting and in sculpture the face seems the nobler for lacking curiosity, alert attention, all that we sum up under the famous word of the realists "vitality." It is even possible that being is only possessed completely by the dead, and that it is some knowledge of this that makes us gaze with so much emotion upon the face of the Sphinx or of Buddha. (p. 280)

The significance of the mask then is twofold: first, it suggests the superhuman; second, as a stylization or abstraction of nature, it reduces human character to some essential quality. For the depths of the mind cannot be represented by the complex tragicomic characterizations of Shakespeare or the psychologically accurate characterizations of Ibsen, because the struggle within the mind is the result of a conflict between spiritual qualities, intense states of being that underlie all complexity of character. In fact, as he began to do in "The Tragic Theatre," Yeats abandons the traditional idea of character altogether in favor of suggestive patterns revealed in the mask; he praises Japanese dramatists who:

In neglecting character which seems to us essential in drama, as do their artists in neglecting relief and depth, whether in their paint- ings or in arranging flowers in a vase in a thin row . . . have made possible a hundred lovely intricacies.   (p. 290)

This extreme stylization of character extends to the chorus, which "describes the scene and interprets their [the principals'] thought, [but] never becomes as in the Greek theatre a part of the action" (p. 285). The chorus functions rather as a buffer between the fabulous event and the audience.

As both Fenollosa and Pound had observed, style must be primarily a matter of some single effect arising out of a subtle unity of overall structure brought to harmony by a single, sus- tained metaphor: "I wonder am I fanciful in discovering in the plays themselves . . . a playing upon a single metaphor, as de- liberate as the echoing rhythm of line in Chinese and Japanese painting" (p. 289). Augmented by subdued musical accompani- ment, the speech must be as subtle in its traditional allusions as in diction and rhythm:

A poetical passage cannot be understood without a rich memory, and like the older school of painting appeals to a tradition, and that not merely when it speaks of "Lethe's Warf" or "Dido on the wild seabanks" but in rhythm, in vocabulary; for the ear must notice slight variations upon old cadences and customary words, all that high breeding of poetical style where there is nothing ostentatious, nothing crude, no breath of parvenu or journalist.   (p. 281)

Above all, style in its most general sense must keep its imagina- tive distance against "a pushing world":

Verse, ritual, music, and dance in association with action require that gesture, costume, facial expression, stage arrangement must help in keeping the door.   (pp. 277–78)

However, keeping a proper distance allows a vivid immediacy, for a stage set in a drawing room puts the fabulous action in the center of ordinary human life; moreover, the choric buffer and the very brilliance of style bring the distant fable to a high vividness.

Finally, the supernatural or spiritual element is to be incorporated in the form, not as something to be assessed on some realistic scale of probability but as part of the dramatic convention itself, no more out of place or arbitrarily introduced than the mask or the chorus. The meeting of man and ghost, of human and daemon, is part of the convention, itself a "given" that must be accepted as a whole and be judged by its coherence and vividness.

Such, in substance, was Yeats's invention, and yet he had no more created an entirely new form than he had adopted the Japanese Nō. He had, rather, discovered in Nō a catalyst which brought his own experiments to their logical conclusion. The Yeatsian Nō was implicit in earlier plays and was, notably in *Deirdre,* becoming more and more explicit in his work.[23] In fact, by 1919, the date of his essay "A People's Theatre," the Nō was wholly assimilated into his critical views as the ideal form in a hypothetical tradition that Yeats imagined for the subjective drama:

I desire a mysterious art, always reminding and half-reminding those who understand it of dearly loved things, doing its work by suggestion, not by direct statement, a complexity of rhythm, colour, gesture, not space-pervading like the intellect but a memory and a prophecy: a mode of drama Shelley and Keats could have used without ceasing to be themselves, and for which even Blake in the mood of *The Book of Thell* [*sic*] might not have been too obscure.[24]

He now envisaged the "mysterious art" entirely in terms of the "Per Amica" conflict of opposites: natural with supernatural, self with daemon or antiself, objective with subjective. Because he was a subjective dramatist living in an objective era, he had to discover his form in opposition: "I seek, not a theatre but the theatre's anti-self" (*Controversies,* p. 215). It was, indeed, in the "theatre's anti-self" that Yeats ended his long quest for a tragic dramatic form; for, though he was to experiment with dramatic structure to the end of his career, every play following *At the Hawk's Well* was in some degree influenced by the conception of the ideal theatre delineated in "Certain Noble Plays of Japan"; in fact, most of these plays closely follow in form the Yeatsian Nō described there.

The quest for dramatic form ended only when Yeats thought that he had solved the problem troubling him from the first plays of his career: that is, how to introduce the supernatural seriously and effectively on an actual stage. His solution was to make the supernatural one dramatic element in a total dramatic convention. Since the "theatre's anti-self" displayed a spiritual struggle in the depths of the mind, the supernatural could participate in the metaphorical representation of this struggle with no strain. Such a solution to the old problem made Yeats's efforts in ornate symbolism and tragicomedy seem heavy-handed by comparison. It remains now to see how successfully the new theory was actually realized in the later tragedies.

THE PRACTICE: AT THE HAWK'S WELL (1916)

In his brief introduction to *At the Hawk's Well,* written and performed in 1916, Yeats affirms his commitment to the Nō model, and, unequivocally rejecting his tragicomic theory of the preceding decade, seems to echo his nineties' attitudes toward the drama:

Whatever we lose in mass and in power we should recover in elegance and in subtlety. Our lyrical and our narrative poetry alike have used their freedom and have approached nearer, as Pater said all the arts would if they were able, to "the condition of music"; and if our modern poetical drama has failed, it is mainly because, always dominated by the example of Shakespeare, it would restore an irrevocable past.[25]

Though the allusion to Pater might suggest a harking back to *The Shadowy Waters,* Yeats's awareness that dependence on the past was fatal indicates that he was perfectly conscious that the dramatist must create in and for his own age, even if he opposes it. Lacking both an opaque body of occult symbols and any suggestion of comedy, *At the Hawk's Well* no more indicates a return to *The Shadowy Waters'* aesthetic than it suggests merely one more compromise with realistic objectivity.

The subject of the new play was one of Cuchulain's adventures, but not one of the great events in the hero's life available in the records of his deeds. Yeats, aiming to penetrate into the depths of the mind, ignored the hero's wonderful feats performed in the objective world and invented, instead, an incident to represent an event in the subjective world of individual spirit, the meeting of mortal and immortal that, taking place in Cuchulain's youth, shapes his later destiny as hero.[26] The action of *At the Hawk's Well* concerns the protagonist's spiritual birth as a tragic hero and has a temporal priority to Cuchulain's later combats with the objective world.

The plot is simple to the point of bareness. On a high, wind-swept, barren place an Old Man is waiting beside a dry well under a leafless hazel. He has been waiting there for years, and each time the well has filled with immortalizing waters he has been too late to drink; so he has wasted his life there, his sole company being a dumb girl, the Guardian of the well. As the play begins, the young Cuchulain comes in search of the waters of immortality, whose existence rumor had brought to his ear. Despite the Old Man's jealous insistence that the hero leave the well, the latter elects to wait by it, depending upon his usual luck for a favorable turn of events. The well suddenly gives a sign that it may fill, and, as usual, the Old Man is foiled. This time he is put to sleep by the Guardian who, emitting the cry of a hawk, has begun a dance which quickly bemuses Cuchulain; when she runs off, the hero pursues her, leaving the well as it fills up. The Guardian is infused, as the Old Man has warned she would be, with the being of the goddess of the place, who earlier, in the form of a hawk, had tried to drive Cuchulain away as he climbed toward the well. His pursuit of the Guardian frustrated, the hero returns and the Old Man awakens; they find the well once more all but dry. For his pains Cuchulain is cursed by the supernatural power that he has directly challenged, and the Old Man predicts a tragic destiny for him. The curse begins to work immediately, for the fierce women to whom the hawk goddess is sacred have been roused to battle against the intruder. It is their queen, Aoife, who later bears Cuchulain's son and trains him for the mortal combat that constitutes the subject of *On Baile's Strand*.

The scene in which this action occurs is bare except for a blue square of cloth representing the well and a patterned screen behind the stage. The musicians, whose comments bracket the action, bring out, unfold, and refold a cloth at the beginning and end of the play.

Characters are stripped of all attributes except those that contribute to the action; this simplification is enhanced by Yeats's stage direction that the actors' movements should suggest those of marionettes.[27] The chorus of three musicians has several functions, the first being to fill the bare stage with an image of the world in which the main action will take place. Thus, the opening chant, sung by the First and Second Musicians as they unfold the square of cloth, summons up the scene for the mind's eye before which the spiritual conflict will take place:

> I call to the eye of the mind
> A well long choked up and dry
> And boughs long stripped by the wind.   (*Well,* p. 208)

In a few simple lines they prepare for the action and introduce dry well and bare tree which, along with the hawk, will merge into the complex of images that constitute what Yeats had noted as an essential characteristic of the Japanese Nō, the "playing upon a single metaphor" that binds the whole form. In the same imaginative creation of scene, the chorus introduces the hero:

And I call to the mind's eye
Pallor of an ivory face,
Its lofty dissolute air,
A man climbing up to a place
The salt sea wind has swept bare.   (p. 208)

The last line completes the scene in which the spiritual reality emblemized by well, tree, and Guardian is set.

    Refolding the cloth (after the Guardian has entered and crouched by the well), the two musicians continue their description of the bleakness, but now generalize from the bare scene to all life:

What were his life soon done!
Would he lose by that or win?
A mother that saw her son
Doubled over a speckled shin,
Cross-grained with ninety years,
Would cry, "How little worth
Were all my hopes and fears
And the hard pain of his birth!"   (p. 208)

To this general assertion of the futility of a mortal life subject to old age, the musicians add a second concerning the divided nature of human desire:

The heart would be always awake,
The heart would turn to its rest.   (p. 209)

This gnomic assertion states the human predicament in the world of the play; that is, the melancholy brevity of all human life makes an initial choice imperative to all men: either to quest passionately and heroically for some sort of meaningful if dangerous destiny, perhaps immortality, or to seek the peace of mediocre withdrawal, insensitivity, or death itself. The choice is open to all men; both alternatives are compelling and divide not only men from men but men from themselves. In these two lines, then, the choices that circumscribe the possibilities of the protagonist are implied.

Another choric function emerges after a slightly more detailed description of the scene. The Second Musician, affected
by the strangeness of what is summoned up, cries, "I am afraid
of this place" (p. 209), suddenly crystallizing the normal human
response to the strangeness of the desolation pictured; here, the
chorus serves as buffer between the fabulous and the audience.
A final function given the chorus is that of interpreting the
actions of the principals at moments when the latter cannot
speak. When the Guardian's dance puts a spell on Cuchulain,
the First Musician cries: "The Madness has laid hold upon him
now,/ For he grows pale and staggers to his feet" (p. 217). The
chorus, then, creates the scene, prepares for the action, explains
or generalizes on both, and naturalizes the incredible, all without entering the action. In all its functions it operates as a human imagination given special insight into the depths of the
mind, yet reacting to the tragic struggle there with a horror
springing from a normal sense of life that exists somewhere
between the heroism of Cuchulain and the abjectness of the
Old Man.[28] Thus, the musicians' last song is the judgment on
the heroic man by those whose "heart would turn to its rest":

> Come to me, human faces,
> Familiar memories;
> I have found hateful eyes
> Among the desolate places,
> Unfaltering, unmoistened eyes.
>
> .   .   .   .
>
> "The man that I praise,"
> Cries out the empty well,
> "Lives all his days
> Where a hand on the bell
> Can call the milch cows
> To the comfortable door of his house.
> Who but an idiot would praise
> Dry stones in a well?"
>
>   (p. 219)

The character of the Old Man is as precisely functional as
that of the chorus. Everything about him is the reverse of the

heroic. His very age sets him in opposition to Cuchulain, not only because of the latter's youth but also because the heroic life is characteristically associated with youth. Moreover, the Old Man's quest for the well is not heroic, but motivated by a personal greed for longevity, a greed that physical decay has reduced to a carping pettiness of spirit:

> Why don't you speak to me? Why don't you say:
> "Are you not weary gathering those sticks?
> Are not your fingers cold?" You have not one word,
> While yesterday you spoke three times. You said:
> "The well is full of hazel leaves." You said:
> "The wind is from the west." And after that:
> "If there is rain it's likely there'll be mud."
> Today you are as stupid as a fish,
> No, worse, worse, being less lively and as dumb.   (pp. 210–11)

Nor can his suffering in the quest lead to transcendence, for he is not only petty and jealous of the true hero but also afraid of the pain necessary for heroism.[29] When Cuchulain asserts that he will keep himself awake to be ready for the well's filling, the Old Man replies, thinking of himself: "No, do not pierce it, for the foot is tender,/ It feels pain much" (*Well*, p. 214). It is characteristic that he is terrified when the Guardian is possessed by daemonic power and that, when she dances, he should sink into an ignominious sleep.

Cuchulain possesses all that is lacking in the Old Man: youth, strength, generosity, courage, and recklessness—in sum, his heroic "luck" that makes him the gods' choice for the working out of their obscure wills. The hero reveals his relationship with them unwittingly as he describes his approach to the well:

> As I came hither
> A great grey hawk swept down out of the sky,
> And though I have good hawks, the best in the world
> I had fancied, I have not seen its like. It flew
> As though it would have torn me with its beak,
> Or blinded me, smiting with that great wing.
> I had to draw my sword to drive it off,

And after that it flew from rock to rock.
I pelted it with stones, a good half-hour,
And just before I had turned the big rock there
And seen this place, it seemed to vanish away.
Could I but find a means to bring it down
I'd hood it. (p. 214)

The hostility of the hawk and Cuchulain's urge to capture it are inextricably linked, as the supernatural will is linked with the heroic human desire for superhuman experience. This hawk, no ordinary bird, is, according to the Old Man, "the Woman of the Sidhe herself" who flits "upon this mountain-side,/ To allure or to destroy" (pp. 214–15). The twofold nature of the goddess —to allure and to destroy—is the counterpart of the twofold development of the hero—to desire the superhuman and to be defeated in that desire by human limitations. Cuchulain's quest for the superhuman (hawk woman and well water) are defeated, but the very defeat gives him his tragic experience—his heroic character and fate,[30] both summoned up in his final words and gesture:

> I will face them.
> (*He goes out, no longer as if in a dream, but*
> *shouldering his spear and calling*)
> He comes! Cuchulain, son of Sualtim, comes! (*Well*, p. 218)

The daemonic spirit that brings Cuchulain to his destiny, the Guardian of the well, becomes an active agent in the play only when possessed by the goddess; then her dance functions to emblemize in its hawklike gesture the presence of the supernatural, its remote beauty and immediate power. Reinforcing the quality of this presence, the First Musician watching the dance cries out:

> O God, protect me
> From a horrible deathless body
> Sliding through the veins of a sudden. (p. 217)

The simplicity of the character of the Guardian appropriately represents the Unity of Being possessed by immortals, in contrast to the relative complexity of humans who live in a divisive world of nature. It is her beautiful and powerful being that draws Cuchulain to her in the ecstasy of trance and finally gives him the "wisdom" that "must live a bitter life" (p. 219).

The bare functionalism of character has its analogue in the play's style. Because the characterization is so narrowed, the verse of both chorus and principals is less complex than that of *Deirdre,* although *At the Hawk's Well* reveals a fairly wide range of human feeling. But if one compares Deirdre's richly varying reaction to her situation with the Old Man's to his, the difference becomes plain:

> I only should be punished.
> The very moment these eyes fell on him,
> I told him; I held out my hands to him;
> How could he refuse? At first he would not—
> I am not lying—he remembered you.
> What do I say? My hands?—No, no, my lips—
> For I had pressed my lips upon his lips—
> I swear it is not false—my breast to his;
> Until I woke the passion that's in all,
> And how could he resist? I had my beauty.
> You may have need of him, a brave, strong man,
> Who is not foolish at the council-board,
> Nor does he quarrel by the candle-light
> And give hard blows to dogs. A cup of wine
> Moves him to mirth, not madness.
>
> What am I saying?
> You may have need of him, for you have none
> Who is so good a sword, or so well loved
> Among the common people. You may need him,
> And what king knows when the hour of need may come?
> You dream that you have men enough. You laugh.
> Yes; you are laughing to yourself. You say,
> "I am Conchubar—I have no need of him."

You will cry out for him some day and say,
"If Naoise were but living"——

   Where is he?
Where have you sent him? Where is the son of Usna?
Where is he, O, where is he?[31]

Compared with Deirdre's passionate and complex speech, the
Old Man's seems relatively subdued and simple:

It was her mouth, and yet not she, that cried.
It was that shadow cried behind her mouth;
And now I know why she has been so stupid
All the day through, and had such heavy eyes.
Look at her shivering now, the terrible life
Is slipping through her veins. She is possessed.
Who knows whom she will murder or betray
Before she awakes in ignorance of it all,
And gathers up the leaves? But they'll be wet;
The water will have come and gone again;
That shivering is the sign. O, get you gone,
At any moment now I shall hear it bubble.
If you are good you will leave it. I am old,
And if I do not drink it now, will never;
I have been watching all my life and maybe
Only a little cupful will bubble up.   (*Well,* p. 215)

The passage, fairly typical for the play, is characterized by
a rhetorical heightening through balance and repetition of word
and of phrase; the effect is almost dreamlike. What distinguishes this effect from that of the plays of the nineties, particularly *The Shadowy Waters,* is a clarity of logic and simple,
almost idiomatic diction. These qualities make the speech of
At the Hawk's Well at once remote in tone and immediate in its
nearness to what it describes. This twofold effect is reinforced
by the contrast of the blank verse spoken by the principals with
the verse of the choric musicians. The principals' speech is
based upon traditional blank verse conventions which elevate

the action out of which that speech grows. Except at the moment of the climactic dance where the choric speech is briefly blank verse, both the song and speech of the musicians are chants, varying from one to four stresses to the line; their almost ballad-like quality enforces the human reaction they are meant to express. Compare the Old Man's gravely formal utterance at finding the well water come and gone again with the apparent simplicity of the musicians' song:

> The accursed shadows have deluded me,
> The stones are dark and yet the well is empty;
> The water flowed and emptied while I slept.
> You have deluded me my whole life through,
> Accursed dancers, you have stolen my life.
> That there should be such evil in a shadow!   (pp. 217–18)

> Folly alone I cherish,
> I choose it for my share;
> Being but a mouthful of air,
> I am content to perish;
> I am but a mouthful of sweet air.   (p. 219)

Yeats, typically, summed up his use of the two styles in historical terms:

There was something in what I felt about Deirdre, about Cuchulain, that rejected the Renaissance and its characteristic metres, and this was a principal reason why I created in dance plays the form that varies blank verse with lyric metres. When I speak blank verse and analyze my feelings, I stand at a moment of history when instinct, its traditional songs and dances, its general agreement, is of the past. . . . The contrapuntal structure of the verse . . . combines the past and present.[32]

The verse style, though bare, is enriched by a symbolic element that pervades the whole play; scene, action, property, character, as well as speech—all are symbolic in that they combine to serve as metaphor or mask for the otherwise inexpressible spiritual conflict. Yet, unlike the symbols of *The Shadowy*

Waters, those of *At the Hawk's Well* are explained by the action
and seldom seem arbitrary or require special knowledge for
their comprehension. Compare the recondite symbolism of

> but love is made
> Imperishable fire under the boughs
> Of chrysoberyl and beryl and chrysolite,
> And chrysoprase and ruby and sardonyx,[33]

with the self-explanatory symbolism of

> You can, it may be
> Lead me to what I seek, a well wherein
> Three hazels drop their nuts and withered leaves,
> And where a solitary girl keeps watch
> Among grey boulders. He who drinks, they say,
> Of that miraculous water lives for ever.[34]

Symbols like the well and tree are so much a part of the common
literary tradition that they no longer seem chosen for their
obscurity; or they come naturally out of human experience.
The primary meaning of such symbols is, therefore, clear and
directly related to the action; any esoteric significance that
Yeats attached to them is secondary and unnecessary for intelligent comprehension of the play.

   Yeats believed that the aesthetic aim of the Nō was to
create a unity of form close to "the condition of music," in
which all the elements illuminated each other by achieving a
wholeness of impression. The unity was chiefly attained through
a pervading cluster of images or a single recurring metaphor
which linked all the other elements of the play. In *At the
Hawk's Well* the binding metaphor is composed of three recurring images—tree, well, and hawk—which serve to link all the
elements of the play. The tree is a natural emblem, suggesting
in its various states the stages of growth, fulfillment, and decay
of all living creatures. Moreover, the hazel tree signifies wisdom
in Celtic mythology.[35] In the play this tree, its boughs stripped

bare of leaves by the wind, represents, among other things, the barren or "bitter wisdom" commented on at the end of the play. The well and its waters are traditional symbols in literature and legend and their meaning is made clear in the play. Cuchulain's failure to drink from the well entitles him to the tree's sad wisdom—the tragic limits of mortality—that the tree, deciduous and subject like men to age, offers those who quest for the immortalizing waters.[36] The significance of the hawk is made perfectly clear in the context of the play; its natural Unity of Being (animals do not suffer from human divisiveness), its fierceness, and its isolation all make it the appropriate embodiment of the supernatural, the Genius of the dry well and leafless tree set on a mountain waste. The hawk, then, possesses natural qualities that lend themselves to the play's symbolic meaning.[37]

Hardly less important than the binding metaphor are other symbolic elements that work to unify the dramatic structure. Masks are a symbolic stage convention actively functioning within the larger convention of the whole drama. In the play masks are worn by Cuchulain and the Old Man, types participating in a spiritual drama. The function of the masks is to simplify the principals to some essential and intense quality defined by the fate that formulates itself in this tragic moment of choice.[38] The faces of the musicians and the Guardian of the well are painted to resemble masks; the musicians are not primarily participants in the action but human observers, and the Guardian is also human until daemonically possessed. Because the musicians require a more flexible expression to indicate a wide range of normal human reaction to the tragic moment, their faces are merely painted to resemble masks; the Guardian's face is also painted because she must be able to undergo the sudden and climactic change from natural to supernatural. The mask (or lack of it) defines identity and relationship without the need of elaborate obtrusive exposition. The stillness of the carved face, remarked by Yeats in "Certain Noble Plays," combined with its vividness, creates a convention resembling the larger one of the play; both conventions allow the spirit to come through some intensely patterned, remotely strange yet vivid structure—the Yeatsian metaphor-mask which expresses the remote through a medium that is itself powerfully immediate. Like all other symbolic elements in the play, the mask achieves its meaning only as part of the dramatic whole.

The aesthetic economy of this whole is perhaps its most impressive quality: even the stage properties are symbolic because they are appropriate to the world of the play. In the "theatre's anti-self" the depths of the mind constitute an enormous concentration of meaning for it is necessary that the whole spiritual reality, when dramatically revealed, make perfect sense; nothing can be gratuitous where ontological essences themselves are the natural participants in the drama. With the perfect matching of tragic theory and form in *At the Hawk's Well* Yeats for the first time in his career had achieved an effective embodiment of his theme. The making of the heroic self, the main theme of the play, is cleanly delineated by all the elements. The scene, at once actual and symbolic, perfectly accommodates the action, which moves clearly and logically from the coming of the Young Man to his defeat; that, in turn, leads to his heroic fate, summed up by the Old Man in his description of the "curse" for those who gaze into the "unmoistened eyes" of the immortal:

> That curse may be
> Never to win a woman's love and keep it;
> Or always to mix hatred in the love;
> Or it may be that she will kill your children,
> That you will find them, their throats torn and bloody,
> Or you will be so maddened that you kill them
> With your own hand.[39]

This passage is a prophecy of Cuchulain's future.[40] The choric musicians, echoing their earlier line about the heart that quests

for heroic fate and the heart that turns to peace, describe Cuchulain's fatal choice of the goddess instead of the waters of immortality, of supernatural intensity of natural long life and perhaps
abundance:

> He has lost what may not be found
> Till men heap his burial-mound
> And all the history ends.
> He might have lived at his ease,
> An old dog's head on his knees,
> Among his children and friends.[41]

The plot, clearly defining this theme, leads to the hero's acceptance of his fate, after the daemonic power has brought him to
his choice.

Character, far from being personification conforming to the
requirements of monolithic allegory, functions as part of a
whole; that whole is the total mental experience of the hero—a
complex of essential and opposing qualities in his nature or of
stylized simplifications of actual human types all of which find
their place in human nature because it is heterogeneous and
divisive. In the play, these types, from hero to coward, work
toward a clarity of relationship that defines the whole mind in
the midst of the tragic experience.

The style, both in the broad and narrow senses, is emi-
nently suited to express the inner combat of man with his daemon; action is kept at an aesthetic distance with the dreamy,
ritualistic remoteness in the speech of the characters, yet given
vivid immediacy by the bare directness of diction and figure in
both the heightened speech of the principals and the human
voice of the chorus. The sense of immediacy is sharpened by
the music of harp, flute, drum, and gong which accompany the
action at high moments (particularly at the opening and closing
of the play and during the dance of the Guardian). The music
is introduced for the same purpose as all other elements: to
create clearly and simply a vivid, elevated wholeness of effect.

Yeats's explanation of his choice of instruments confirms this purpose:

In order to apply to the music the idea of great simplicity of execution underlying the whole spirit of the performance, it was necessary to use instruments that anyone with a fair idea of music could learn in a few days.[42]

The costumes, in line with the whole style of the play, simplify and heighten: each character is clothed in a dress that marks him off as a participant of types or essences. Thus the Guardian is "entirely covered by a black cloak," [43] her dark garb emblematic of her mysterious nature; Cuchulain appropriately glitters in gold apparel; [44] and the Old Man is pictured in *Four Plays for Dancers* in a tattered gown that expresses the failure of his long vigil.[45] Again, the aim is to bring the least detail into clear relationship with the whole.

But perhaps the most significant achievement of the play is that it accommodates the supernatural with no strain on dramatic structure. The war of spiritual on natural—an internal combat in the depths of the mind—is externalized through the metaphor-mask, a conventionalized fable, static by traditional dramatic standards but rich in gesture, pattern, rhythm, and vivid speech, all made credible by their relation with the whole. Unlike the doubtful vision of Paul Ruttledge in *Where There is Nothing*, the Guardian's supernatural possession, symbolized by her dance, arises out of the world of the play; credibility here must be assessed in terms of that world, itself a metaphorical representation of a locale that cannot be shown by literal adherence to objective reality. The supernatural thus becomes an actual part of the play's landscape, that "given" which, once the dramatic convention is accepted, proves to be as functional as mask, actor, or costume.

Yet, to grant all these unquestionable merits is not to claim that *At the Hawk's Well* is without serious weaknesses. As a first experiment it suffers perhaps from an overzealousness to exclude anything that might have seemed excessive to the total convention of the play. With the Japanese Nō such formal purity is relieved by the richness of poetic allusion, by traditional associations connected with scene and action. The courtly audience in Japan could be expected to catch all such subtleties, in fact, would demand them from the playwright; in this way audience imagination enriches the play itself at the cue of an allusion, until the convention blossoms into something far more emotionally ample than the literal action could communicate. *At the Hawk's Well* could not be expected to achieve this blossoming because Yeats, even among the highly select audience of the rich drawing room, was not able to find auditors sufficiently literate and experienced in catching subtle changes of inflection that echoed literary classics. Yet, as if indifferent to the need for a compensating device, he failed to compromise with his audience; he even went beyond the Japanese dramatists in excluding allusion and richness of reference, so that what remains is an action that, while not prosaic, seems flat. For this reason *At the Hawk's Well* seems coldly unsuggestive, lacking in depth of feeling, a result of the "mere economy" [46] that Yeats thought he had escaped.

Later, though, he registered his own dissatisfaction in the terse comment: "I felt, however, during the performance of 'The Hawk's Well' . . . that there was much to discover." [47] What he had to discover was how to make the combat between man and daemon more comprehensible to the feelings. The combat in *At the Hawk's Well* is at such an abstract level that audience sympathy is not sufficiently aroused. For, though the conflict in the depths of the mind is a combat of essential characteristics or types, the participants must stir sympathy or antagonism sufficiently to command the attention of an audience. Because the Guardian is so remote a figure that she hardly seems adequate opposition for the hero, Cuchulain's choice to assume his destiny appears mechanical, almost automatic. The depths

of the mind revealed in *At the Hawk's Well* are somewhat pale
and rigid. Earl Miner goes further, asserting that "the verse is
not sufficiently dramatic, the play lacks a real beginning, middle, and end, and the place of Cuchulain in the play is somewhat uncertain." [48] The first criticism is certainly accurate,
though the second and third are wide of the mark, for the structure of the play is clear; so too is Cuchulain's position in the
play. Yet *At the Hawk's Well* is by no means a completely satisfying drama that could produce, as ideal tragedy should, that
"lofty emotion" that one feels "most alive." [49]

Although *At the Hawk's Well* was only a beginning, an
impressive first try at a new form, it was clear to Yeats that he
had found what he wanted:

I need a theatre; I believe myself to be a dramatist; I desire to show
events and not merely to tell of them. . . . I am certain . . . I have
found out the only way the subtler forms of literature can find
dramatic expression.[50]

What his first experiment taught him is revealed in his next
plays, which achieve all that *At the Hawk's Well* did and often
more: the richness and depth that the first experiment lacked.

RANGE OF DRAMATIC EXPRESSION: THE GREAT CYCLE

Both the apparent eccentricity of his ontology and his narrowly defined conception of the Nō form might well have reduced Yeats's possibilities as a tragic dramatist to the obviously
limited expression of *At the Hawk's Well*. All seven of the
tragedies written in this last period of his career (1916–39) are
based upon this ontology, and, in varying degrees, all employ
Nō conventions.[51] These facts argue that the long search for a
dramatic form was over, but might also seem to imply that he
had boxed himself in a mode that would permit little room for
variety in style or subject. Yet, his final settling upon carefully
defined theories of reality and dramaturgy did not have the
effect of limiting Yeats to one dramatic formula. The explicit

awareness of what his ontology implied and the severity of the Nō convention had the opposite result, and, in fact, gave him an instrument capable of working effectively in any subject; the last seven plays cover almost every area accessible to the dramatist: mythology, theology, history, politics, and society. Now, he could even successfully confront the reality of the realists, approached before with such unhappy results. A general scrutiny of the last plays not only confirms the argument that Yeats had indeed "found" his form but also demonstrates that the form quite literally released the Yeatsian theme from a tendency to the severely limited and repetitive dramatic expression potential in what seems to be confining theory.

Perhaps the clearest way to discover both the great variety and family resemblance in these tragedies is to perceive them as types in an intelligible pattern that subsumes them all. Categories such as mythology and theology are a little misleading because individual plays sometimes deal with more than one category. One useful way of grouping the last tragedies is to see them as Yeats might have: that is, as dramatic moments in the great cycle of being that he metaphorically defined in *A Vision* as the 28 phases of the moon, the full round of which is the emblem for both historical and personal life cycles.[52] Though each lunar phase has its own characteristics, the phases tend to group into two great divisions, the subjective (8–22) and the objective (23–7). Men, both during and after their lifetimes, as well as cultures pass through each phase and fall, at any particular time, into one of the two great divisions. Their location in either subjective or objective being shapes their fates. Moreover, the individual's phase can be significantly different from that of the culture in which he is born. Thus Yeats, because he was a subjective type living in an objective era, regarded himself as out of phase with his culture and the "theatre's anti-self" as his reaction to this incongruity.[53] However, types in themselves are incomplete (except for that of Phase 15). The result then is that, outside of the fulfilled Phase 15, each phase desires its opposite, each type wills its *Mask* [54] or, in terms of "Per Amica," each self seeks completion through its daemonic opposite. This dramatic dialectic of thesis, antithesis, and synthesis is in the very nature of being, and Yeats seized upon this dialectic for his tragedies, treating there either subjective or objective being in conflict with its opposite.

One further distinction in Yeats's lunar system needs to be made. Objectivity from Phases 1–7 is different from that of Phases 23–28. The first is pristine, beginning the new cycle and ultimately moving into subjectivity (8–22). The objectivity of Phases 23–28 is the disintegrative end of the cycle.[55] Yeats sums up these categories within the larger categories in a way that helps define the last tragedies:

Phase 8 and Phase 22 are phases of struggle and tragedy, the first a struggle to find personality, the second to lose it. After Phase 22 and before Phase 1 there is a struggle to accept the fate-imposed unity, from Phase 1 to Phase 8 to escape it.[56]

This slightly elliptical definition is illuminated somewhat by a second:

The *Mask* before Phase 15 [moving toward pure subjectivity] is described as "revelation" because through it the being obtains knowledge of itself, sees itself in personality; while after Phase 15 [moving toward pure objectivity] it is a "concealment," for the being grows incoherent, vague, and broken, as its intellect (*Creative Mind*) is more and more concerned with objects that have no relation to its unity but a relation to the unity of society or of material things known through the *Body of Fate* ["fact as it affects a particular man"].   (*Vision*, p. 85)

In the subjective phase, being tragically struggles toward completeness or tries to hold completeness by self-generated heroic choice or by an imaginative transcendence of incompleteness. Past its completion, being in objectivity moves toward disintegration and is determined by external circumstance until the first phase and a radical change to the pristine objectivity of a new cycle in which being exists in a sort of innocent naturalness; there, its destiny is imposed from the outside as in the objective phases of the old cycle. In short, the history of all being, individual or cultural, describes a circle, half of which is subjective, half objective. Yeats interprets all history and personality in terms of that circle, and his last tragedies are, as a group, perhaps most clearly comprehensible within it.

All of these plays embody some meeting between subjective and objective being, the spiritual conflict of opposites constituting the dramatic action. The specific nature of the conflict makes the distinction between the basic kinds of tragedies. On the one hand, there are those plays in which the subjective nature is at the center of dramatic interest, the theme being heroic transcendence that realizes the tragic ecstasy (the "revelation" open only to being in the subjective phase); on the other hand, there are those plays in which the objective nature is the center of dramatic attention and the theme is the failure of heroic transcendence, failure that results in horror without affirmation, unqualified pathos (the objective "concealment" which cuts being off from its full realization). More specifically, in the meeting of subjective with objective, if the context is subjective (that is, if the age or personality in which the conflict occurs is passing through subjective phases), tragic heroism and completion of being are possible. *At the Hawk's Well* and *The Only Jealousy of Emer* (1918) provide such an instance; so do *The King of the Great Clock Tower* (1934) [57] and its revision, *A Full Moon in March* (1935). However, if the conflict occurs in an objective context, in a phase of history or personality dominated by the qualities associated with objectivity, then tragic heroism and completion of being are impossible; in the objective phases heroism and completion are replaced, at best, by a desolating awareness of the loss of freedom to choose, and, by implication, a sense of the lost opportunity for completion of self or for perfect harmony and ecstatic beauty. *Calvary* (1921), *The Resurrection* (1927), *The Dreaming of the Bones* (1919), *The Words Upon the Window-Pane* (1934), and *Purgatory* (1939) fall into this category. A further subcategory is necessary to distinguish between the pristine objectivity of *Calvary* and *The Resurrection* and the degenerate objectivity of *The Dreaming of the Bones, The Words Upon the Window-Pane,* and *Purgatory.* One final play which tends to fall into both the major categories, *The Death of Cuchulain* (1938), shows not only the completion of being of its subjective hero but also the changing of historical phase from subjective to objective cycle so the result is both horror and heroic joy, which might put the play in the subjective category except that emphasis upon the horror is so great. Aside from this one doubtful instance, the other plays can be seen as falling into one or the other of the two major groups.[58]

The subjective group is notably smaller in number than the objective, a not very surprising fact if it is recalled that Yeats believed himself to be a subjective dramatist writing in and, therefore, profoundly influenced by an objective age moving towards its final disintegration. *At the Hawk's Well* has been discussed; it is only necessary to repeat here that its theme is the making of a hero, that is, of a being with the capacity for tragic transcendence, a process which works itself out through Cuchulain's career of superhuman deeds, as exemplified by the action in *On Baile's Strand. The Only Jealousy of Emer,* because it represents, independent of the present consideration, a notable achievement in the Nō form, is discussed in some detail in Chapter V; it is sufficient to say for now that this play takes place in the depths of the mind and imposes upon its central figure, Emer, a heroic choice that, accepted, performs for Emer what such a choice did for Cuchulain in *At the Hawk's Well.* The dramatic form is almost identical with that of the earlier play, but with significant improvements based upon what Yeats had learned in his first experiment with the Nō form.

The last play of this group, *The King of the Great Clock Tower*, also employs all the Nō conventions—bare stage, choric attendants, masks, dance, binding metaphor—to reveal completion of being. The plot is extremely simple. After an introductory song by the attendants, the King of the Great Clock Tower is found complaining to his wife that she has not spoken since she suddenly walked into his house a year before and was taken to wife by him. A Stroller enters, who says that he was commanded by the gods in a vision to come and see the Queen of the Great Clock Tower. Moreover, he asserts that the gods promised him that the Queen would kiss him on the stroke of midnight. This insolence provokes the King to command that the Stroller be beheaded. Unruffled, the Stroller promises that all he has come to see and do will be accomplished. At this, the Queen begins to dance and sing. Having meanwhile set the Stroller's head on the throne, the King challenges it to fulfill its promise with a song. To his horror it begins to sing, and on the stroke of midnight at the climax of the Queen's dance she kisses it. The King kneels before this spectacle, and the attendants sing a concluding song.

The theme of ecstatic fulfillment after conflict and death is revealed not only in the action but by the attendants' songs, which employ for binding metaphor contrasting images of time and timelessness. In the timeless is perfection of being, subjective fulfillment, imaged in the dancing lovers of Tir-nan-oge (Irish fairyland):

SECOND ATTENDANT. They dance all day that dance in Tir-nan-oge.

FIRST ATTENDANT. There every lover is a happy rogue;
And should he speak, it is the speech of birds.
No thought has he, and therefore has no words,
No thought because no clock, no clock because
If I consider deeply, lad and lass,

> Nerve touching nerve upon that happy
> ground,
> Are bobbins where all time is bound and
> wound.[59]

The clockless land of the immortals contrasts with the temporal realm of the King of the Great Clock Tower; his authority is ignored by the Queen, whose mysterious origin is supernatural and who needs to complete herself through her opposite found in the human love of the Stroller. The binding metaphor is completed by one of the last songs of a choric attendant singing for the severed head:

> What's prophesied? What marvel is
> Where the dead and living kiss?
> *What of the hands on the Great Clock face?*
> Sacred Virgil never sang
> All the marvel there begun
> But there's a stone upon my tongue.
> *A moment more and it tolls midnight.*   (*Tower*, p. 640)

The place in which "the dead and living kiss" is the spiritual reality of being; the time is midnight, at the height of the subjective phase.[60] Then personality is at Phase 15 or the middle of its cycle, if the day is seen to reach its climax at noon, high point of the sun or the objective phase. The kiss of Queen and Stroller, her opposite, completes her being.

Yeats's treatment is much the same as in *At the Hawk's Well*. Supernatural elements, such as the singing head of the Stroller, are validated by the whole dramatic convention. However, Yeats introduced an unusual device into the play to strengthen the credibility of the presence of the supernatural. The very fact that the Stroller can prophesy what the Queen will do after his beheading has the effect of making believable what actually happens. The working out of a sort of oracular logic satisfies the aroused expectations of the audience and makes the incredible seem appropriate in the world of the play.

Yeats was not satisfied with his treatment of the theme in

this work. The product of his dissatisfaction was a revision, *A Full Moon in March,* which makes the theme of fulfillment of being far clearer by simplification. The King is eliminated, because his function is not essential to the action; the Queen, now an active agent, is clearly defined as a virgin goddess, cruel and beautiful, needing human love to achieve her full identity, needing, in fact, all that is opposite to her virgin beauty. Thus, the Stroller becomes a filthy arrogant Swineherd, whose sacrifice "fertilizes" the Queen's barren virginity so that it can achieve fulfillment at the full moon in March:

> I sing a song of Jack and Jill.
> Jill had murdered Jack;
> *The moon shone brightly;*
> Ran up the hill and round the hill,
> Round the hill and back.
> *A full moon in March.*[61]

The binding metaphor is again found in the introductory choric voice; but instead of dwelling on images of time and timelessness, more pertinently the song of the chorus expresses the opposition of types that achieve fulfillment: *"Crown of gold or dung of swine"* (*Moon,* p. 622). This refrain is both explicated and its significance completed by the First Attendant's reply, at play's end, to the inquiry as to why the "holy, haughty feet" of the Queen must descend to the mire of swine: "For desecration and the lover's night" (p. 629).[62] The Queen's completion requires that she be fulfilled by her opposite. Again, as in *The King of the Great Clock Tower,* the supernatural is perceived as part of the whole convention and, also, enforced, as a presence, by the sense of ordinarily incredible events fulfilling some prophecy, some mysterious logic of events that is inevitable and rooted in the very nature of the relationship of Queen and Swineherd:

THE QUEEN.   Pray, if your savagery has learnt to pray,
               For in a moment they will lead you out
               Then bring your severed head.

THE SWINEHERD.	My severed head. (*Laughs.*)
	There is a story in my country of a woman
	That stood all bathed in blood—a drop of blood
	Entered her womb and there begat a child.
THE QUEEN.	A severed head! She took it in her hands;
	She stood all bathed in blood; the blood begat.
	O foul, foul, foul!
THE SWINEHERD.	She sank in bridal sleep.
THE QUEEN.	Her body in that sleep conceived a child.

(March, p. 626)

All of the plays in this group, along with *The Death of Cuchulain,* have mythological subject matter for the obvious reason that Yeats believed that the age of myth was a subjective age and also that at such a time natural and supernatural were closer together; thus, the meeting of the two orders, necessary for completion of being, was an immediate possibility. *The Death of Cuchulain* marks the end of the age of myth; as such, the play provides a convenient bridge between the subjective and the objective tragedies.

Appropriately, the action is introduced by an angry Old Man who represents the values and attributes of subjective nature. He curses the objective world in which he must live:

I am old, I belong to mythology. . . . I spit three times. I spit upon the dancers painted by Degas. I spit upon their short bodices, their stiff stays, their toes whereon they spin like peg-tops, above all upon that chambermaid face. They might have looked timeless, Rameses the Great, but not the chambermaid, that old maid history. I spit! I spit! I spit! [63]

His departure signals the beginning of another action in the depths of the mind, with the usual Nō conventions of bare stage, dance, music, and choric song. The absence of masks may be attributed to the fact that the play was still in the process of revision when Yeats died.[64]

The action is based upon the final episode in Cuchulain's life, his last and fatal battle with his old enemy, Maeve.[65] The plotting is somewhat in the manner of *Samson Agonistes* or Yeats's own *The King's Threshold:* the protagonist, Cuchulain, is confronted with a series of antagonists, all of whom have played some role in his past life. Just before the battle with the forces of Maeve, his mistress, Eithne Inguba, comes to him and, apparently under Maeve's spell, would send him to his death against impossible odds, though she bears in her hand a letter from Emer telling Cuchulain to wait until reinforcements arrive. Cuchulain, discovering Eithne Inguba's "treachery," assumes that she has ceased to love him, but ready to die he generously forgives her. In fact, it was his own plan to join battle immediately. When the war goddess, the Morrigu, appears between the hero and his mistress, visible only to her, it is clear to Eithne Inguba that her lover, softened, no longer quick to vengeance, is doomed and in despair she threatens to denounce herself to the lowest servants so that they will punish her. Cuchulain, the doom upon him, shrugs off her bitter railing and arranges for her future well-being with the abstracted tenderness of a magnanimous man preoccupied by some greater matter; she is left to her awareness that there is nothing she can do but accept the will of the gods:

> I might have peace that know
> The Morrigu, the woman like a crow,
> Stands to my defence and cannot lie,
> But that Cuchulain is about to die.   (*Cuchulain*, p. 698)

The stage darkens; when the lights go up, Cuchulain enters, wounded and obviously dying. He tries to bind himself to a stone pillar so that he may die standing up. Another old enemy, Aoife, the mother of Cuchulain's only son, enters seeking revenge. She is now white-haired, yet still single-mindedly bent on killing Cuchulain. But before she can accomplish her aim, she is forced to hide [66] because of the entrance of the Blind Man of *On Baile's Strand,* who has been offered twelve pennies by

Maeve for bringing back the head of Cuchulain. The hero assumes that the Blind Man, because he is the agent of fate, understands the dark forces underlying Cuchulain's tragic life, but he is told by the old man (who, it will be remembered, was the base double or "shadow" of Conchubar in *On Baile's Strand*) that it is only "good sense" which motivates him, not knowledge that he is agent in the great mystery of a hero's death and end of an age: "How could I have got twelve pennies for your head/ If I had not good sense?" (*Cuchulain*, p. 702) Cuchulain, seeing his own shade floating before him, says simply: "I say it is about to sing" (p. 703). The stage then darkens and the Blind Man beheads him. When the action begins again, the Morrigu is seen holding the hero's head (a black parallelogram); six other "heads," those, the Morrigu explains, of the warriors who had mortally wounded Cuchulain and were killed by him, are seen at the back of the stage. The war goddess also declares that she has arranged for the climactic dance by Emer, who enters as the Morrigu goes out. Emer "moves as if in adoration or triumph," indicating that the apotheosis is complete. She then hears "a few faint bird notes" (p. 704).[67]

The stage darkens, and music is heard "of some Irish Fair of our day" (*Cuchulain*, p. 704). When the lights go up, three musicians are seen in ragged street singers' clothes. One sings the final choric song, that of a harlot to a beggar; this song is the equivalent of the Queen's song to the Swineherd in *A Full Moon in March,* or of any heroic woman's song to her man in the subjective age; but this passionate song has now been reduced by modern objectivity to the spiritual counterpart of prostitution and poverty. In such an age, the harlot who adores the great heroes

> can get
> No grip upon their thighs.
> I meet those long pale faces,
> Hear their great horses, then

Recall what centuries have passed
Since they were living men.

But she remembers

That there are still some living
That do my limbs unclothe,
But that the flesh has gripped
I both adore and loathe.   (p. 704)

Though the syntax of this passage offers some difficulties, it seems
that the last four lines imply that the harlot finds in some living
men, perhaps men like the inspired revolutionists referred to in
the next part of the song, heroic qualities that arouse her passions. She then raises the Yeatsian question: Is what "men adore
and loathe/ Their sole reality?" (p. 704) [68] That is, can reality
only be found in the heroic, immortal passions of love and hate,
or in her terms—the terms of objectivity—lust and aversion for
the human embodiment of those heroic, immortal passions? The
answer, of course, is yes. For what men adore and hate is their
opposite, the daemonic antithesis that brings them through suffering to fulfillment. The filthy, insolent Swineherd brought the
virgin Queen to her fulfillment, or, more generally, the objective brings the subjective to its completion by being its absolute
opposite in all respects. Even in an objective age, the age of
harlot and beggar, the immortal subjective passions, if only as
embodiments of artistic imagination, affect human experience:

No body like his body,
Has modern woman borne,
But an old man looking on life
Imagines it in scorn.
A statue's there to mark the place,
By Oliver Sheppard done.
So ends the tale that the harlot
Sang to the beggar-man.   (*Cuchulain*, p. 705)

The play has come full circle: the image of the bitter Old Man
is summoned up again, his subjective being imagining in scorn

(for the impoverished prostitution of an objective age) the heroic figures that can give modern men a model for heroic greatness only completely realizable in a subjective age.[69]

The binding metaphor in *The Death of Cuchulain* is a composite of images from the arts; the Old Man speaks of the dance that he must have in the play and spits on the "realist" paintings of Degas. The harlot of the musicians' song speaks of the heroic figures of the Old Man's imagination and links them with Oliver Sheppard's statue of Cuchulain. Underlying these images is an implied contrast between the vulgar imitative art of an objective age (Degas' chambermaids) and the noble products of a subjective imagination (dancer and statue). Taken together, the images composing the binding metaphor reinforce the theme of the spiritual apotheosis of heroism at the very moment of the triumph of historical objectivity, the victory of the Blind Man's "good sense" over Cuchulain's passionate quest for superhuman intensity in his mortal life.[70]

Critics have argued about Cuchulain's death, Peter Ure insisting that it is the very opposite of transfiguration or apotheosis,[71] Helen H. Vendler, that it reveals only "weariness and indifference,"[72] F. A. C. Wilson, that it is a transfiguration but on a subdued note.[73] It seems to me that what Yeats meant by heroic destiny and tragedy throws some light upon just what Cuchulain's death signifies, how, that is, it is supposed to be taken. If one expects all the fireworks of popular conceptions of bluff and hearty heroic endings, then one is bound to be disappointed by Cuchulain's death. But Yeats was far more traditional than popular conceptions; indeed, he was Homeric. Achilles' most tragic moment in *The Iliad* is not on the battlefield, but in his own quarters when, violating all "popular" notions of the hero, he gives Priam back the greatest spoil of the war, his dead son, Hector. This generous gesture is accompanied by a deeply moving, rather quiet speech which shows Achilles' compassionate grasp of the human condition. Not even Priam truly understands what has happened, but for the first time in the epic someone has been courageous enough to feel and act on the profound and unpopular idea that, in E. M. W. Till-yard's words, "in the utmost extremities the things that unite men are stronger than those that divide them." [74] Like Achilles, Cuchulain, in the face of his fate, exhibiting heroic generosity and heroic calm, is misunderstood. And he assumes that tone of reverie, which Yeats believed marked the tragic ecstasy, to say "I say it is about to sing"; this prophecy suggests transfigura-tion for the hero, if only in the words of the poet who sings of his heroism. It is enough. Cuchulain's end is forbidding because Yeats was too honest to deny that failure and defeat and death are human realities. It is the hero's triumph that he sees and accepts, and yet can prophecy a singing beyond his death.[75]

Yet, even though it suggests a profound understanding of heroism, *The Death of Cuchulain* strains the dance play con-vention, as if Yeats were attempting to crowd too much into the form. The treatment of the supernatural in the play is identical with that in the other mythological plays; the supernatural pres-ence is treated as part of the world of the play in which the Morrigu and Cuchulain's vision of his soul after death are nat-uralized by the convention itself. Yet, because of the sense of crowding, the supernatural presence seems perfunctory. It is almost as if, in trying too much, Yeats vitiated that effect of con-centration which is one of the strongest features of the Nō form. Other characteristics of the play tend to support such a con-jecture. For instance, the binding metaphor carries a burden of explicit didacticism that goes beyond (perhaps too far beyond) the defining or reinforcing theme. The furious Old Man of the Prologue, while railing against modern education, is actually offering an educative model for the audience by insisting that they cannot understand his drama unless they know Irish epics and Yeats's plays about them. The harlot's song offers the ob-jective unheroic age another model in her description of Irish heroes.

Still, though possibly undramatic, the didacticism has its

reason. It appears in a play which shows the death of heroism and the triumph of meretriciousness. The best that a subjective dramatist can do in the light of events is to show an objective age a vision of greatness. This vision, while it cannot provide the means of tragic transcendence, might, at least, provide a mask or image that would give the age fullness and dignity or perhaps prevent it from choosing its worst possibility, the dreadful condition shown in *Purgatory*. The didacticism in *The Death of Cuchulain* is, then, the result of Yeats's sense of duty to his time, a sense almost concealed under the fierce pride of a subjective man in an alien objective age.[76]

It is this objective age that Yeats treats of in the bulk of his last plays, and treats of literally from beginning to end, from its inception in the career of Christ to its grim conclusion in the murderous and debased Old Man in *Purgatory*.[77] With one exception, *The Words Upon a Window-Pane,* all of these plays, like those of the first group, employ many of the Nō conventions. Aside from *The Words Upon a Window-Pane* and *The Resurrection,* the plays have stylistic qualities resembling those of *At the Hawk's Well:* the lyric chant of the choric voice, the heightened traditional verse of the principals, and the binding metaphor.

It is appropriate to begin with the play that deals with the initiation of the objective Christian age, also one of the earliest of the objective plays, *Calvary.* In this play, the already crucified Christ relives in the depths of his mind the walk to Calvary.[78] As in the plays of the subjective category, the supernatural is also at the center of action and part of the given dramatic convention. After the choric song, the plot unfolds, somewhat in the manner of *The Death of Cuchulain,* as a series of confrontations between Christ and his antagonists. The play begins with the choric song immediately introducing the binding metaphor which consists of images of birds—the symbols, according to Yeats in his Notes to the play,[79] of subjectivity. The action begins as Lazarus confronts Christ with a bitter attack on His pity for one who preferred the loneliness of the tomb to resurrection. The three Marys then come and worship Him, the First Musician commenting:

Take but His love away,
Their love becomes a feather
Of eagle, swan or gull,
Or a drowned heron's feather
Tossed hither and thither
Upon the bitter spray
And the moon at the full.[80]

Remove Christ's objective pity from them and these women would fall back into the fragmented subjectivity of the cycle just past (a "drowned" subjectivity now). Their appearance is shadowy, and they are given no lines because, to rephrase Dante, their peace is in His Will. The Marys are driven away by the approach of Judas, who gleefully tells Christ that His betrayal was calculated by a mind that wished to retain its freedom in the face of perfect objectivity. Judas' intention is to resist external domination and the loss of personal will in the objective nature of Christ who is here to do His "Father's will" (*Calvary*, p. 452). Having planned his freedom when no living thing was near him "but a heron/ So full of itself that it seemed terrified" (p. 454), Judas rejects Christ, as had Lazarus, because as a man of the old cycle with vestiges of its subjectivity still clinging to his nature he regards choice as the essence of being; this capacity to choose can give him his fulfillment by accepting the most difficult challenge that the daemon proposes. It is Judas' horrible misfortune to be living at a time when objectivity and its values dominate, so that his choice, instead of being the suffering that brings him to tragic vision, leads to being abhorred by all those who share in the objective world.[81]

The last confrontation is with three Roman soldiers whom Yeats described as "a form of objectivity that lay beyond His help." [82] They, like Lazarus and Judas, seem to be remnants of the decayed classical age which has disintegrated into objectivity. Claiming to be merely "three old gamblers that have asked for nothing" (*Calvary*, p. 456), they worship chance, now separated from choice at the divisive end of the old cycle.[83] As such, they are indifferent to Christ and a world determined by His will. Their polytheism, though they are themselves objective types, indicates their allegiance to an order alien to Christ's objectivity. Their rejection culminates in the climactic dance, after which Christ cries out in His isolation, "My Father, why hast Thou forsaken Me?" (*Calvary*, p. 456) The irony of the soldiers' concluding dance is that this ritual act, which usually suggests Unity of Being, is given to those who, indifferent to such unity, emblemize its opposite. Now, the choric song fittingly concludes with images of lonely seabirds to whom "God has not appeared" (p. 457), a gier-eagle and a swan, creatures of subjectivity and of nature, beyond the torment of men confronted by their daemon. The meeting of Christ, the spirit of the new cycle, with those beyond His pity and saving is horrible in its fruitlessness. It is a meeting which reveals only the terrible isolation in store for those who seek the self-fulfilling solitude of subjectivity but receive in the new cycle the sterile loneliness of individuals in a mob. The horror is compounded by Christ's loneliness as a man; though His divine nature is objective, His human nature, derived from the dying subjective cycle, experiences the agony of a man out of phase and deprived of the possibility —in His isolated state—of completion.[84] He is a protagonist agonizingly fixed in His historical role and has no hope of a fulfilling tragic experience. Living His experience over again means only *that,* not a purgatorial cleansing. Appropriately, the play ends on a note of unmitigated horror.

The next play in this series, *The Resurrection,* is concerned, like *Calvary,* with one of the momentous incidents in Christ's biography and with the transition between subjective and objective historical cycles, between the dying objectivity of the Greek civilization and the pristine objectivity of its Christian counterpart. The play opens with a choric song that states the larger theme, the changing of phase, the death of one historical era and the birth of a new, as symbolized in the Dionysian ritual:

> I saw a staring virgin stand
> Where holy Dionysus died,
> And tear the heart out of his side,
> And lay the heart upon her hand
> And bear that beating heart away;
> And then did all the Muses sing
> Of Magnus Annus at the spring,
> As though God's death were but a play.
>
> Another Troy must rise and set,
> Another lineage feed the crow,
> Another Argo's painted prow
> Drive to a flashier bauble yet.
> The Roman Empire stood appalled:
> It dropped the reins of peace and war
> When that fierce virgin and her Star
> Out of the fabulous darkness called.[85]

The action, more complex in structure than *Calvary,* opens upon a room in which a Hebrew and a Greek are guarding the eleven disciples the third day after Calvary. The guards, presenting radically different interpretations of Christ, argue over the nature of the experiences of the last few days. Meanwhile, an orgiastic Dionysian rite is progressing in the streets outside, and a mob is hunting down Christians. It is soon evident from the argument that the Hebrew is a commonsensical man who finds in Christ simply the best of good men deluded at a weak moment into believing himself the Messiah. A follower of Christ's goodness, and an objective man himself, the Hebrew is not ready to accept the possibility of a Messiah because it would mean giving up all human hopes in the objective natural world, since all reality, if Christ were indeed the Messiah, would become supernatural, a state beyond the imagination and desire of normal men. The Greek is a rationalist, the last manifestation of the old cycle's subjective high point,[86] and regards Christ as an idea or phantom, not a flesh-and-blood human whose suffering would hardly be a fit object to worship. As a subjective man, the Greek looks out upon the Dionysian revelry with contempt; he sees it merely as a way in which the poverty-stricken lose their personal identity and escape their wretchedness. He gives a brilliantly clear exposition of the relationship between natural and supernatural in the last subjective phase:

I cannot think all that self-surrender and self-abasement is Greek, despite the Greek name of its god . . . . They [the gods] can be discovered by contemplation, in their faces a high keen joy like the cry of a bat, and the man who lives heroically gives them the only earthly body that they covet. He, as it were, copies their gestures and their acts. What seems their indifference is but their eternal possession of themselves. Man, too, remains separate. He does not surrender his soul. He keeps his privacy.[87]

A Syrian, sent by the Greek to look at Christ's tomb, returns with the news that it is empty and that the Marys have seen the risen Christ. The Hebrew is incredulous, the Greek confident that Christ the phantom is certainly abroad since no crucifixion could kill him and no stone keep him imprisoned. The Syrian, a creature of the transition from age to age, not only accepts the mystery of Christ but revels in the irrationality of the present. At this moment, the Dionysian revelry gathers momentum, increasing the dramatic tension as the participants cry, "God has arisen!" (*Resurrection*, p. 592) In a wild, ancient dance, described by the Greek (which takes the place of the usual Nō dance), they approach the house in which the eleven disciples and the guards wait out events. Suddenly, falling into silence, the revelers fix their stares upon the house until the pitch of intensity is unbearable. It is then that Christ enters; the bewildered Hebrew kneels, and the Greek confidentally thrusts his hand at the presence only to cry, "The heart of a phantom is beating!" (p. 593) Christ goes in to the disciples and His meeting with them is described by the Syrian. The Greek, stunned and horrified, announces the end of subjective civilization:

O Athens, Alexandria, Rome, something has come to destroy you. The heart of a phantom is beating. Man has begun to die. Your words are clear at last, O Heraclitus. God and man die each other's life, live each other's death. (p. 594)

Man as personality is dying into God's life, or man's personal will is dying into God's impersonal, universal will.

The web of images relating to the heart and heart's blood functions as the binding metaphor of the play; the image is first developed in the Dionysian ritual of the initial song, then becomes the beating heart of the supernatural Christ, and is completed in the musicians' last song. The scent of the irrational heart's blood, not Dionysus', but Christ's, blood of a far more enduring, more alien god, overwhelms subjectivity:

Odour of blood when Christ was slain
Made all Platonic tolerance vain
And vain all Doric discipline. (p. 594)

And the final stanza of the song defines the tragic nature of the human heart, capable of immortal, eternal recurring passions that are always exhausted by the heart's mortal limitations:

Everything that man esteems
Endures a moment or a day:
Love's pleasure drives his love away,
The painter's brush consumes his dreams;
The herald's cry, the soldier's tread
Exhaust his glory and his might:
Whatever flames upon the night
Man's own resinous heart has fed. (p. 594)

Dialogue in *The Resurrection* consists of a remarkably direct prose for the burden of exposition and ideas it must carry. The characters are differentiated more by the ideas they express than by personal inflection, but the slightly elevated speech is appropriate to the formality of the whole convention and to the fact that the characters represent types of thinking rather than individuals. Yeats uses the technique he exploited so well in *On Baile's Strand* of having a character onstage describe an action offstage, the effect being to create a tension through heightened response of the observing narrator. A fair sample of both the prose style and of this method is seen in the Syrian's description of Christ's reception by the disciples:

He is standing in the midst of them. Some are afraid. He looks at Peter and James and John. He smiles. He has parted the clothes at his side. He shows them his side. There is a great wound there. Thomas has put his hand into the wound. He has put his hand where the heart is.   (p. 593)

In *The Resurrection,* as in *Calvary,* the supernatural of objective reality meets the human of subjective reality, and the opposition produces a terrible recoil; Greek is isolated from Hebrew, who is forced to accept the objective reality of Christ, from Syrian, who accepts the irrational and miraculous because he regards these as the heart of reality, and from the disciples, who in their objective simplicity rejoice at the appearance of their Saviour. The enormous confidence of the Greek, his superiority to the vulgar mystery cult and its orgy, is utterly destroyed as the Christian mystery transcends anything that his subjective background prepared him for, or even the Dionysians imagined possible. The horror that he expresses is the emotion commensurate with the stunning event taking place before him: the death of his kind of being and the birth and triumph of an alien and terrible being beyond his comprehension.

The remarkable effectiveness of the play arises out of this dramatic collision of the orders of reality. The irrational supernatural exerts increasingly tense pressure on both the practical scepticism of the Hebrew and the Greek's rationalism, until the new reality, prefigured by the Dionysian rites, bursts through in its full power. Yeats's ability to create so dramatic a tension is a sure measure of the success with which he could, at this time, bring the supernatural on the stage. His authoritative handling of the Nō convention in *The Resurrection* established the credibility of what transcended the normal range of human experience. Within that convention he was even able to use most tellingly an Elizabethan device: characters in the play, suddenly confronted by the supernatural, are forced not merely to accept it; in the very intensity of their reaction to its presence they reinforce the sense of its reality. Marlowe in *Doctor Faustus* and Shakespeare in *Macbeth* used the same means to bring the supernatural into the drama. Yeats's use of the device escapes T. S. Eliot's well-known criticism of the Elizabethan dramatists—that their confusion between realistic and conventional led to equivocation about the supernatural.[88] In Yeats's earlier plays such confusion and its resulting equivocation is certainly present; but *The Resurrection* sustains an unmarred consistency of convention in which the reality of the risen Christ seems wholly logical, all the more so because of the staggering shock His appearance causes in two types—sceptic and rationalist—who, while they live properly in the world of the play, share with the audience a normal wonder or terror in the presence of the supernatural. In *The Resurrection* Yeats had reached such a mastery of his convention that he could bring into it with good effect techniques of another tradition.

The next tragedies in the objective category deal with the objectivity that supersedes subjective phases of the Christian cycle, which itself, according to Yeats, was now drawing to a close. These plays fittingly take for their subject modern Ireland, and they represent Yeats's efforts to deal with his own time. In *The Dreaming of the Bones* and in *Purgatory* he confronted the reality of the realists through the Nō form; in *The Words Upon the Window-Pane* he confronted the same reality, but in the manner that the realists themselves did, through imitation of the objective world.

In form *The Dreaming of the Bones* is perhaps the closest of all Yeats's later plays to typical Japanese Nō. After the choric introduction, the action unfolds as the meeting of a traveler with ghostly lovers who must receive his prayers or help in order to consummate their love. It is the lovers' misfortune that the traveler is an Irish Revolutionist fleeing from victorious enemies. For, as they lead the Revolutionist to a hiding place in a ruined abbey which they haunt, they gradually reveal that they are Diarmuid and Dervorgilla, archtraitors to Ireland who seven hundred years before had "brought the Norman in" [89] and put the land forever under foreign domination. The Revolutionist, though nearly swept up in their poignant suffering as eternal wanderers who cannot kiss or touch hands because of remorse for their sin, finally denies them his forgiveness. He cannot forget that his life is right now in jeopardy fighting what the lovers, in the impulse of bitterness, have brought on Ireland. The ghosts dance their anguished dance and vanish unforgiven, fated to endless wandering until they meet someone more compassionate.

The subject of the play is not the experience of any one of the characters, but the spiritual life of Ireland as a nation. For the Revolutionist, who represents modern Ireland,[90] in refusing to forgive his own past refuses to give modern objective Ireland its heroic mask, its fullness of being. Because now "the moon is covered up" (*Bones*, p. 434), that is, the historical character of the nation is in the objective phase, and because the lovers belong to a mythic age, an earlier subjective phase, there is at least a chance for fruitful completion of being. But the objective man cannot rise to the occasion, cannot don a mask.[91] The lovers are doomed to haunt the divided spirit of the land; they are unreconciled with the present, therefore with themselves; and the present cannot accept the past. The theme of *The Dreaming of the Bones,* then, is the protagonist's refusal or incapacity to assume the tragic mask. The result of such a refusal is horror, a horror that returns the spirit lovers to their terrible fate and leaves the young Revolutionist unchanged, full of cruel bitterness that is his fruitless answer to a seven-hundred-year-old cruel bitterness. The bones of lovers must go on "dreaming" their suffering, their beings incomplete because unpurged of unfulfilled emotions, which will haunt the living until satisfied: [92]

> They dream that laughed in the sun.
> Dry bones that dream are bitter,
> They dream and darken our sun. (*Bones,* p. 445)

As the young Revolutionist is not roused by the daemonic spirits to tragic choice, so Ireland fails (as Cuchulain was willing) to accept the "curse" that would ultimately bring it Unity of Being through the tragic experience.

The binding metaphor is built, with appropriate irony, from images of sexual fulfillment or sexual power and from those contrasting night and day.[93] The First Musician in the opening song suggests that power:

> And many a night it seems
> That all the valley fills
> With those fantastic dreams.
> They overflow the hills,
> So passionate is a shade,
> Like wine that fills to the top
> A grey-green cup of jade,
> Or maybe an agate cup. (*Bones,* p. 434)

The image of a wine-filled cup is augmented by the repeated image of the red cock crowing in the potent and fulfilling month of March.[94] The musicians end the play with images that suggest a sort of primal sexual power meant to foil the impotence of the lovers who, tortured by fruitless proximity, cannot consummate their love:

My heart ran wild when it heard
The curlew cry before dawn
And the eddying cat-headed bird;
But now the night is gone.
I have heard from far below
The strong March birds a-crow.
Stretch neck and clap the wing,
Red cocks, and crow!   *(Bones,* p. 445)

The unsatisfied sexuality of the lovers becomes, in terms of the action, the fruitless meeting of opposites, objective and subjective, of night's spirits and day's dreamers who do not know they dream, in a divisive, sterile world.

As in the Japanese Nō, all elements are part of the "given" of the convention, and Yeats did not resort to the devices that he used in other dramas of this period to vivify the supernatural presences in the play, possibly because this is a comparatively early effort and was written before he had developed the techniques used for this purpose in *The Resurrection* and *A Full Moon in March.*

If *The Dreaming of the Bones* is a revelation of a real, though fruitless, meeting of objective and subjective, then *Purgatory* (discussed in the next chapter) is the revelation that, beyond a certain point, a genuine meeting of the two phases is impossible. The Old Man, who is the play's protagonist, bears witness to the last and degenerate expression of objectivity. With his bastard son, he watches the repeated degradation of the spirit of his aristocratic mother, reliving in purgatorial torment the debasing last days of her life with her drunken groom-husband. In keeping with the protagonist's horrible incapacity to rise above the depraved scene, the style is the barest, the form the most radically simple and stringent of all of Yeats's last plays, going even beyond *At the Hawk's Well* in its severity. For an almost brutal candor about the objective world, the play is unsurpassed in Yeats's work and hardly less harsh than Gorki's *The Lower Depths.*

Another and almost equally brutal picture of the objective world is found in *The Words Upon the Window-Pane,* which, however, is an exception among the last plays. On the surface its dramaturgy is the closest thing in Yeats's late plays to a realist approach to modernity; certainly, it shared with Ibsen's drama, and more particularly with Shaw's, a preoccupation with ideas and a tendency to let discussion loom large in the plot. Yet, even this departure from the other late tragedies depends considerably on Nō convention, and, as Earl Miner asserts, upon Japanese Nō plot. Miner, who has traced the connections between *The Words Upon the Window-Pane* and the Japanese drama, is well worth quoting in full on the subject:

Words Upon the Window-Pane is in prose, and in many other ways is not one of Yeats's "Noh Plays." But it is clearly the product of the form of theatre he had developed from the nō. Like Kumasaka, one of the nō which he republished, it is a supernatural play on a historical subject—the appearance of Jonathan Swift, Vanessa, and Stella to a séance in a house where Stella had once stayed. The motif of the ghostly lovers brought together years after their death is the same *Nishikigi*-motif employed in *The Dreaming of the Bones,* but here there are two women who love Swift instead of the one in the earlier play—a triangle posing a problem of dramatic focus which Yeats solves brilliantly through the device of the séance where only one of the dead can speak at a time, first the impetuous Vanessa, and then Swift. Stella does not speak a word in the play, but her presence is implied throughout by Swift's address to her and by the "Unifying Image" of the words upon the window-pane taken from the poem which she wrote for Swift's fifty-fourth birthday. The group at the séance is a medley of ignorance and sensitivity and, as a group, are the equivalent of the priest in *Nishikigi* or the revolutionary in *The Dreaming of the Bones;* like these characters, they experience a revelation of the central, supernatural characters in the play. This play is one of Yeats's finest and, in spite of its completely English subject matter, shows how well he was able to refine and adapt to the modern stage the conventions of the form which he borrowed from the nō.[95]

The basic theme of the play, as with all tragedies in the second category, is the sterile incapacity of being, as it moves into disintegrating objectivity, to complete itself. Embodied by the character of Swift, "the chief representative of the intellect of his epoch," shattered being becomes emblematic of a whole civilization: "Was Swift mad? Or was it the intellect itself that was mad?" [96] asks John Corbet, the Cambridge student who, with Dr. Trench, serves as the expository "chorus" for ideas underlying the play; these two prepare, in their long discussion before the séance, for Swift's unexpected and shocking emergence. Dr. Trench reveals that the house in which they are now gathered was that of Grattan or Curran, and that Stella had left her poem to Swift on one of its windowpanes. However, when he calls Swift's life "tragic," because all the great ministers who had been his friends were banished and broken, Corbet, a scholar working on Swift's life for a doctorate, corrects him, pointing out that the tragedy was deeper, a case of a whole epoch moving rapidly toward disintegration and chaos:

His ideal order was the Roman Senate, his ideal men Brutus and Cato. Such an order and such men had seemed possible once more, but the movement passed and he foresaw the ruin to come,—Democracy, Rousseau, the French Revolution   (*Words*, pp. 601–2)

the complete triumph that is, of the worst attribute of objectivity —undifferentiated and undifferentiating mob mentality. After Swift's tragic experience is clarified, Dr. Trench provides the spiritual explanation for the purgatorial agony to follow in the séance:

Some spirits are earth-bound—they think they are still living and go over and over some action of their past lives, just as we go over and over some painful thought, except that where they are thought is reality. . . . Sometimes a spirit relives not the pain of death but some passionate or tragic moment of life.   (p. 604)

The agony comes as an interruption of the séance by the voices of Swift and Vanessa; she begs Swift to marry her, to have children that would spare him from the horrible loneliness of old age. But, fearful of passing on his intellectual disintegration (emblematic of the historical one) or of promulgating merely healthy fools and knaves, he refuses her. A hymn, sung by those at the séance intending to "bring good influence" (p. 611), has the effect of summoning for Swift's voice a new object, Stella, whom he praises for having learned the meaning of beauty of the spirit; he recites her poem (the words on the windowpane) as evidence of her profound understanding, but there is no reply from Stella.[97] It is then the séance ends, the medium, Mrs. Henderson, is exhausted by Swift's agony. Though those who came to hear or see their loved ones are disappointed, Corbet is astonished and delighted, but believes that the medium is "an accomplished actress and scholar." [98] He is quickly disabused of this illusion when he learns that she has never heard of Swift, only knows him as she saw him: "His clothes were dirty, his face covered with boils. Some disease had made one of his eyes swell up, it stood out from his face like a hen's egg" (*Words*, p. 616). After the departure of her clientele, and surely in one of the most stunning stage effects in modern drama, Mrs. Henderson, as she draws herself a cup of tea, lapses into the voice of Swift. The medium thus serves the same function as the musicians in *The King of the Great Clock Tower* and *A Full Moon in March* who sing for the severed heads of Stroller and Swineherd. After reciting the names of the great ministers, his friends, now gone, Swift cries from Mrs. Henderson's mouth, "Perish the day on which I was born!" (p. 617)

The tragedy then, as Corbet implies, is that of a man heroically devoted to subjective virtues—freedom, spiritual fullness, individuality—living in an increasingly objective age; whatever remnant of subjectivity survives is now drowned in the climactic tide of disintegrative objectivity. Swift, who sought a mask in heroic Roman nobility, could not personally achieve it, or only partially so in his creations: on the one hand, his satires, and on the other, the two women who loved him and were made more beautiful by his labors. He himself sank into the age's madness and now wanders the spiritual purgatory of shades who, like the lovers in *The Dreaming of the Bones*, remain incomplete because they cannot burn off self-shattering mortal impurities. In his relationship with Vanessa his personal failure is most clearly seen. She is his daemon, his opposite in all respects, a creature of the senses, a fruitful, motherly woman with no intellectual ambition. And when Swift exclaims at her urgent request for marriage, "My God, I am left alone with my enemy" (p. 611), he reveals the true relationship. That he resists her is a kind of heroism, a kind of transcendence, but ultimately unsatisfactory and fruitless, as his spiritual agony testifies. In an objective phase at the end of the cycle of being, heroism does not lead to completion, but at best to a bitter, arrogant integrity of what remains of being.

The Words Upon the Window-Pane shares with all the late tragedies the theme of spiritual conflict—daemonic struggle of self and its antithesis—and shares with the plays of the objective phase the horror of incompletion; but it is clearly a stylistic departure for Yeats. For though the play, as Miner has shown, relies more than is superficially evident on Nō conventions, it is realistic in setting and external detail. Why, if the Nō form was entirely satisfactory to Yeats, did he depart from it in this work? Yeats himself answers this question by prefacing the play with an explanation of this singular departure from his typical mode:

I collect materials for my thought and work, for some identification of my beliefs with the nation itself, I seek an image of the modern mind's discovery of itself, of its own permanant form, in that one Irish century that escaped from darkness and confusion. I would that our fifteenth, sixteenth, or even our seventeenth century had been the clear mirror, but fate decided against us.[99]

The Words Upon the Window-Pane represents the compromise between Yeats's personal belief and "the nation itself"; the play is an image which, in its realistic surface, makes the concession to objectivity that is "the nation itself." A concession to the realism that he had so long battled was the only means, he now believed, to make his view understandable to an audience that would find his "anti-theatre" incomprehensible. Through surface realism, then, he attempted to penetrate to the nation's spiritual being, the depths of its mind, at that period—the eighteenth century—when there was still hope for national greatness through assuming a mask.

Intellect and its products—aristocracy modeled on Roman ideals—Yeats thought to be the best mask for a nation falling into the decay of a cycle's end. Such a mask would constitute the closest thing to subjective realization of being, to a political and intellectual unity imposed from the outside through some great model. Swift reminds Vanessa, whom he found as an ignorant girl:

I taught you to think in every situation of life not as Hester Vanhomrigh would think in that situation, but as Cato or Brutus would, and now you behave like some common slut with her ear against the keyhole. (*Words*, p. 609)

His failure with Vanessa is the failure of the mob-ridden, irrational Irish nation to come to terms with its own heroic past or to find some noble model to emulate.

Even though *The Words Upon the Window-Pane* seems to despair of hope for Ireland, the didactic impulse (a quality also of *The Death of Cuchulain*) was so strong in Yeats that he still attempted to provide Ireland with a model; in the process, he sacrificed most of what he now valued in dramatic form, giving up the "theatre's anti-self" this one time for the sake of teaching the objective theatre's audience its heroic and necessary duty. In his introduction to *The Words Upon the Window-Pane*, he suggested

to the Cellars and Garrets [the artists] that though history is too short to change either the idea of progress or the eternal circuit into scientific fact, the eternal circuit may best suit our preoccupation with the soul's salvation, our individualism, our solitude. Besides we love antiquity, and that other idea—progress—the sole religious myth of modern man, is only two hundred years old.[100]

Taking a cue from Shaw, Yeats used his introduction further to explain the didactic purposes of his play: to teach a proper theory of history, and, within that, proper theories of politics and art. This play is a final compromise with the objectivity of the times, Yeats's last direct effort in the drama to rectify the failure of the Irish to attain greatness as a nation.[101]

In this very compromise, however, Yeats revealed how wholly he had mastered the problem of introducing the supernatural into the drama, for here, in a realistic modern setting, he faced a challenge that the mythological plays, completely compassed by the Nō convention, did not present. In *The Words Upon the Window-Pane,* with only a bare suggestion of the convention available to him, and that carefully submerged in the pattern of the action, Yeats had to bring the supernatural onto the stage. His solution was the one used in *The Resurrection:* the character least likely to believe in the supernatural, the sceptical John Corbet, bears strong witness to the fact of its presence. Moreover, the character who is totally ignorant of Swift and his life, Mrs. Henderson, speaks for him and Vanessa. The ghostly presence of Swift becomes a dramatic fact when Mrs. Henderson must reveal it against her will; she does so, at the last, in a state of daemonic possession, all the more compelling and terrible because it occurs after the séance and while she is alone in the "ordinary" circumstances of her daily life. What Yeats had not been able to do in *Where There is Nothing,* written thirty years before, he was able to do in this, his only other tragedy in the realistic mode. In the earlier play, he had equivocated about the reality of the supernatural by leaving in question the sanity of the hero and the actual nature of his vision. Here, using the method employed in *The Resurrection*

three years before, he boldly brings the supernatural on stage
and allows the reactions of human characters to establish its
undeniable presence. The effect is powerfully heightened in
The Words Upon the Window-Pane by the incongruity between
the placid usualness of the realistic setting and the sudden intrusion of a dialogue between unseen, but vividly present,
spirits.

Yeats's triumph in *The Words Upon the Window-Pane* indicates that his earlier failure with tragicomedy was by no means
complete and irreversible. For the thought and training of thirty
years had prepared him now to use the natural world of Dickens
for reaching through to a reality which, heretofore, he had been
able to discover only in the depths of the mind. Thus, *The
Words Upon the Window-Pane,* the one striking exception
among Yeats's tragedies of the last period, testifies that, while
his tragic theme had hardly changed, his skill as a dramatist had
immeasurably increased, and that the bold use of the supernatural developed in the "theatre's anti-self" could be applied
to material that previously had proved intractable to his purposes.

But, for all this, it is clear that the Nō convention was still
the most effective medium for the central theme that informs
all the last tragedies: the inherently tragic striving and suffering
of unfulfilled being. This theme, rationalized by Yeats as a dynamic cycle of distinct phases through which all being must pass,
opened the way for the great range of subjects found in the last
tragedies. And, despite its apparent limitations, the Nō convention proved to be remarkably flexible as a means for realizing his
full dramatic range. On the one hand, its remote ritualistic
qualities permitted him to present the heroic age of myth, or
being, in its subjective phase when fulfillment was a vivid possibility. On the other, the Nō convention's direct and concentrated power, deriving from its aesthetic economy and severity,
permitted him to present periods hostile to heroism or to being

in some phase of objectivity when unity or fulfillment was impossible. The fine nobility of Cuchulain's heroic acceptance, the horrible loneliness of Christ discovering beings beyond His help, the hopeless degradation of the Old Man in *Purgatory*—the range is astonishing, roughly comparable to what the range of a traditional dramatist would be if he could successfully write heroic tragedies, mystery plays, and realistic dramas, all in the same stylistic form.

The Climax: Two "Noble Plays"

No playwright, as even Shakespeare's work testifies, can be expected inevitably to equal his highest achievement in whatever he does after it; it is no surprise that Yeats's last tragedies are not all equally effective. *The Resurrection* is a remarkable achievement; but its companion work, *Calvary,* bears in a concentrated form too much abstraction, too much elliptical theory. *Calvary* embodies some of the basic ideas found in *The Resurrection,* but compresses them so much that the expressed motives of the principals sound like flat exposition and, even to an extremely learned audience, are incredible. Nor did Yeats solve the problems of dramatic focus and audience sympathy in *Calvary.* Who is the protagonist? Christ's lonely sorrow is real, but sympathy with it would be misplaced; in His divine nature He triumphs—even if, ironically, it is not over those beyond His reach, except to cut them off from historical meaning now that His era is rising. Lazarus and Judas are too unprepossessing to arouse sympathy, and they are on the periphery of Christ's central experience. One might see the pristine objective spirit as "hero," but such a protagonist seems abstract and remote; the play is thus too philosophical, or philosophical in the wrong way: an unclear abstract of a conception not fully embodied. In *The Dreaming of the Bones,* both the young Revolutionist and the lovers have an immediacy that arouses sympathy, though it is divided and finally dissipated by the frustrating conclusion; but the play is moving because it has a vital immediacy for the audience.

Perhaps the charges of abstractness and overcompression directed against *At the Hawk's Well* and *Calvary* might be leveled, as well, at *The King of the Great Clock Tower* and its revision, *A Full Moon in March.* The remoteness of action in both versions is not compensated for by any vividness of character, although costume, music, and the poetry go some way in achieving such vividness. Despite the necessary austerity of the "theatre's anti-self," the playwright must still somehow touch the audience; and even *A Full Moon in March,* though well-constructed, puts too much aesthetic distance between itself and its audience.[1]

Such a weakness cannot be attributed to *The Death of Cuchulain.* Since it was completed just before Yeats died, the play is not as perfectly finished as it might have been had it received the benefit of a later, cool consideration. Actually only a brief one-act play with three scenes, *The Death of Cuchulain* seems too cluttered in action and too tangled in development, and these weaknesses are not rectified by the play's unusually numerous dramatis personae (seven). The Nō convention is here merely strained by the overcrowding of action and character.

The Words Upon the Window-Pane is an achievement that belongs with *The Resurrection, The Dreaming of the Bones, The Only Jealousy of Emer,* and *Purgatory* as the triumphs of the final period. The last two plays, perhaps Yeats's finest accomplishments in the "theatre's anti-self," not only came up to his own standards but may be enduring contributions to the tradition of English tragedy. They are worth a careful scrutiny aimed at providing a conclusive demonstration of what Yeats's ideal of tragedy could achieve in actual practice. The success of these plays is due in great measure to Yeats's brilliant solutions to his problem of how to make the supernatural a central element of the dramatic form. The plays are prime examples of his final answers to this old and crucial problem, answers that are typical for all the tragedies of the last period, if never so effectively worked out as in these two representative plays.

The Only Jealousy of Emer is the finest example among those plays—*Calvary, The Dreaming of the Bones, The King of the Great Clock Tower,* and *A Full Moon in March*—which adhere scrupulously to the Nō convention and bring the supernatural into the action as part of the given of that convention. *Purgatory,* at least, is one of the finest examples of those plays— *The Resurrection* and *The Words Upon the Window-Pane*—in which the Nō convention is loosened or all but abandoned, until Yeats seemed to be adopting the methods of realism. In these plays the supernatural is given life by the shocking contrast between the normal, common-sense reality of the surface world and the presence of a superhuman so vivid that the dramatis personae in the common-sense world must acknowledge it, though as much against their wills as it might be for members of an audience in the same situation. *The Only Jealousy of Emer* and *Purgatory* are at once typical of Yeats's last tragedies and, in themselves, powerful plays.

THE ONLY JEALOUSY OF EMER:
SUBJECTIVE TRAGEDY (1916–1934)

The Only Jealousy of Emer, whose versions span a period from 1916 to 1934, is a singular example of Yeats's dramatic methods over almost the entire last period of his career. The idea for the play had already begun working in his mind in 1916, when, in a letter to Lady Gregory, he considered the pos-

sible changelings who might enter Cuchulain's "dead" body
after the hero's fight with the sea: "Who should it be—Cuchulain's grandfather, or some god or devil or woman?" [2] Again,
as in *At the Hawk's Well,* Yeats fabricated an incident in the
life of Cuchulain: his wife's effort to rescue the hero from death
after his fight with the waves on Baile's Strand.[3] In a note to
an early version, he briefly suggested the ontological theory that
informed the play and was to culminate in *A Vision.* This mere
hint at theory is sufficient, in the light of the foregoing analysis,
to perceive what the major theme of *The Only Jealousy of Emer*
will be. Thus, when Yeats asserted that "physical beauty, only
possible to subjective natures, is described as the result of emotional toil in past lives," [4] he meant that tragic struggle ("emotional toil") in the subjective phases results in perfection of
being ("physical beauty" emblemizing Phase 15). Such remarks
indicate that Yeats was consciously employing his theory in the
play. Yet theory does not function in this drama as an abstract
dogma arbitrarily bending action and character to formula.

The Only Jealousy of Emer, in its earliest version, has a
relatively simple plot hardly suggesting the elaborate scheme
that helped give it shape. After their initial song, whose theme
is the suffering required to produce beauty, three choric musicians summon up the scene of action, "a poor fisher's house," [5]
in which, Cuchulain, dressed in his graveclothes, has been laid
after his fight with the sea. Seated by the curtained bed on which
the body lies is Emer, the hero's wife; crouched near the front
of the stage is a figure, invisible to the humans in the play,
dressed exactly like the body of the hero. As the action opens,
Eithne Inguba, Cuchulain's present mistress, stands timidly at
the entrance of the house, the sea at her back, until Emer, who
has sent for her, bids her enter. After describing Cuchulain's
fight with the waves, Emer tells Eithne Inguba that she suspects
some changeling of having gained possession of the body, though
she does not believe that Cuchulain is yet dead. Eithne Inguba

suggests that, since the dead are believed to haunt "the scenery of their lives" (*Emer,* p. 32) for a time after death, the wife ought to call out to her husband; but Emer asks that Eithne Inguba do the calling since it is she who now has the hero's love. Emer then prepares for the summoning by closing the bed curtains so that Cuchulain aroused will not be able to view the sea (out of which can come daemonic possession) and by building the hearth fire because "enchantments of the dreaming foam/ Dread the hearth-fire" (p. 33).

Reproached by Emer for her first timid summons, Eithne Inguba calls out passionately to the hero, only to arouse a changeling, Bricriu, the withered-armed "maker of discord" (p. 35) among the gods.[6] Eithne Inguba having run off in terror, Emer is left to face Bricriu, who informs her that only if she foregoes the hope of ever regaining her husband's love can he be brought back. In order to show her from what she may save Cuchulain, Bricriu touches Emer's eyes and makes visible the Ghost of Cuchulain, the crouching figure, now stirred by the human voices into a state of dreaming customary to newly dead shades still attached to memories of their human existence. Emer then witnesses the temptation of Cuchulain by the Woman of the Sidhe, the goddess Fand, who dances around the Ghost of Cuchulain and seems, because of her movements and bronze attire, "more an idol than a human being" (p. 41).[7] In the dialogue between hero and goddess, Cuchulain recognizes Fand as the Guardian of the hawk's well who lured him away from the immortalizing waters. Now the goddess, needing a mortal's love to attain completion of being, promises the hero the perfect freedom of oblivion with a single kiss. Deeply troubled by images out of his past life, Cuchulain desires the goddess' kiss because he wants final liberation from the suffering and frustrations of the human condition. At this moment, Emer surrenders her hope of his love and, in so doing, assures his return to life.

The ensuing dialogue between Fand and Cuchulain reveals that the hero's humanity is stronger than the temptations of the supernatural, for Cuchulain acknowledges the overpowering strength of natural attachments, especially those tinged with suffering that no immortal can comprehend:

> How could you know
> That man is held to those whom he has loved
> By pain they gave, or pain that he has given,
> Intricacies of pain.   (*Emer*, p. 46)

Fand, on the departure of the hero's Ghost, lashes out in her disappointment at Bricriu, who defends himself as being by nature a maker of discord; then the two immortals fly off to present their cases to Manannán, the king of the sea. Cuchulain awakens at this moment and calls out, not for Emer, but for Eithne Inguba who has just returned. The play concludes with the song of the choric musicians whose theme is the suffering and frustration attendant upon all effort to complete being:

> O bitter reward
> Of many a tragic tomb!
> And we though astonished are dumb
> Or give but a sigh and a word,
> A passing word.   (p. 50)

The staging of *The Only Jealousy of Emer,* like that of almost all the late tragedies, is a bare place "against the wall of any room" (p. 27), and the properties, with the exception of the curtained bed, are also characteristic of the Yeatsian Nō: simple musical instruments, black cloth for the unfolding and folding ritual at the beginning and end of the play, and masks. Yeats follows his usual procedure with respect to the allotment of masks. The musicians' faces are painted to resemble masks, as are those of the other two human principals, Emer and Eithne Inguba, who, however, can also be masked, since they, unlike the musicians, are actual participants in a spiritual drama. Fand,

Bricriu, and the Ghost of Cuchulain, all supernatural, are masked. Cuchulain, before and after possession by Bricriu, is masked, as in *At the Hawk's Well,* because he is also a participant in a spiritual struggle.

Characterization escapes the chilly abstractness found in *At the Hawk's Well* and *Calvary* through a complexity and variety that yet work toward a strong definition of theme. It is perhaps because of the richness of characterization that Yeats is able to diminish the role of the choric musicians whose multiple function in *At the Hawk's Well* particularly is overcomplicated for dramatis personae who do not participate in the action. The choric voice in *The Only Jealousy of Emer,* functioning in a finely balanced pattern, opens and closes the play with songs that state the tragic theme and set the scene by a remarkably vivid and terse summoning up of the fisher's house to the mind's eye:

> I call before the eyes a roof
> With cross-beams darkened by smoke;
> A fisher's net hangs from the beam,
> A long oar lies against the wall.
> I call up a poor fisher's house.   (p. 29)

Aside from an occasional musical accompaniment, the chorus is quiet during the action, its role simply to enclose a vivid struggle, much more humanized than that of *At the Hawk's Well* and, therefore, able to speak more directly for itself.

The principals of *The Only Jealousy of Emer* are developed, as is usual in the Yeatsian Nō, through a series of contrasts and oppositions, but far more emotionally compelling ones than those of *At the Hawk's Well,* whose uncompromising strictness, unenriched by allusion and the traditional associations available to the Japanese drama, was its major weakness. Yeats's problem in *The Only Jealousy of Emer,* since he could not avail himself of the literary allusion of the Japanese dramatists, was to find means of enriching the form without losing its remoteness or "stillness"; his solution was to make Emer the focus of multiple conflicts that elicit a profound sympathy lacking for the coldly distant Cuchulain of *At the Hawk's Well* or for the inhumanly remote Christ of *Calvary*. Yet, because these conflicts are spiritual ones in the depths of Emer's mind, the static quality of the action is preserved.

Emer's character is revealed through metaphorical conflict, not through what Yeats would have regarded as mere realistic busyness. She is seen first in contrast to Eithne Inguba, whose timidity and selfishness are opposed to the courage and selflessness that Emer must exercise to redeem Cuchulain. Emer is also set against the wicked, daemonic Bricriu, whose inhuman destructiveness arouses her to her full humanity. She is set against Fand, whose nearly perfect Unity of Being manifests itself, from the mortal point of view, in a remorseless, self-absorbed beauty which has the power to lead men into an oblivious rejection of their human responsibility; Fand's opposition rouses Emer to a sacrifice that signifies a full sense of that responsibility. Finally, Emer is seen in contrast to Cuchulain, whose love shifts to any object that will bring him closer to the ideal of perfect beauty. Thus Fand is more desirable to him than Eithne Inguba because the goddess is closer to that ideal; Emer's love fixes only upon the object that brings her to her full womanhood.

Other oppositions and contrasts of character work within those that unfold the personality of Emer. The contrast of Cuchulain and Bricriu, of noble hero and ignoble daemon, sets the "virtue" of the human world against the apparent evil of the superhuman. It is a contrast that makes clearer why Fand receives far less sympathy than Emer; the brilliant idol-like nature of the goddess is too cold and remote to inspire audience identification. Fand, close to completion of being, is set in opposition to Bricriu and Cuchulain, the first a symbol of a superhuman dissolution of being, the second of the mortal's incapacity to rise for long above its attachment to the natural world. Finally

Fand and Bricriu are set in opposition to Emer and Cuchulain, an opposition that expresses Yeats's old conviction that gods for their purposes use mortals but are indifferent to them. In this play the spiritual is clearly at war with the natural and the consequence for the natural is a nearly unrelieved anguish. In short, the complex of oppositions and contrasts creates a remarkable richness and unfolds through action the theme stated by the musicians: that the quest for completion of being demands perpetual suffering and frustration. At the center of extreme opposites, Emer moves through the tragic rhythm of the achievement of selfhood by being brought to heroic choice by daemonic Bricriu, and she must ironically be "cursed" (p. 37), as was Cuchulain in *At the Hawk's Well,* for the very virtues which would in some ideal world seem ultimate blessings: courage, integrity, constancy, and a sublime capacity to rise above selfish desires. In exercising these virtues, she achieves her identity. It is a perilous achievement both for the fate it brings her and because she has—one more somber irony—"rescued" Cuchulain, as Peter Ure suggests, from immortality.[8]

The richness of characterization is reflected in the play's verse which is more varied than in any of the other Nō tragedies. The blank verse, used chiefly by Emer, Eithne Inguba, and Bricriu, functions on many more levels than it does in *At the Hawk's Well,* moving from Emer's succinctly telling exposition,

> Towards noon in the assembly of the kings
> He met with one who seemed a while most dear.
> The kings stood round; some quarrel was blown up;
> He drove him out and killed him on the shore
> At Baile's tree, and he who was so killed
> Was his own son begot on some wild woman
> When he was young, or so I have heard it said;
> And thereupon, knowing what man he had killed,
> And being mad with sorrow, he ran out;
> And after, to his middle in the foam
> With shield before him and with sword in hand

> He fought the deathless sea. The kings looked on
> And not a king dared stretch an arm, or even
> Dared call his name, but all stood wondering
> In that dumb stupor like cattle in a gale,
> Until at last, as though he had fixed his eyes
> On a new enemy, he waded out
> Until the water had swept over him;
> But the waves washed his senseless image up
> And laid it at this door   (*Emer*, pp. 30–31)

to the passionate outcry of Eithne Inguba calling Cuchulain
from death,

> O my beloved, pardon me, that I
> Have been ashamed and you in so great need.
> I have never sent a message or called out,
> Scarce had a longing for your company
> But you have known and come; and if indeed
> You are lying there, stretch out your arms and speak;
> Open your mouth and speak, for to this hour
> My company has made you talkative.
> What ails your tongue, or what has closed your ears?
> Our passion had not chilled when we were parted
> On the pale shore under the breaking dawn.   (p. 34)

Against this verse is set that of the musicians' speech and song,
ranging from two to five stresses per line:

> A man lies dead or swooning,
> That amorous man,
> That amorous, violent man, renowned Cuchulain,
> Queen Emer at his side
> At her own bidding all the rest have gone.   (p. 29)

Finally, a third type, unique in Yeats's plays, is used in the exchange between the Ghost of Cuchulain and Fand. This verse
takes the form of octosyllabic couplets that remove the superhuman exchange to a different level from that of the other characters. The effect of these couplets is a chant so heightened by
its metrical convention as to suggest a realm of discourse alien
to the others of the play: [9]

Time shall seem to stay his course;
When your mouth and my mouth meet
All my round shall be complete
Imagining all its circles run;
And there shall be oblivion
Even to quench Cuchulain's drouth,
Even to still that heart.   (*Emer,* p. 43)

Emer is lifted into this realm once when she gives up Cuchulain's love to redeem him; after Emer's renunciation, even Fand and the Ghost of Cuchulain speak blank verse, the tension of Fand's temptation having subsided. Thus, within the small compass of the play three different states of being are expressed by clearly marked differences of style: the choric, the intermediating voice between actors and audience; the heroic, the voice of noble humanity in a subjective age; and the supernatural, the voice of being in its metaphysical state.

The complex of images constituting the play's binding metaphor grows naturally out of the subject itself. The prevailing image of the sea, especially as encroaching upon the land, is native to the very locale of the action—the seashore which has been the scene of Cuchulain's fight with the waves. The opening song of the First Musician immediately establishes the characteristic qualities of the image:

A woman's beauty is like a white
Frail bird, like a white sea-bird alone
At daybreak after stormy night
Between two furrows upon the ploughed land:
.   .   .   .
A strange unserviceable thing,
A fragile, exquisite, pale shell,
That the vast troubled waters bring
To the loud sands before day has broken.
The storm arose and suddenly fell
Amid the dark before day had broken.
What death? what discipline?
What bonds no man could unbind

Being imagined within
The labyrinth of the mind,
What pursuing or fleeing,
What wounds, what bloody press
Dragged into being
This loveliness?

.   .   .   .

Beyond the open door the bitter sea,
The shining, bitter sea, is crying out,
(*singing*) White shell, white wing!
I will not choose for my friend
A frail unserviceable thing
That drifts and dreams, and but knows
That waters are without end
And that wind blows.   (pp. 27–29)

The sea, which Yeats had earlier defined as "the drifting indefinite bitterness of life," and, like all images of water, "the signature of the fruitfulness of the body and of the fruitfulness of dreams," [10] is an active presence throughout the play. Emer chides Eithne Inguba's timidity in summoning Cuchulain, insisting, "We're but two women struggling with the sea" (*Emer*, p. 34). Eithne Inguba, addressing the body of Cuchulain, speaks of their passion "on the pale shore" (p. 34). Both Fand and Bricriu are creatures of the sea, and when Emer redeems Cuchulain, Fand sends him to the "Country-Under-Wave" to demand his life (pp. 45–46). These images of the sea are not only repeated with variations throughout the play; they are also enriched by subordinate but related images, chiefly those of bird, wind, and moon.

The lovely white sea bird is cast up by the force of the sea onto a "ploughed land," that is, a land ordered by human purpose. The sea here is like the fruitful but cruelly indifferent anima mundi casting up living images or reincarnated spirits onto the anima hominis. The bird—subjectivity and female beauty— is "stranded" on a human shore where beauty has no function, indeed, is a source of its own and others' suffering.[11] Immediately following Emer's redemption of him, Cuchulain refers to the "frail bird heard and seen/ In the incredible clear light love cast" (p. 45). The bird image is not the only one related to that of the sea; wind is also associated with water as in the First Musician's opening song. The wind also recurs in Fand's promise of forgetfulness in exchange for Cuchulain's kiss: "For all have washed out of their eyes/ Wind-blown dirt of their memories" (p.44). Here the reference is to earthly attachments stirred into blinding chaos by passions. Though not as frequent an image as the others, the wind is as important as sea or bird. Yeats treated wind as "a symbol of vague desires and hopes, not merely because the Sidhe are in the wind . . . but because wind and spirit and vague desire have been associated everywhere." [12] Wind is, then, twofold in significance: it embodies both supernatural identity and human passions, particularly those aroused by the Sidhe.

The moon image is used with overt reference to Yeats's system of personality. Thus the Ghost of Cuchulain cries out to the newly entered Fand:

Who is it stands before me there
Shedding such light from limb and hair
As when the moon, complete at last
With every labouring crescent past,
And lonely with extreme delight,
Flings out upon the fifteenth night?   (*Emer,* p. 41)

Emer associates the moon and sea in her renunciation of Cuchulain, asserting that she will be content if Cuchulain looks upon her with "Eyes that the cold moon [Fand], or the vague sea [the anima mundi] [has] made indifferent" (p. 45). Fand, in her wrath at Bricriu, reveals that he is her opposite because he has dropped "From a last leprous crescent of the moon" (p. 46), the last phase before the completely objective phase.

The images of sea, bird, wind, and moon function to unify, define, and vivify the tragic action taking place in the depths of the mind. The binding metaphor, along with other unifying elements like mask, dance, music, and general pattern of gesture and scene design, build to a convention which provides a powerful and vivid world for the meeting of natural and supernatural. The supernatural in *The Only Jealousy of Emer* can in no sense be considered an incredible intrusion or mechanical personification.

After years of experimenting, Yeats had discovered a way to bring the war of orders onto the stage. The spiritual combat of the "theatre's anti-self" presupposed principals who were superhuman since the drama in the depths of the mind brings into play spiritual forces. Bricriu, Fand, and the Ghost of Cuchulain have an unquestionable dramatic necessity, participating in a spiritual experience that is expressed by the conflict between the human and the daemonic. Fand's dance, for example, unlike the dance in *At the Hawk's Well,* grows out of the action and is an accurate symbol for the beautiful and remote superhuman that draws Cuchulain to its near perfection. As Miner asserts:

the dance and the central figure are both part of the drama, since the masked, metallic dancer's ritualistic motions represent the force against which Emer struggles and are, so to speak, the counterpoint to the surgings of her own heart." [13]

There are, however, weaknesses in the first version of the play which Yeats criticized in his characteristic fashion: through significant revision. The version in *Four Plays for Dancers* is curiously troubling. Emer seems to hold the center of the stage for the first half of the action, and her choice up to then seems central. Bricriu's demand that she give up the hope of Cuchulain's love fulfills exactly the description of the tragic function of the daemon already cited in "Per Amica":

The Daemon, by using his mediatorial shades, brings man again and again to the place of choice, heightening temptation that the choice may be as final as possible, imposing his own lucidity upon events, leading his victim to whatever among works not impossible is the most difficult.[14]

Emer's situation is identical with Cuchulain's in *At the Hawk's Well;* she is brought to the agonizing choice that gives her a tragic identity. Or as Bricriu taunts her: "You dare not be accursed, yet he [Cuchulain] has dared" (*Emer,* p. 37). That Emer chooses to put herself, as had Cuchulain, in the fatal powers of the gods and, therefore, assures her heroic mask seems to be the theme of this tragedy. Bricriu's daemonic touch illuminates the choice that she must face.

There are elements in this version of the play that distract from the theme, or, at least, hardly serve it. For instance, Cuchulain's memory of Emer during his temptation by Fand does not clearly establish a real opposition to the beautiful goddess. Cuchulain's first memory is that of his son's death, not of the wife whose image ultimately keeps him from accepting the goddess' offer. What is more confusing is that after Emer's speech, giving up all hope of ever regaining her husband's love, the continued converse of Fand first with the Ghost of Cuchulain and then with Bricriu appears to make the play's subject the disappointment of the goddess in failing to complete her being. This sudden concern with Fand diminishes the tragic irony of Cuchulain's turning, in the end, not to the woman who sacrificed for him all that she valued but to his timid mistress who ran from the tragic meeting of heroic spirit and its daemon. The sense that the play is shifting its attention to Fand is reinforced by the musicians' last song, most of which seems to apply only to the frustration of the goddess:

> Although the door be shut
> And all seem well enough,
> Although wide world hold not
> A man but will give you his love
> The moment he has looked at you,

He that has loved the best
May turn from a statue
His too human breast.   (p. 49)

In fact, the construction of the play prompts Birgit Bjersby to
adopt the view that Fand is the play's heroine. Bjersby concentrates her attention upon the goddess, finding her failure to
complete herself chiefly an autobiographical revelation—Yeats's
failure with Maude Gonne: "In the drama the rôles are reversed,
but the main theme is there: the impossibility of union between
two souls not kindred to one another." [15] Both F. A. C. Wilson
and Helen H. Vendler follow Bjersby in giving the play to Fand
and regard Emer as a sort of conscience for Cuchulain or a poor
domestic counter for Fand's divine power. But these interpretations characteristically tend to explain the play as a code for
Yeats's system or his life and ignore or distort the actual text by
which *The Only Jealously of Emer* must stand or fall.[16]

Although interpretations that give Fand the play might be
valid for the earlier drafts, the final revision leaves little doubt
that the play belongs to Emer, is her tragedy. For in the version
appearing in *The Collected Plays* (1935), Cuchulain remembers,
in his exchange with Fand, only Emer and his disloyalty to
her.[17] More important, in the revision, Emer's choice is made
a far more dramatic moment. In the earlier versions, Emer,
interrupting the kiss that will give Cuchulain oblivion and
Fand perfection, expresses her tragic choice in a set speech
whose tone seems merely tired resignation after no evident
struggle: [18]

If but the dead will set him free
That I may speak with him at whiles
By the hearth-stone, I am content—
Content that he shall turn on me
Eyes that the cold moon, or the vague sea,
Or what I know not's made indifferent.[19]

In the revision Cuchulain pursues the goddess, begging for the
kiss, and Bricriu challenges the unwilling Emer to save her

husband. The daemon builds tension by picturing the goddess in her chariot, the hero ready to mount beside her, until Emer cries, "I renounce Cuchulain's love for ever." [20] The single line speaks far more vividly for Emer's human passion than the too logical and considered speech of the earlier versions. Finally, after Emer's decision, Yeats insures that the play remains hers by excising the unbalancing exchange between Fand and Cuchulain as well as that between Fand and Bricriu.[21] This excision brings in Eithne Inguba immediately, who, instead of a few timid lines, takes full credit for summoning back Cuchulain and is rewarded by Cuchulain's crying out for her. The tragic irony of Emer's decision is now properly the center of dramatic attention.

That Yeats diminished Fand's role suggests that he meant also to diminish the overt use of his phase theory of personality. And, in fact, he excises all references to the lunar phases except in the exchanges between Fand and the Ghost of Cuchulain and in the closing song, both instances where references to the system would be most appropriate. Certainly, this repressing of theory is consonant with Yeats's habit throughout his career of keeping philosophy in his creative work submerged below the surface of action. His youthful comment to Katharine Tynan that he had deliberately disguised meaning in the second part of *The Wanderings of Oisin* [22] is echoed a year before his death in a comment to Ethel Mannin on the philosophy of *The Death of Cuchulain:*

My "private philosophy" is there but there must be no sign of it; all must be like an old faery tale. It guides me to certain conclusions and gives me precision but I do not write it.[23]

However, his failure to change the musicians' last song seems to shift the dramatic focus from Emer, for the song refers chiefly to the goddess who is now diminished in importance.

Yet the revision clarifies another pattern that the early versions had not made clear, and it is this pattern which puts the final song into dramatic balance with the rest of the play.

In the earlier versions, the musicians' final song seemed merely
an extension of the concern with Fand's frustration that occupied the last half of the play. With Fand's role cut so that
Emer's part dominates the action, the last song can be seen for
what it was meant to be, antistrophe, so to speak, to the play's
opening song, which was devoted to introducing the beautiful
Eithne Inguba, comparing her to a frail sea bird, useless product
of untold suffering, cast upon the shore of human life. As Eithne
Inguba, one extreme form of woman, receives the musicians'
first tribute, so Fand, the other extreme, receives their last:

> Why does your heart beat thus?
> Plain to be understood,
> I have met in a man's house
> A statue of solitude,
> Moving there and walking;
> Its strange heart beating fast
> For all our talking.
> O still that heart at last.
>
> O bitter reward
> Of many a tragic tomb!
> And we though astonished are dumb
> And give but a sigh and word,
> A passing word.
>
> Although the door be shut
> And all seem well enough,
> Although wide world hold not
> A man but will give you his love
> The moment he has looked at you,
> He that has loved the best
> May turn from a statue
> His too human breast.
>
> O bitter reward, *etc.*
>
> What makes your heart so beat?
> Is there no man at your side?

When beauty is complete
Your own thought will have died
And danger not be diminished;
Dimmed at three-quarter light
When moon's round is finished
The stars are out of sight.

O bitter reward, *etc.*[24]

The sorrow of Eithne's frail human beauty and the frustration of Fand's superhuman beauty represent opposite extremes of emotion that widen the range of Emer's suffering as she stands between the two types. Thus, the songs broaden the theme to encompass all beauty and its tragic fate: the childlike, almost animal beauty of Eithne Inguba, the human beauty of Emer, and the supernatural beauty of Fand. Yet the choric songs are still subordinate to the main action in which Emer is the central figure.[25]

Miner's view, then, is surely the right one, that the play is primarily about

Emer's tragic choice . . . to lose Cuchulain to the supernatural forces against which she struggles, or to win him back to life at the cost of renouncing his love forever.[26]

In more Yeatsian terms, Emer, in the depths of her mind, meets her daemonic opposite who arouses her to the agonizing tragic choice. Her triumph, like Cuchulain's in *At the Hawk's Well,* is that, in defeat, she assumes the heroic mask which is necessary to the completion of being, the aim of all unrealized selves. Emer, purified by suffering, the "curse" that is part of the tragic experience, rises for a moment to impersonal greatness, to universal stature. If Emer after her sacrifice is not permitted any obvious show of tragic joy—that calm exaltation that Yeats felt to be the quality of heroic transcendence—it should not be inferred that she is reduced to dumb pathos. Her simple statement followed by a stillness indicates the calm after great anguish. The "joy" in subjective tragedy is not in any overt expression of it (as in comedy), but the act of acceptance and the absolute and unequivocal absorption of character in the heroic gesture and all it implies. And the quality of this joy wholly bound up with a heroic act is defined by the poetic heightening inherent in the dance-play convention itself.

The Only Jealousy of Emer is a more precise dramatic embodiment of Yeatsian tragedy than the best play of the previous decade, *On Baile's Strand,* for the tragic gesture of Cuchulain in the earlier play, his assault on the sea itself, is ambiguous in implication and, therefore, a doubtful tragic resolution. Emer's gesture has tragic intensity and meaning within the world of the play, for it arises out of the action and leads to consequences that make her fate clear. And, perhaps most important, this clarity is achieved without the audience knowing, though such knowing enriches the play, the abstract system of lunar phases that Yeats was, at this time, developing.[27] The tragedy is rich with a self-generated meaning that flows from action and defines itself in terms of action.

PURGATORY: OBJECTIVE TRAGEDY (1939)

Planned early in 1938 as a "scene of tragic intensity," [28] *Purgatory* is perhaps the most tightly constructed of all the late tragedies, surpassing even *At the Hawk's Well* in the austere bareness of convention. Yeats claimed to "have put nothing into the play because it seemed picturesque." [29] The scene of action is simply "A ruined house and a bare tree in the background," [30] and the dramatis personae a Boy and an Old Man. As befitting a play set in the objective phases of a dying cycle in which men become reduced to fragmented beings, no character is masked and there is no ecstatic dance; nor is there any chorus to interpret an action that takes place in the depths of a mind that is incapable of spiritual transcendence and hence needs no interpretation. The speech and actions of the two characters must carry the full burden of the dramatic convention.

The plot is equally severe in its simplicity. The action, taking place in the nineteenth or early twentieth century, opens with two peddlers, the Boy and the Old Man, his father, coming upon a ruined mansion at night. The Old Man commands the Boy to study the ruin, "Because there is somebody in that house" (*Purgatory,* p. 682). The Boy sneers at this, insisting that the ruin is empty. The Old Man reveals, then, that the house was his mother's, burned down in a fit of drunkenness by her husband, a blackguardly groom who squandered his wife's fortune and debased her family name. The Old Man further confesses that during the fire he killed his groom-father, ran away to escape punishment, and became a peddler. It is at this point that he hears the beat of a horse's hoofs, and remembers that this very night is the anniversary of his mother's wedding, "Or of the night wherein I was begotten" (p. 685). Then, though the Boy can see nothing, the Old Man (and the audience) can perceive a girl in the suddenly lighted window of the ruined mansion. The hoofbeats are the signal of the groom's returning home drunk. The Old Man is then forced to watch with horror the shades of his mother and father conceiving him. He cries out to his mother, but knows that he calls in vain.

Meanwhile, his own son, thinking him mad, attempts to run off with their money. Caught, the Boy plays with the idea of killing the Old Man, but is brought up short, seeing what he has not heretofore been able to see, a light in the window and someone standing there, although "The floorboards are all burnt away" (p. 687). The Old Man explains that:

> There's nothing leaning in the window
> But the impression upon my mother's mind;
> Being dead she is alone in her remorse.   (pp. 687–88)

Frightened, the Boy covers his eyes, and the Old Man takes this opportunity to kill him with the very same knife that years ago he had used to murder his father, the groom. The window then darkens, and the Old Man believes that by killing his son he has stopped the consequences of his mother's evil marriage and, therefore, ended her remorse, her tortured, compulsive reliving of her ruinous passion. But he is immediately disabused when, with the sound of the phantom hoofbeats of his father's horse, the whole tormenting scene begins again:

> Twice a murderer and all for nothing,
> And she must animate that dead night
> Not once but many times!   (p. 689)

His last words are a prayer growing out of the horror of double murder, the general debasement of the life that he knows, and the agony of both the impure living and the impure dead:

> O God,
> Release my mother's soul from its dream!
> Mankind can do no more. Appease
> The misery of the living and the remorse of the dead.   (p. 689)

Characterization, like the plot, is pared down to suggestive essentials that are delineated clearly by the speech and action of the principals. The mixed nature of the Old Man, a compound of the base inheritance from his father and the aristocratic inheritance from his mother, is embodied in his speech. Sometimes he is brutally direct and, if not colloquial, achieves an effect of the colloquial, as in his contemptuous reply to his son's question:

> BOY.   What education have you given me?
> OLD MAN.   I gave the education that befits
>   A bastard that a pedlar got
>   Upon a tinker's daughter in a ditch.   (p. 684)

Sometimes the Old Man reflects his mother's cultivation; after stabbing his son, he sings with a terrible irony:

> "Hush-a-bye baby, thy father's a knight,
> Thy mother a lady, lovely and bright."
> No, that is something that I read in a book,

> And if I sing it must be to my mother,
> And I lack rhyme.   (p. 688)

The Boy, inheriting only that side of the Old Man's nature that derives from a grandfather who was a crude and uneducated servant, has one coarse voice:

> My God, but you had luck! Grand clothes,
> And maybe a grand horse to ride.   (p. 684)

The Boy's thievery and half-threat to murder his father complete his character, as his father's character is completed by the ruthless killing of his son, an act which paradoxically reveals something fine in the Old Man's nature, because this last murder was motivated by a wish to end his mother's terrible suffering. The Old Man's brutalized fineness is the only direct expression in the play of the lineal aristocratic superiority thrown away by his mother.

The verse style of *Purgatory* has a hard and sinuous bareness befitting its function as the utterance of an objective world in which experience has a fragmented and opaque surface. The absence of mask, music, and dance concentrates all attention on the verse, a fact which challenged Yeats to achieve a style that would not err either on the side of overcompensation in a grandiose richness or on the side of austerity in a cold flatness like that of *At the Hawk's Well*. Yeats was equal to the challenge, and boldly departed from the traditional blank verse of his earlier poetic tragedies. He chose, instead, another verse convention, a line predominantly iambic tetrameter, loosened with many anapaest substitutions, so many that it could be argued that the verse consists simply of four stresses with unstressed syllables varying considerably from point to point. The following is a fair example:

> Looked at him and married him,
> And he squandered everything she had.
> She never knew the worst, because

> She died in giving birth to me,
> But now she knows it all, being dead.
> Great people lived and died in this house;
> Magistrates, colonels, members of Parliament,
> Captains and Governors, and long ago
> Men that had fought at Aughrim and the Boyne.   (p. 683)

A characteristic variation appears in the first foot of the second line, two unaccented syllables followed by a strong stress. This type of foot is frequently found in an ultimate position as in lines five and six. Such variations are almost the norm. Yeats had experimented in *The Only Jealousy of Emer* with octosyllabic couplets in the exchange between the Ghost of Cuchulain and Fand; these rigorously iambic couplets worked surprisingly well as heightened speech. Here, Yeats uses as the norm the four-stressed or tetrameter line, unrhymed and flexible with regard to the number and position of unstressed syllables. The result is a rhythmic convention, coupled with a diction that keeps mostly to an informal or middle range, close to that of idiomatic speech. In contrast to the elevated blank verse of the other tragedies, this verse pattern seems genuinely conversational, although tractable enough to bear the rhetorical elevation of the play's last lines. Yeats, in fact, had discovered a verse medium that could exactly express an almost unrelieved coarseness—the chief characteristic of the two personalities in the play—and that yet maintained the sense that their speech is the heightened expression of a type of spiritual reality which is always the "setting" in the "theatre's anti-self." Hence, the verse can stoop to brutality, then lift to a brief nobility without an inconsistency that breaks the unity of expression. The style, thus, absorbs everything from the philosophical explication of the half-learned Old Man,

> But there are some
> That do not care what's gone, what's left:
> The souls in Purgatory that come back

To habitations and familiar spots.

. . . .

                      Re-live
Their transgressions, and that not once
But many times; they know at last
The consequence of those transgressions
Whether upon others or upon themselves;
Upon others, others may bring help,
For when the consequence is at an end
The dream must end; if upon themselves,
There is no help but in themselves
And in the mercy of God   (p. 682),

to the simplest, crudest emotion,

What if I killed you? You killed my grand-dad,
Because you were young and he was old.
Now I am young and you are old.   (p. 687)

Though in *Purgatory* Yeats abandoned many of the Nō conventions, one that he maintains is the binding metaphor, that vivid image or group of images that thematically links elements in the play. The binding metaphor is introduced in the first few lines of *Purgatory* (its usual place in the plays with choric musicians):

OLD MAN.   The moonlight falls upon the path,
              The shadow of a cloud upon the house,
              And that's symbolical; study that tree,
              What is it like?
BOY.   A silly old man.
OLD MAN.   It's like—no matter what it's like.
              I saw it a year ago stripped bare as now,
              So I chose a better trade.
              I saw it fifty years ago
              Before the thunderbolt had riven it,
              Green leaves, ripe leaves, leaves thick as butter,
              Fat, greasy life.   (pp. 681–82)

The fruitless, stricken tree, which the boy rightly associates with the old age of manhood, is also an emblem of the ruined house that was once rich and of the family line that was once healthy and fruitful. The nature of the play's action links tree, house, and familial line in the wider implication of a general bastardization, coarsening, and decay of life. Moreover, the tree is not only a natural symbol for the last stage in a cycle of birth, growth, and decay; this particular tree is ruined, riven by a thunderbolt, and will not blossom again. Finally, in the position usually assigned to the final chorus, the Old Man completes the binding metaphor; on a dark stage, "except where the tree stands in white light" (p. 688), he commands:

> Study that tree.
> It stands there like a purified soul,
> All cold, sweet, glistening light.
> Dear mother, the window is dark again,
> But you are in the light because
> I finished all that consequence. (p. 688)

The tree is now identified with his mother's spirit, purged both of "fat, greasy" human life and of that life's corruption and ruin. But the illusion of this identification is quickly dispelled when he learns that his mother is not purged by the murder of his son. Thus the tree loses a saving meaning, indeed, cannot signify anything but its present reduced self to a mind trapped in its own and history's objectivity, and fixed in a desolating and opaque isolation where experience is reduced to minimal meaning or utter meaninglessness. In this state, the tree is a fit symbol for the Old Man himself; the connection is immediately clear to his son, a child of the age. Like the Old Man, the tree is reduced to its least significance—a barren, isolated ruin, only suggestive of another kind of life by what it once was or signified in the past. Now, as the Old Man says, "Mankind can do no more" (p. 689). And it is appropriate for him to pray to the God of Calvary, the deity whose will is the surrogate for the individual Choice and infinite Chance of a subjective phase.[31]

The Old Man's prayer to a God whose very existence presupposes human helplessness is appropriate for a further reason. Fruitful contact with the supernatural is impossible in the world of the play. Reality in this world is so fragmented that one kind of being cannot reach out to, cannot meet, other kinds of beings. Yeats achieved this awful sense of isolation by introducing into the play a supernatural presence which is kept at such a distance that the human principals can only witness it, helpless before its agony, much as those present at the séance in *The Words Upon the Window-Pane* were helpless before Swift's spiritual suffering. As in *The Resurrection* and *The Words Upon the Window-Pane,* the supernatural is given dramatic reality by the reaction of humans on the stage; yet, aiming to keep a distance between the natural and the supernatural, Yeats confined the latter to mere glimpses, through a lighted window, of a young girl and a man pouring whiskey. These presences are developed by the Old Man's comments, but could conceivably be his illusions. Wishing to preserve this ambiguity, Yeats withheld until the play's climax the Boy's shocked confirmation that the Old Man does, in fact, see actual ghosts. This ambiguity is deliberately sustained throughout the play, is, indeed, reinforced by the play's very title and setting. For purgatory, aside from its specifically Yeatsian meaning, would suggest to an audience a supernatural locale in which the dead purge themselves of earthly sins before entering Heaven. The desolate scene in which the action opens suggests the possibility that the play may in fact be placed in the Christian purgatory. Though it becomes apparent soon enough that such is not the case, the expectation of the initial possibility is by no means dissipated; the natural world of the play is so purified of circumstantial clutter, so reduced to its grim elementals, that the scene remains touched with the remote and strange. The ambiguity of the locale serves as an appropriate context for the ambiguous relationship of natural and supernatural.

The fact of supernatural presence is no more important

than the fact of its hopeless distance from human life. Yeats, in achieving both effects, perhaps surpassed even his brilliant treatment of the supernatural in *The Resurrection* and *The Words Upon the Window-Pane*. For in *Purgatory* he was trying to show a world fallen further into objectivity than that of *The Words Upon the Window-Pane*. Such a world had to be seen as determined or shaped by its very loss of contact with the spiritual reality. Yeats chose to reveal this loss of contact by showing its result on both the natural and the supernatural world. But the latter had to be shown not only in some dramatically effective way; it had also to be shown as beyond the reach of the natural world. Yeats, by keeping both worlds a little ambiguous—in themselves [32] and in their relationship to each other—until the last moments of the play, achieved his end. On the surface a simple play, *Purgatory* proves, after all, to be remarkably complex, a daring and profound treatment of the supernatural in dramatic form.

This tragedy, like the stripped tree at its symbolic center, embodies a dying or dead reality. In the world of *Purgatory*, man cannot reach his own opposing daemon, cannot transcend his own paralyzing limits. The Old Man is unable to reach the isolated and tormented spirit in the depths of his mind; he is as helpless before this lost spirit as the Boy who must also bear witness finally to the awful ritual and whose uncomprehending mind is brutalized, disinherited, violent, and ignorant. The play, in revealing ways, is analogous, but antithethical, to Yeats's mythological tragedies, and reads on occasion almost like a shocking parody of them, for if the sacrificial murder of the Swineherd leads to the Queen's fulfillment in *A Full Moon in March*, the son's murder in *Purgatory* leads to an ultimate and pointless death, the extermination of a line. Like Cuchulain in *On Baile's Strand*, the Old Man kills his own son. But whereas Cuchulain does so unwittingly and the killing is heroic, leading to tragic transcendence, the Old Man knows whom he kills and the murder leads to nothing beyond itself but further debasement. Cuchulain kills in heroic combat with a sword; the Old Man murders treacherously with the knife used to kill his father years before and to cut his food with still. The Old Man's counterpart in *The Only Jealousy of Emer* is a protagonist whose heroic choice is able to summon Cuchulain back to life. The Old Man's sacrificial gesture is not only horrible, but utterly fails to relieve his mother's suffering. In short, there is, at the end of the play, not the slightest hope for natural regeneration, heroic transcendence, or even the peace of oblivion.

As the play's convention is appropriately limited, so its theme reduces the possibility of human dignity to almost nothing. *Purgatory* is without question one of the most horrifying of all the later plays, leaving no room for the joy that Yeats, even in his last definition of the tragic emotion, found necessary to full tragedy. He declared to the last that the

arts are all the bridal chambers of joy. No tragedy is legitimate unless it leads some great character to his final joy . . . but I add that "will or energy is eternal delight," and when its limit is reached it may become a pure, aimless joy, though the man, the shade, still mourns his lost object.[33]

Little of "pure, aimless joy" is detectable in *Purgatory;* yet Yeats spoke of his play as having "tragic intensity." The contradiction is only apparent; for though full tragic ecstasy is beyond the reach of being in its objective phase, still, in *Purgatory* —certainly an extreme example of the objective category—the genuine intensity of the Old Man in his final agony may be compared with Cuchulain's just before his fight with the sea; and though the Old Man's suffering leads nowhere but to a sterile isolation, his very capacity for passion attaches him for one moment to a fuller condition of being. So, too, the Greek's passion in *The Resurrection,* Swift's in *The Words Upon the Window-Pane,* and the Revolutionist's in *The Dreaming of the Bones* redeem and relieve the sterile context of far-gone objectivity. This redeeming passion is especially essential to *Purgatory* in which none of the vivid immediacy available to the Nō convention can be brought to bear. As the extreme instance of *Purgatory* shows, the objective plays at their best achieve something like Yeatsian tragic joy in the very exercise of passion that transcends the objectivity of their protagonists' fates. So Yeats could regard the somber plays of the objective category just as truly tragedies as those of the subjective category without inconsistency and in consonance with his own theory. Though lacking in the fullness and richness of *The Only Jealousy of Emer*, *Purgatory* has no less immediacy and depth.

A Place in the Tradition

Yeats, in one of his last critical pronouncements, speaks of a perpetual war "where opposites die each other's life, live each other's death." [1] This is no less than the war of "spiritual with natural order," the subject of *The Secret Rose* nearly forty years earlier—the war at the heart of human experience and therefore, so Yeats believed, the most serious subject for the drama. On the strength of that belief, he labored, often in bitterly discouraging circumstances, to find a dramatic form that would suit a living stage. The intensity of Yeats's desire to find a suitable embodiment for his chosen subject can be measured by his ruthless self-criticism; he was, both as poet and playwright, a constant and careful reviser. From the beginning he got little enough help from the English theatre where the only war was between the proponents of a dying traditional drama and the advocates of the realistic problem play. In this situation the temptation for a literary man, with an inclination for playwriting, would be closet drama or, perhaps, dramatic monologue. But Yeats wanted to write plays for a living theatre, "character in action," not "action in character"; [2] the result was years of experiment that began in the shadowy precincts of Pre-Raphaelite moodiness and ended in the lucid depths of the individual mind, scene of a relentless but sometimes ennobling conflict between spirit and nature.

I have argued that the last period in the long search contains the best plays because in them Yeats had for the first time satisfied his own dramatic requirements. When the supernatural order appeared on stage in *The Only Jealousy of Emer* it could not by any rationalization be passed off as a symbol for psychological or sociological realities; the supernatural, in the last plays, is the supernatural or the spiritual reality either in the self or beyond it, no more and no less. This achievement cannot be claimed for the earlier plays.

It is perhaps indicative of their failure to offer a serious presentation of the supernatural that *The Land of Heart's Desire, The Countess Cathleen,* and even *On Baile's Strand* are so easily accepted into the traditional repertory. If *Purgatory* is also accepted, I think that must be laid to the fact that the play looks a little like *Waiting for Godot,* that is, seems to fit into the new fashion.

The question then is this: Do the last plays, understood as serious embodiments of spiritual reality, have any place in the tradition of plays that deserve a stage, or are they brilliant closet dramas at best, despite Yeats's intention? One easy answer is to "interpret" these plays in some way so that they do become psychological after all. Another such answer, a better one, is to invoke the "willing suspension of disbelief," to say, in substance, that in their own terms the plays are valid, as *The Divine Comedy* is valid for non-Catholics or unmedieval Catholics.

The first answer will not do; the second is somewhat evasive and fails to do justice to what I have called Yeats's philosophical seriousness as a playwright. For Yeats demands belief, if not in his system, then in the reality the system names and orders. Just how much belief he demanded is indicated by the requirements for staging his dance plays: better than fair actors, unremitting adherence to the convention,[3] and an audience that comes with no expectation of daily reality or some noble form of it. Yeats saw to it, in short, that his last words in the drama would not be easily domesticated to the modern stage. And naturally enough the reaction from those not willing to make concessions to so stubborn an eccentric has been indifference, baffled irritation, or patronizing dismissal.[4] It is one thing to admit the "theatre of the absurd" into the repertory; it is quite another to admit what looks very odd but lays claim to being just the opposite. Yeats is perhaps *too* clear to misinterpret on this score. So he can be safely left to the bravery of college theatres which may not be quite so devoted to fashion and so much the victims of box office. Or the plays can be studied in class as literature, an adjunct to the poems but less important than some of the secondary texts used.

Yeats understood the consequences of his position but was willing to take the risks. He never expected, at least in our era, that he would be regarded as another in a long line of tragic playwrights of the western tradition and that his last plays would be familiar to a wide audience, so perhaps any justification of these plays as part of the great tradition is beside the point. In *On the Boiler* he sums up his awareness with a fine clarity:

The theatre has not . . . gone my way or in any way I wanted it to go, and often looking back I have wondered if I did right in giving so much of my life to the expression of other men's genius. According to the Indians a man may do much good yet lose his own soul. Then I say to myself, I have had greater luck than any other modern English-speaking dramatist; I have aimed at tragic ecstasy and here and there in my own work and in the work of my friends I have seen it greatly played. What does it matter that it belongs to a dead art and to a time when a man spoke out of an experience and a culture that were not of his time alone, but held his time, as it were, at arms length, that he might be a spectator of the ages.[5]

Yet I think there is reason to regard the best of the last plays as fit for the modern stage, even if one grants their obvious and demanding limitations. *Purgatory* and *The Only Jealousy of Emer* are moving works not because they fit neatly into categories like the psychological or social that give moderns a way of interpreting even the strangest kinds of art but because they treat man's fate with the ruthless honesty and convincing dignity open to the tragic dramatist, more especially open, if history is any proof at all, to the tragic dramatist who is also a great poet. Nor are the honesty and dignity alien to moderns. Yeats's last plays restate, in a new way, the traditional position of tragedy: man, divided and complex, vulnerable both to the world and to himself, is forced to make choices that give him his destiny. Built into this very situation is the possibility—almost probability—that he will bring down suffering on his head and injure others in the process. The total reality of his condition compels him to make his choice; this reality involves a mystery that goes beyond the "natural" or the social, and one cannot account for this mystery by reducing it to psychological, sociological, or historical categories. It is a vital, sometimes terrible presence that man recognizes in moments when his passions seem to break out of the circle of the human. Call the presence anything you like, Apollo or daemon, it is a fact of experience and, in the drama, a fact that inspires belief. The hero is a man who draws this presence to him; it arouses him, by its opposition, to great passion and to action that leads to calamity and suffering in which he discovers his destiny and the wonder of his humanness. In this discovery there can be something like joy, or at least that high, resonant calm in which the whole being accepts what must be and finds its part in the nature of things. If, as in *Purgatory*, the passion falls back on itself without achieving the calm of acceptance, at least the audience has been in the presence of an intensity that is a revelation of one great human possibility.

> O bitter reward
> Of many a tragic tomb!
> And we though astonished are dumb
> Or give but a sigh and a word,
> A passing word.

Abbreviations and Notes

ABBREVIATIONS OF FREQUENTLY CITED WORKS BY YEATS

Agate	*The Cutting of an Agate.* New York, 1912.
Autobiography	*The Autobiography.* New York, 1938.
Blake Poems	*Poems of William Blake.* Yeats ed. New York, 1938.
Blake Works	*The Works of William Blake.* Yeats and Edwin J. Ellis eds. 3 vols. London, 1893.
Boiler	*On the Boiler.* Dublin, 1939.
Bones	*The Dreaming of the Bones,* in *The Collected Plays* of W. B. Yeats. London, 1952.
Calvary	*Calvary,* in *Plays.* London, 1952.
Cathleen	*The Countess Cathleen,* in *Poems.* London, 1895.
Controversies	*Plays and Controversies.* London, 1923. (All quotes are from this edition.)
Cuchulain	*The Death of Cuchulain,* in *Plays.* London, 1952.
Dancers	*Four Plays for Dancers.* London, 1921.
Deirdre	*Deirdre,* in *Plays.* London, 1952.
Discoveries	*Discoveries,* in *Essays.* London, 1929.
Early Poems	*Early Poems and Stories.* New York, 1925.
Emer	*The Only Jealousy of Emer,* in *Dancers,* early version only. Other versions in *Plays.* London, 1934 and 1952.

Essays	*Essays.* London, 1924. (All quotes are from this edition.)
Heart's Desire	*The Land of Heart's Desire.* London, 1894.
Introductions	*Essays and Introductions.* London, 1961.
Irish Theatre	*Plays for an Irish Theatre.* 3 vols. London, 1903. Later edition 1 vol. London, 1911.
Kathleen	*The Countess Kathleen: A Miracle Play,* in *The Countess Kathleen and Various Legends and Lyrics.* London, 1892.
Letters	*The Letters.* Allan Wade ed. London, 1954.
Moon	*Full Moon in March,* in *Plays,* London, 1952.
New Island	*Letters to the New Island.* Horace Reynolds ed. Cambridge, Mass., 1934.
Nothing	*Where There is Nothing,* in *Irish Theatre,* Vol. I. London, 1903. Revised and published under a different title in 1908—see *Unicorn.*
Oisin	*The Wanderings of Oisin,* in *The Wanderings of Oisin and Other Poems.* London, 1954.
Oxford	*The Oxford Book of Modern Verse, 1892–1935.* Yeats ed. New York, 1937.
Plays	*The Collected Plays of W. B. Yeats.* London, 1934; 2d ed. with additional plays, London, 1952 and New York, 1953.
Poems	*Poems.* London, 1895.
Purgatory	*Purgatory,* in *Plays.* London, 1952.
Reeds	*The Wind Among the Reeds.* London, 1899; 4th ed., 1903.
Responsibilities	*Responsibilities,* in *Responsibilities and Other Poems.* London, 1916.
Resurrection	*The Resurrection,* in *Plays,* London, 1952.
Secret Rose	*The Secret Rose.* London, 1897.
Strand	*On Baile's Strand,* in *Irish Theatre,* Vol. III. London, 1903.
Strand, 1907	*On Baile's Strand,* revised version in *The Poetical Works of W. B. Yeats,* Vol. II. London, 1907.
Tables of Law	*The Tables of the Law and the Adoration of the Magi.* London, 1904.
Tales	*Irish Fairy and Folk Tales.* Yeats ed. New York, Modern Library.
Threshold	*The King's Threshold,* in *Plays.* London, 1952.

Tower	*The King of the Great Clock Tower,* in *Plays.* London, 1952.
Twilight	*The Celtic Twilight.* London, 1893; 2d ed., 1902.
Unicorn	*The Unicorn from the Stars,* revised version of *Nothing,* in *The Unicorn from the Stars and Other Plays,* in collaboration with Lady Gregory. London, 1908.
A Vision	*A Vision.* London, 1937.
Waters	*The Shadowy Waters.* London, 1900; 2d ed., 1901.
Well	*At the Hawk's Well,* in *Dancers.* London, 1921. Revised version in *Plays,* London, 1952.
Wheels	*Wheels and Butterflies.* London, 1934.
Words	*The Words Upon the Window-Pane,* in *Plays.* London, 1952.
Works	*The Collected Works in Verse and Prose of W. B. Yeats.* 8 vols. Stratford on Avon, 1908.

NOTES

Introduction. Drama and the Dynamics of Reality

1. Yeats, "The Four Winds of Desire," *The Celtic Twilight* (London, 1893), p. 200. This essay is excluded from the second edition of *The Celtic Twilight,* published in 1902.

2. Yeats, *The Secret Rose* (London, 1897), p. vii.

3. Yeats and E. J. Ellis, eds., *The Works of William Blake* (3 vols., London, 1893), I, 238–50. For an intensive study of the relationship between Blake's and Yeats's theories, see Hazard Adams, *Blake and Yeats: The Contrary Vision* (Ithaca, 1955).

4. In the nineties, "mood" was an important word in Yeats's vocabulary. For a detailed discussion of the meaning of the word, see Richard Ellmann, *The Identity of Yeats* (London, 1954), Chap. 3, Sec. 3. The word usually signified the immortal or divine substance that creates and underlies human nature. The "great Moods are alone Immortal, and the creators of mortal things." "The Wisdom of the King," *Secret Rose,* p. 21. Myth, legend, fairy and folk tales, and the arts embody the moods and are, so to speak, emanations from the immortal mood, the divine substance. The artist, because his imagination comprehends them, is able "to discover immortal

moods in mortal desires." "The Moods," *Essays* (New York, 1924), p. 240.

5. Yeats, untitled comments, *Beltain, an Occasional Publication*, II (Feb., 1900), 24.

6. Yeats, *The Tables of the Law and The Adoration of the Magi* (London, 1904), p. 35.

7. Yeats, *Secret Rose*, p. 23.

8. *Ibid.*, pp. 111–12.

9. Yeats, *Tables of Law*, p. 35.

10. *Ibid.*

11. Yeats, "To the Secret Rose," *Secret Rose*, pp. ix–x. For an extension of this metaphor, see also "Out of the Rose," p. 63.

12. Yeats, "A Symbolical Drama in Paris," *Bookman* (London), VI (April, 1894), 15.

13. Yeats, "Ideas of Good and Evil," *Essays*, p. 112.

14. Yeats, "William Blake and His Illustrations to *The Divine Comedy*," *Essays*, p. 170.

15. Madame Blavatsky, the leader and philosopher of the theosophists, based her criticism of orthodox religions upon their neglect of the moral nature of man. See H. P. Blavatsky, *Key to Theosophy* (London and New York, 1889), p. 25.

16. Yeats, "Magic," *Essays*, pp. 60–61. The doctrine of correspondences underlying this passage is based on Yeats's occult studies, and after 1903, according to Virginia Moore in *The Unicorn* (New York, 1954), pp. 55–56, on Arbois de Jubainville's study of Irish mythology, *The Irish Mythological Cycle and Celtic Mythology*, trans. by R. I. Best (Dublin, 1903). But Yeats again found in Blake what he regarded as a clear statement of the theory of correspondences in which "As natural things correspond to intellectual, so intellectual things correspond to emotional." Yeats and Ellis, *Blake*, I, 239. In his essay "The Three Persons and the Mirror" (*ibid.*, 246–50) Yeats charts the Divine Macrocosm and the Human Microcosm in a Table of Correspondences that shows the various degrees from highest to lowest and the connections between macrocosm and microcosm. The important literary implication in this system is the ontological validity of symbol which can operate on two levels and carry the weight of both human and divine realities at once. The discovery of this metaphysical symbolism by Yeats preceded, and influenced him more than, the symbolism he was to encounter in continental thought and literature.

17. Yeats, *Letters to the New Island*, Horace Reynolds, ed. (Cambridge, Mass., 1934), p. 216.

18. Yeats, "The Return of Ulysses," *Essays*, pp. 246–48.

19. Yeats, "The Theatre," *Essays*, p. 209.

20. Moody Prior, *The Language of Tragedy* (New York, 1947), p. 289.

21. Alfred Tennyson, *The Poetic and Dramatic Works*, H. E. Scudder, ed. (Boston, 1898), p. 677.

22. Henry Arthur Jones, *The Tempter* (London, 1898), p. 100.

23. William Archer, *English Dramatists of Today* (London, 1882), p. 40.

24. For discussion and excerpts from *Vanderdecken,* see Clement Scott, *The Drama of Yesterday and Today* (2 vols.; London, 1899), II, 78–84.

25. Yeats, *The Autobiography* (New York, 1938), p. 105.

26. Yeats, *New Island*, p. ix. This passage was written in retrospect, but it is in accord with the general tone of Yeats's opinions of the earlier period. See, for instance, "The Autumn of the Body" (first published 1898), *Essays*, pp. 232–38.

27. Yeats, *New Island*, p. 213.

28. Yeats, "Discoveries," *Essays*, p. 338.

29. Yeats, *New Island*, pp. 217–18.

30. Yeats's antagonistic attitude toward Ibsen changed somewhat over the years. Even in his early mentions of the Norwegian dramatist, he was never unequivocal in his judgment. For instance, in his review of *Brand*, "The Stone and The Elixir," *Bookman* (London), VII (Oct., 1894), 20–21, he praised Ibsen's *Peer Gynt* and *Brand,* characteristically in occult terms, but qualified the praise by noting that Ibsen sees man not as an end in himself but as a means "for the expression of broad generalisations."

Later he described Ibsen as one who though he "has made us so many clear-drawn characters, has made us no abundant character, no man of genius in whom we could believe" and further "even the most momentous figures are subordinate to some tendency, to some movement, to some inanimate energy, or to some process of thought whose very logic has changed it into mechanism—always to 'something other than human life'." "Preface to the first edition of *The Well of the Saints*" (first published 1905), *Essays*, p. 374.

31. Yeats, *New Island*, pp. 112–18.

32. Yeats, *Essays*, pp. 244–49.

Chapter 1. The First Stage

1. Yeats, *New Island.*

2. Yeats, "The Four Winds of Desire," *Twilight,* p. 210. (See also "A Teller of Tales," pp. 6–7.) This essay is revealing for the insight it provides regarding Yeats's attitude toward the supernatural. His habitual tendency to offer alternative explanations for phenomena that he took to be supernatural is here much in evidence. For he speaks of the peasant's "need" (p. 205) for the dreams embodied in folklore. There are good grounds for regarding Yeats's offering both supernatural and natural explanations for phenomena as the equivocation of a young and still uncertain writer much under the influence of his father's scepticism and adopting the unorthodox position with only enough conviction to shock or to appear eccentric. However, there are equally good grounds for regarding the second alternative, the natural explanation, as the afterthought of prudence. In a letter, dated Dec. 21, 1888, to Katharine Tynan, he discussed a series of articles that he was to write for the *Scots Observer* on the difference between Scottish and Irish fairies. Regarding the acceptability of the articles, he asserted: "All will go well if I can keep my own unpopular thoughts out of them . . . I must be careful in no way to suggest that fairies, or something like them, do veritably exist, some flux and flow of spirits between man and the unresolvable mystery." Yeats, *The Letters,* Allan Wade, ed. (London, 1954), pp. 96–97. A less serious view of folklore, from Yeats's point of view, was necessary if he was to expect publication. Virginia Moore sees Irish legend as furnishing Yeats's "conceptual thought with a colorful background." Virginia Moore, *The Unicorn,* (New York, 1954), p. 46. This view is perhaps too mechanical.

3. Yeats, *Twilight* (2d ed.; London, 1902), p. 193. This essay was added in the second edition.

4. Yeats, "That Subtle Shade," *Bookman* (London), VIII (August, 1895), 144. See also Yeats, "Our Lady of the Hills," *Early Poems and Stories* (New York, 1925), pp. 265–67.

5. Yeats, "William Blake and the Imagination," *Essays,* p. 138.

6. According to Richard Ellmann, there are evidences of an even earlier attempt than those under discussion to wed outlook and dramatic form. He found among some of Yeats's unpublished *juvenilia* "several attempts at playwriting usually with Spenserian

characters (knights, shepherds and shepherdesses, enchanters and enchantresses) and scenery (gardens, islands) and often with Shelleyan attitudes." Ellmann cites as typical "An Old and Solitary One." Here, significantly, the characteristic Yeatsian themes of the next fifteen years appear: two orders of experience are at issue, the infinite and unchanging with the limited and transistory:

> They say I am proud and solitary yes proud
> Because my love and hate abideth ever
> A changeless thing among the changing crowd

Revealing is the assertion of the old protagonist that he has been "cursed with immortality" though "molden with a human nature." Although this contrast could have been suggested by Tennyson's "Oenone," the mere fact that such a notion fascinated Yeats in his eighteenth year (Ellmann's dating) is indicative of how early he was concerned with the tragic experience. Richard Ellmann, *Yeats: The Man and the Masks* (New York, 1948), pp. 30–32.

7. Ellmann dates this as April, 1884. *Man and Masks*, p. 36.

8. Ellmann remarks: "Early in 1886 he [Yeats] was working on a draft of a new tragedy, entitled variously *The Blindness, The Epic of the Forest*, and *The Equator of Wild Olives*. This play he says he had located in a crater of the moon, but his memory or mythmaking sense deceived him, for the scene in the manuscript is Spain." *Ibid.*, p. 48.

9. Ellmann's dating of *Vivien and Time*, is January 8, 1884 (*ibid.*, p. 34); the play appears in *The Wanderings of Oisin and Other Poems* (London, 1899), under the title of *Time and the Witch Vivien*. The original differs chiefly from the second version in having a queen as heroine instead of a witch (see Ellmann, *Man and Masks*, pp. 34–36). *Mosada* was written in 1884 (*ibid.*, p. 37) and published in the *Dublin University Review* (June, 1886), as were *The Island of Statues* (April–July, 1885) and *The Seeker* (September, 1885).

10. *Ibid.*, p. 36.

11. Yeats, *The Island of Statues*, the *Dublin University Review* (April, 1885), pp. 56–57.

12. See, for example, Mosada's Shelleyan incantation to the magic powers in scene one.

It should be noted that Yeats reworked this play to the form in which it appears in *Oisin*, explicating the nature of the conflict between the Moors and Catholic orthodoxy at greater length. Also, by lengthening the play, Yeats gained more room for a clarification of motive in the characters. Fundamentally, however, the play is unchanged. Ellmann dismisses it as "Byronic melodrama." Richard Ellmann, *The Identity of Yeats* (London, 1954), p. 14.

13. Joseph Hone, *W. B. Yeats, 1865–1939* (New York, 1943), p. 47.

14. Yeats, *Autobiography*, p. 100.

15. Yeats showed very little interest in *The Cenci*, possibly because Shelley frankly aimed at psychological realism. Yeats was much more interested, as his early work shows, in *Prometheus Unbound*, and yet his style owes less to it than might be expected. For though Yeats admired *Prometheus Unbound*, its tendency to allegory implied the clear outline and abstract statement that Yeats avoided in the formation of his own style.

16. Yeats, *Letters*, p. 114. See also letter to John O'Leary, Feb., 1889, p. 108.

17. Ellmann, *Man and Masks*, p. 131.

18. Yeats, *Letters*, pp. 153–54.

19. Yeats, *The Countess Kathleen: A Miracle Play,* in *The Countess Kathleen and Various Legends and Lyrics* (London, 1892), pp. 7–8.

20. Yeats, *Letters,* to O'Leary, May 7, 1889, p. 125. Here Yeats announced that he had made two prose versions before writing a line of verse, certainly an indication of his desire to be lucid.

21. *Ibid.,* p. 211. Yeats's use of the word "intellect" is Blakean. The "intellect" arises out of the separation of man from God. It is to be equated with human reason and is opposed to divinely inspired imagination. Reason is the limited faculty that can comprehend only the natural world and manifests itself in argument, pedantry, and false personal pride. Imagination is the opposite of "intellect"; the imaginative faculty comprehends the universal, is linked with divine essence, manifests itself through inspired art or emotion, and is impersonal. For a clear summary of Yeats's position on this dualistic theory of psychological faculty, see Thomas Parkinson, *W. B. Yeats: Self-Critic* (Berkeley, 1951), pp. 13–14.

22. Allan Wade notes that the following verse was found inscribed in a copy of *Kathleen:*

God loves dim ways of glint and gleam
To please him well my rhyme must be

A dyed and figured mystery,
Thought hid in thought, dream hid in dream.
W. B. Yeats, May 27th, 1893

Allan Wade, *Bibliography of the Writings of W. B. Yeats* (London, 1951), p. 25. This verse claims, like the letter to O'Leary, a metaphysical significance for the play.

23. See Yeats, ed., "The Countess Kathleen O'Shea," *Irish Fairy and Folk Tales* (New York, Modern Library, n.d.), pp. 248–51. Yeats imagined that he was using purely Irish material, but later discovered the doubtfulness of the story's source. See Yeats, *Plays and Controversies* (London, 1923), p. 285.

24. Yeats, *Kathleen*, p. 13.

25. Gilbert Murray, *Euripides and His Age* (2d ed.; London, 1946), p. 40.

26. T. R. Henn, *The Harvest of Tragedy* (London, 1956), p. 206.

27. Ellmann, *The Identity*, p. 120.

28. See J. A. MacCulloch, *The Celtic and Scandinavian Religions* (London, 1948), pp. 66–75.

29. Yeats, *The Wind Among the Reeds* (4th ed.; London, 1903), p. 77.

30. MacCulloch, *The Celtic and Scandinavian Religions*, p. 90.

31. The obvious autobiographical significance of Yeats's feeling toward the Countess Kathleen cannot be overlooked. He saw Maude Gonne's career as a long sacrifice of a great soul to a bad world (see Hone, *W. B. Yeats*, pp. 92 and 100). Yet the autobiographical facts do not entirely explain the failure of the play to attain his ideal standard.

32. Henn, *Harvest of Tragedy*, p. 206.

33. Yeats, *New Island*, p. ix.

34. Ellmann, *The Identity*, p. 120.

35. Yeats, *Controversies*, p. 89. Kathleen became Cathleen in the 1895 revision of the play.

36. Yeats, *Autobiography*, p. 356.

37. Moore, *The Unicorn*, p. 82.

38. Yeats, *Letters*, p. 319.

39. See Peter Ure, *Yeats the Playwright* (London, 1963), pp. 9–30, for an acute discussion of *Kathleen* and its later revisions.

40. See Parkinson, *Self-Critic*, p. 59.

41. Yeats, *The Countess Cathleen, Poems* (London, 1895), p. 71

42. Yeats, *Autobiography*, pp. 399–400.

43. Ellmann, *Man and Masks*, p. 131.
44. Yeats, *The Land of Heart's Desire* (London, 1894), p. 23.
45. Yeats, *Controversies*, p. 300.
46. Yeats gives several interpretations of the shee, the fairy folk, in his *Irish Fairy and Folk Tales*, pp. 1–3. They are believed by some to be fallen angels who were capable of being neither saved nor lost. Others regard them as the gods of the earth or of pagan Ireland; this view is supported by the fact that the chiefs of the fairies bear names of the heroes of the Tuatha De Danann and the fairy gathering places are the burial grounds of the Tuatha De Danann. Yeats seems to favor the latter view and might well have preferred to the fallen angels of a Christian mythology these mysterious primal creatures who suggest a more ancient source for Irish culture than Christianity. He also proposed a view of them, however, that suggests his later theory of incarnations: "They are, perhaps human souls in the crucible—these creatures of whim" (p. 2).
47. Yeats, *Letters*, p. 434.
48. Ellmann, *Man and Masks*, p. 131.
49. Yeats, *New Island*, p. 113.

Chapter 2. Aestheticism and The Shadowy Waters

1. Thomas Parkinson, *W. B. Yeats: Self-Critic* (Berkeley, 1951), p. 60.
2. Yeats, "The Symbolism of Poetry," *Essays*, p. 201.
3. See Richard Ellmann, *The Identity of Yeats* (London, 1954), pp. 119–27.
4. In James Hall and Martin Steinmann, eds., *The Permanence of Yeats* (New York, 1950), R. P. Blackmur, "The Later Poetry of W. B. Yeats," p. 58.
5. Yeats, *Autobiography*, p. 257.
6. Blackmur, in Hall and Steinmann, p. 58.
7. Louis MacNeice, *The Poetry of W. B. Yeats* (London, 1941), pp. 22–24.
8. Yeats, ed., *The Oxford Book of Modern Verse, 1892–1935* (New York, 1937), p. ix. The effect of Pater's ideas on Yeats was strongly augmented by his friend and Pater's disciple, Lionel Johnson, who was deeply immersed in his master's views and, to judge

from Yeats's comment, was entirely articulate about them. See Yeats, *Autobiography*, pp. 254–68, and Richard Ellmann, *The Man and the Masks* (New York, 1948), p. 148.

9. Walter Pater, *Marius the Epicurean* (New York, Modern Library, n.d.), p. 113.

10. Walter Pater, *The Renaissance* (New York, 1919), pp. 198–99.

11. Yeats, "Rosa Alchemica," *Secret Rose*, pp. 221–65; also Ellmann, *Man and Masks*, p. 148.

12. Joseph Hone, *W. B. Yeats, 1865–1939* (New York, 1943), pp. 70–73.

13. Yeats, *Essays*, pp. 117–35. For a direct reference to Pater see p. 128.

14. Walter Pater, *Appreciations with an Essay on Style* (London, 1944), pp. 211–12.

15. Yeats, *New Island*, p. 217.

16. Yeats, *"Aglavaine and Sélysette,"* *Bookman* (London), XII (Sept., 1897), 155.

17. Yeats, *Essays*, pp. 248–49.

18. Yeats, "The Reform of the Theatre," *Controversies*, pp. 47–48.

19. Pater, *The Renaissance*, p. 196.

20. See Pater, *Marius the Epicurean*, especially the whole of "Animula Vagula," pp. 101–18, and "Second Thoughts," pp. 210–21.

21. *Ibid.*, p. 117.

22. Yeats, *New Island*, p. 174.

23. Yeats, "The Irish Literary Theatre, 1900," *Beltain*, II (Feb., 1900), p. 24.

24. For a clear statement of Yeats's method of testing see A. B. Stock, *W. B. Yeats: His Poetry and Thought* (Cambridge, 1961), pp. 83–84.

25. Yeats, *Secret Rose*, pp. 223–24. Pater, in *Marius the Epicurean*, p. 199, discusses Marius in the same vein:

Had he not come to Rome partly under poetic vocation, to receive all those things, the very impress of life itself, upon the visual, the imaginative, organ, as upon a mirror; to reflect them; to transmute them into golden words? He must observe that strange medley of superstition, that centuries' growth, layer upon layer, of the curiosities of religion (one faith jostling another out of place) at least for its picturesque interest, and as an indifferent outsider might, not too deeply concerned in the question which, if any of them, was to be the survivor.

26. Yeats, *Reeds*, 4th ed., p. 74.

27. Although the parallel here to the conclusion of *Marius the Epicurean* is worth noting, it cannot be pushed very far. The experience that drove the hero of Yeats's story to the church was not possible in the world of Marius.

28. Yeats, *Autobiography*, p. 257.

29. Yeats, *Essays*, pp. 230–31. This passage seems to echo Maurice Maeterlinck's book of essays, *The Treasure of the Humble*, which Yeats reviewed in July, 1897. In the essay, "The Awakening of the Soul," Maeterlinck's theme was that "a spiritual epoch is perhaps upon us," Maurice Maeterlinck, *The Treasure of the Humble*, trans. by Alfred Sutro (New York, 1900), p. 25. Yeats' own essay, though dated in *Essays*, 1897, appeared in part in *Cosmopolis* (June, 1898). The dating suggests that Yeats's essay could easily have followed his reading of Maeterlinck's. Maeterlinck's influence upon Yeats, however, will be taken up in its proper place.

30. Yeats, *Letters*, letter dated "after Sept. 6, 1888," p. 88.

31. William Tindall, "The Symbolism of W. B. Yeats," in Hall and Steinmann, pp. 264–77.

32. Yeats's major essays on the subject are "The Philosophy of Shelley's Poetry" (1900), pp. 79–116; "William Blake and the Imagination" (1897), pp. 136–41; "William Blake and his Illustrations to *The Divine Comedy*" (1897), pp. 142–78; "Symbolism in Painting" (1898), pp. 180–87; and "The Symbolism of Poetry" (1900), pp. 188–202, *Essays*.

33. Arthur Symons, *The Symbolist Movement in Literature* (London, 1899), p. 10.

34. Arthur Symons, *Studies in Prose and Verse* (New York, 1922), p. 234.

35. Yeats, "Symbolism in Painting," *Essays*, p. 183.

36. Yeats, *"The Return of Ulysses,"* *Essays*, p. 248.

37. There is no doubt of the significance of Symons' role in bringing Yeats to a clearer understanding of his own position. Yeats himself affirms Symons' role in *The Autobiography:* "Arthur Symons, more than any man I have ever known, could slip as it were into the mind of another, and my thoughts gained in richness and in clearness from his sympathy" (p. 272).

38. Yeats, *Letters*, to Lady Gregory, March of 1900, p. 337.

39. Yeats, *Essays*, pp. 192–93. Although, characteristically, Yeats proposed alternative explanations for the nature of the emotions that symbols evoke, his "I prefer" puts him on the side of the super-

natural explanations. But even with his equivocation, he goes beyond Symons who would have favored the naturalistic explanation provided by impressionism that the emotions are evoked "because of long association." See Symons, *The Symbolist Movement,* pp. 9–10.

40. Yeats's aim in using symbol seems to have been identical to Baudelaire's in his poem "Correspondances." This is clearly an instance of closely parallel intention. For a discussion of the symbolism in "Correspondances" see Charles Baudelaire, *One Hundred Poems from Les Fleurs du Mal,* C. F. MacIntyre, trans. (Berkeley, 1947), pp. 336–37.

41. See Maeterlinck, *The Treasure of the Humble,* pp. 30–33.

42. *Ibid.,* pp. 128–29.

43. *Ibid.,* pp. 106–7.

44. *Ibid.,* pp. 108–9.

45. Yeats, *"The Treasure of the Humble,"* *Bookman* (London). XII (July, 1897), 94.

46. Maeterlinck, "The Awakening of the Soul," *The Treasure of the Humble,* p. 29.

47. Yeats, "The Tragic Theatre," *Essays,* p. 298.

48. Maeterlinck, "The Tragical in Daily Life," *The Treasure of the Humble,* p. 119.

49. Yeats, "The Tragic Theatre," *Essays,* pp. 302–3. Yeats in a comment crediting his father's taste in the drama with helping to shape his own, uses the Maeterlinckian term "somnambulistic." When the elder Yeats read to his son from some play, the passages chosen were carefully selected: "All must be an idealisation of speech, and at some moment of passionate action or somnambulistic reverie," *Autobiography,* p. 59.

50. Tindall, in Hall and Steinmann, p. 273. Tindall has noted this problem and states:

Some of the plays of William Butler Yeats resemble those of the French symbolist stage not only because they are also transcendental reactions against the realistic stage but because he had Villiers and Maeterlinck in mind when he wrote them. The debt of *The Shadowy Waters* to Villiers is clear. *The Countess Kathleen* (1892), however, which has all the atmosphere of Maeterlinck, was written before Yeats knew of him. It is difficult to say what part of Yeats' other plays comes from the French and what from the so-called Celtic twilights or the English romantic tradition.

It is, however, necessary to qualify Tindall's remark concerning *Kathleen.* Of all Yeats's early plays, this one was the least shadowy in motive and outline, and the least like Maeterlinck's work.

51. Yeats, *Letters*, p. 255.

52. It is worth noting, however, that Yeats rather freely interpreted Maeterlinck's remarks in *The Treasure of the Humble*. See Yeats, "The Return of Ulysses," *Essays*, pp. 244–45.

53. Yeats, *"Aglavaine and Sélysette,"* *Bookman* (London), XII (Sept., 1897), 155.

54. Yeats, *Letters*, p. 255. The remark referred to *Les Aveugles*, but was entirely apposite to Yeats's feelings about *Aglavaine and Sélysette*. A comparison of Yeats's remarks concerning both plays reveals his belief that they suffered from the same basic faults.

55. Tindall, in Hall and Steinmann, pp. 265–66.

56. Yeats, *Essays*, p. 233.

57. Walter E. Houghton, "Yeats and Crazy-Jane: The Hero in Old Age," in Hall and Steinmann, pp. 369–71.

58. The best summary of Villiers' play is found in Edmund Wilson, *Axël's Castle* (New York, 1948), pp. 259–64.

59. Yeats, "A Symbolic Artist and the Coming of Symbolic Art," *The Dome* (December, 1898), p. 233.

60. Yeats, "The Queen and the Fool," *Twilight,* 2d ed., p. 192.

61. Yeats, *Autobiography*, p. 272.

62. Yeats, "A Symbolical Drama in Paris," *Bookman* (London), VI (April, 1894), 15.

63. Hone, *W. B. Yeats*, p. 112.

64. Yeats, *Twilight,* 2d ed., p. 192.

65. Yeats, "Christian Rosencrux," *Essays*, pp. 242–43.

66. Villiers de l'Isle-Adam, *Axël*, H. P. R. Finberg, trans., Yeats, Preface (London, 1925). In his preface, Yeats asserts that the play is too long.

67. Tindall, in Hall and Steinmann, p. 273.

68. Yeats, "The Moods," *Essays*, p. 240.

69. Yeats, *Letters*, p. 343.

70. Yeats, *"The Return of Ulysses,"* *Essays*, p. 248.

71. Yeats, "Symbolism in Painting," *Essays*, p. 183. It should be noted that Yeats never made clear the distinction between magician (one who controls by supernatural power) and the mystic (one who identifies with the supernatural). Evidently he did not separate them in his own mind. See Margaret Rudd, *Divided Image* (London, 1953).

72. Yeats, "Mr. Rhys' Welsh Ballads," *Bookman* (London), XIV (April, 1898), 14–15.

73. Yeats, "Lady Gregory's Translations," *The Cutting of an Agate* (New York, 1912), pp. 7–8.

74. Yeats, "Symbolism in Painting," *Essays,* p. 183.

75. Yeats, "The Theatre," *Essays,* p. 209.

76. Ellmann states that *The Shadowy Waters* was the result of an old idea conceived as early as 1885 and taken up again in 1894. *Man and Masks,* p. 134.

77. Parkinson, *Self-Critic,* p. 60.

78. Yeats, *Letters,* p. 280.

79. Ellmann, *Man and Masks,* p. 134.

80. See Yeats, *Letters,* p. 237, footnote 4 in which a synopsis of the play's genesis is given.

81. Yeats, *Letters,* p. 322.

82. Ellmann, *The Identity,* pp. 80–81. Ellmann's citation reads: *The Arrow,* November 24, 1906, in Henderson Collection, National Library, Dublin.

83. Parkinson, *Self-Critic,* p. 61.

84. Yeats, *Letters,* p. 324.

85. Ellmann, *The Identity,* p. 81. Ellmann quotes an unsigned program note for the July 9, 1905 performance, regarding the passage as Yeats's own.

86. *Ibid.,* p. 313.

87. Yeats leaves his audience this alternative when he states in his notes "Forgael and the woman drifted on alone following the birds, awaiting death and what comes after." See n. 82 above.

88. Yeats, *Reeds* (London, 1899), p. 72.

89. Ellmann, *The Identity,* p. 81. For a penetrating analysis of the symbolism of *The Shadowy Waters,* see pp. 80–84. For a more generalized discussion of the play and its revisions, see Parkinson, *Self-Critic,* pp. 59–75.

90. See Thomas Parkinson, "The Sun and the Moon in Yeats's Early Poetry," *PMLA,* L (August, 1952), 54.

91. Yeats, "William Blake and His Illustrations to *The Divine Comedy*," *Essays,* p. 149.

92. Ellmann, *The Identity,* p. 82. The quoted remarks within the quotation from Ellmann are taken from the first edition of *Waters* (1900). Fiona Macleod (William Sharp) in *Poems and Dramas* (New York, 1914), pp. 318–19, defines the fairy fool, the Dalua, of whom Yeats spoke in his letter to Russell concerning symbolism in *Waters,* in the following way:

He is the Amadan-Dhu, or Dark Fool, the Faery Fool, whose touch is madness or death for any mortal: whose falling shadow even causes bewilderment and forgetfulness. The Fool is at once an elder and dreadful god, a mysterious and potent spirit, avoided even of the proud immortal folk themselves: and an abstraction, "the shadow of pale hopes, forgotten dreams, and madness of men's minds."

See also Yeats's own essay on the subject, "The Queen and the Fool," (first published 1901), *Twilight*, 2d ed., pp. 186–94.

93. Yeats, *The Shadowy Waters* (2d ed.; London, 1901), p. 44.

94. Ellmann, *The Identity*, pp. 82–83.

95. See Ellmann, *The Identity*, pp. 83–84; Parkinson, *Self-Critic*, pp. 59–75. Louis MacNeice, *W. B. Yeats*, however, regards the play as a total failure, pp. 98–99.

96. Parkinson, *Self-Critic*, p. 65.

97. *Ibid.*, p. 66.

98. *Ibid.*, p. 62.

99. Ellmann, *The Identity*, p. 81.

100. Yeats, "The Queen and the Fool," *Twilight*, 2d ed., p. 192.

101. The idea that immortals require mortal help for their actions was advanced by Yeats in his essay "Mortal Help," *Twilight*, 2d ed., pp. 12–14, and may have some connection with the hostility or apparent hostility of the gods; for it would seem logical that once they had served the purpose for which the immortals needed them, mortals would either be destroyed or be made miserable by having to return to the common level of human experience—this, from the human point of view, is the cruelty of the gods. Men, then, are mere tools in the hands of a divine purpose, they are marvelously but briefly elevated, only to be cast aside after they have fulfilled their function.

102. Ellmann, *The Identity*, p. 84.

Chapter 3. Tragicomedy, 1900–1908

1. See, for instance, Louis MacNeice, *The Poetry of W. B. Yeats* (London, 1941), Chap. V; Joseph Hone, *W. B. Yeats, 1865–1939* (New York, 1943), Chap. VIII; James Hall and Martin Steinmann, eds., *The Permanence of Yeats* (New York, 1950), F. R. Leavis, "New Bearings in English Poetry," p. 172.

2. See particularly Richard Ellmann, *The Identity of Yeats*

(London, 1954), Chap. V, in which he properly treats the change as one of gradual development.

3. Arthur Mizener, "The Romanticism of W. B. Yeats," in Hall and Steinmann, p. 140.

4. See Una Ellis-Fermor, *The Irish Dramatic Movement* (London, 1939), and Lennox Robinson, *Ireland's Abbey Theatre* (London, 1951), for background of the Abbey Theatre and Yeats's connection with it.

5. Yeats, *Letters,* p. 99.

6. Yeats, *Essays,* p. 265.

7. See Thomas Parkinson, *W. B. Yeats: Self-Critic* (Berkeley, 1951), p. 78. Parkinson defines tragicomedy in the Yeatsian sense as a tragedy that starts "off in the area of the known world" and leads men slowly to ecstasy.

8. See Yeats, *"The Return of Ulysses," Essays,* p. 244.

9. Yeats, "Irish Dramatic Movement, 1902," *Controversies,* p. 22.

10. Parkinson, *Self-Critic,* p. 67.

11. Yeats, "The Reform of the Theatre," *Controversies,* p. 48.

12. Parkinson, *Self-Critic,* p. 70.

13. *Diarmuid and Grania* (performed Oct. 21, 1901) is not discussed in this book since Yeats never included it in his collected works nor was it published during his lifetime. (It was published in the *Dublin Magazine,* April–June, 1951.) The play was written in collaboration with George Moore, a spirit, unlike Lady Gregory, hardly kin to Yeats. Yeats did not evidently consider the play his and planned to reshape it later into something more to his own taste. See Yeats, *Letters,* to Frank Fay, dated Nov. 13, 1904, p. 443.

14. Yeats, *Responsibilities* (London, 1916), p. 188.

15. See Yeats, *Letters,* to Frank Fay, dated Aug. 8, 1903, p. 409.

16. Yeats, *Plays for an Irish Theatre* (London, 1911), p. 219.

17. Ellmann, *The Identity,* p. 104.

18. Yeats, *Poems, 1899–1905* (London, 1906), p. xii. See also Parkinson, *Self-Critic,* for a thorough discussion of the revisions of *The Shadowy Waters,* pp. 51–75.

19. Yeats, *Letters,* p. 386.

20. *Ibid.,* p. 379. Following this comment, Yeats described the difficulty that he had completing the hero's sermon in *Where There is Nothing,* a sermon clearly influenced by Yeats's reading in Nietzsche. See Giorgio Melchiori, *The Whole Mystery of Art* (London, 1960), p. 41.

21. Friedrich Nietzsche, "The Birth of Tragedy," *The Philosophy of Nietzsche* (Modern Library, New York, n.d.), p. 1002. The discussion of Nietzsche's theory is based on this version of his essay.

22. Ellmann, *The Identity*, p. 95. It should be noted that the theme of transcendence of the law had appeared in Yeats's work— notably in "The Tables of the Law" (1897)—before Nietzsche's influence. However, Nietzsche's theories, added to Blake's, provided Yeats with a more aggressive and affirmative program of transcendence than he had had in the nineties.

23. Yeats, *Where There is Nothing*, in *Plays for an Irish Theatre* (London, 1903) I, 25. Yeats used the title of his play, *Where There is Nothing*, for a short story published in *The Secret Rose*. Except that the title there is a full statement, "Where There is Nothing There is God," the short story has little in common with the play. One resemblance is to be found in the fact that the hero of the short story, a saint, has, like Paul Ruttledge in the play, attempted to attain a state of nothingness in order to reach God.

24. "Reason" is here meant in its Blakean sense, at least as Yeats interpreted Blake, as "argument from the memory and from the sensations of the body [which] binds us to Satan and opacity, and is the only enemy of God." Yeats, ed., *Poems of William Blake* (New York, 1938), p. xxviii.

25. Yeats, *Nothing*, pp. 44–46.

26. Yeats's preface to his selection of Blake's poetry helps explain the hero's need to do what by common standards is "sinful," as, for instance, Paul's marrying Sabina Silver by the simple expedient of "leping a budget," *Nothing*, p. 47. Blake, he declared, believed that "sin awakens imagination because it is from emotion, and is therefore dearer to God than reason, which is wholly dead" (*Blake Poems*, pp. xxviii, xxix).

27. The reference in the play is to the twenty-second Psalm, but the actual Psalm sung is the twenty-third.

28. Yeats, *Nothing*, p. 90.

29. Richard Ellmann, *The Man and the Masks* (New York, 1948), p. 136. See, however, Ellis-Fermor, *Irish Dramatic Movement*, p. 104, who defends it and holds it superior to its final version, *The Unicorn from the Stars*.

30. Ellmann, *Man and Masks*, p. 135.

31. For the story of the play's composition, see *Autobiography*, pp. 386–88.

32. Ellmann, *Man and Masks*, p. 135.

33. It is not improbable that the character of the hero of Ibsen's *Brand,* which Yeats had reviewed in 1894, suggested the somewhat similar character of Paul.

34. Yeats, *Letters,* pp. 405–6. It is revealing to see that when the Ibsenesque sense of fate (that Yeats believed arose out of realistic form and setting) began to close in, Yeats was willing to sacrifice dramatic structure for the sake of his hero's vitality, a choice that indicates how far in spirit he was from the realists when he wrote *Where There is Nothing.*

35. Yeats and Lady Gregory, *The Unicorn from the Stars and Other Plays* (New York, 1908), p. ix. A later and harsher judgment is found in *The Autobiography,* p. 388: "*Where There is Nothing* is a bad play; I had caught sight of Tolstoy's essay about the Sermon on the Mount lying on a chair and made the most important act pivot upon pacifist commonplace." The reference to Tolstoy possibly accounts for the radical and inexplicable change in Paul's attitude toward the means of salvation from act to act.

36. See Yeats, *Letters,* to Arthur Griffith, July 16, 1901, p. 353.

37. *Ibid.,* p. 397. It was close to this time (spring, 1903) that he was much preoccupied with the Nietzschean distinction of Apollonian and Dionysian forms (pp. 402–3).

38. Yeats, *In the Seven Woods* (New York, 1903), p. 33.

39. See *The Countess Kathleen and Various Legends and Lyrics,* pp. 100–5, titled there "The Death of Cuchulain."

40. Walter Pater, *Appreciations with an Essay on Style* (London, 1944), p. 196.

41. Yeats, "At Stratford-on-Avon," *Essays,* p. 129.

42. Lady Augusta Gregory, *Gods and Fighting Men* (London, 1904), and *Cuchulain of Muirthemne* (London, 1907).

43. Yeats, *Agate,* p. 9. Yeats's prefaces to Lady Gregory's books appear reprinted in this volume under the title "Thoughts on Lady Gregory's Translations."

44. Yeats, in the Notes to *Reeds,* 4th ed., p. 93, asserted that Professor Rhys called Cuchulain a "solar hero." See A. Norman Jeffares, *W. B. Yeats: Man and Poet* (London, 1949), p. 105. Other meanings of the sun for Yeats at this time, and probably reflecting the influence of Nietzsche, included "sensitive life, and of belief and joy and pride and energy, of indeed the whole life of the will, and of that beauty which neither lures from far off, nor becomes beautiful in giving itself, but makes all glad because it is beauty" ("Shelley's Poetry," *Essays,* p. 114).

45. Yeats, *Strand, Irish Theatre,* III, 69.

46. The names Conchubar and Cuchulain are variously spelled in the many printings of the play. Since orthography in this case apparently does not influence pronunciation, for the sake of consistency the spelling used in this book is that of *The Collected Plays* (New York, 1953).

47. In the legend Conchubar has his druid, Cathbod, put a spell on Cuchulain so that he will fight the sea to prevent his killing everyone in his rage. Yeats does not use this material in the play, although he had used it in the earlier poem on the subject. See Gregory, *Cuchulain of Muirthemne,* p. 319.

48. For discussions of the function of Fool and Blind Man, see T. R. Henn, *Harvest of Tragedy* (London, 1956), pp. 137, 208; Peter Ure, *Towards a Mythology: Studies in the Poetry of W. B. Yeats* (London, 1946), p. 18; Ellmann, *Man and Masks,* p. 170. These authors refer only to the 1906 version of the play.

49. Yeats, *Letters,* p. 425. Yeats's use of sun and moon in this passage is perhaps confusing. It is hard to see the sun as signifying the passive, if Yeats meant that Cuchulain embodied characteristics of the sun. The moon would better fit that description, especially in its character as symbol of the "emotion of multitude." If Yeats meant that Cuchulain is to be identified with the moon, even though he is an offspring of the sun-god, the contradiction is even sharper. The probable explanation is that Yeats's use of these terms, particularly in remarks not meant for publication, was fluid. His habit of seeing polar opposites caused him here to see the two figures in terms that do not quite fit into the context of the play and other of his critical comments.

50. Ure, *Towards a Mythology,* p. 17.

51. The Fool's act suggests Yeats's story, "The Wisdom of the King" (1897), in which the hawk's feathers growing in the hero's hair were a sign that he was a child of the gods.

52. Parkinson, *Self-Critic,* pp. 83–84.

53. Yeats, *Letters,* pp. 424–25.

54. Yeats, *Strand,* p. 99.

55. E. M. W. Tillyard, *Poetry, Direct and Oblique* (London, 1948), p. 99.

56. Yeats, *Letters,* to Lady Gregory, Nov. 24, 1904, p. 444.

57. These writings were later (1923) collected in *Plays and Controversies.*

58. Yeats, *Controversies,* p. 92.

59. Yeats, *Twilight,* 2d ed., p. 192.

60. Yeats, *Controversies,* pp. 104–5.

61. Yeats, *Essays,* pp. 331–32.

62. See Yeats, *Autobiography,* especially "The Trembling of the Veil," pp. 475–76.

63. Yeats, "Discoveries," *Essays,* p. 367. Yeats named some of the masters of the lofty isolated art with which he had identified his own work in the nineties: Shelley, Landor, and Villiers de l'Isle-Adam. Those names are set against such masters of a Dickensian art as Homer, Villon, and Verlaine who sing "of life with the ancient simplicity" (p. 344).

64. Yeats, *Letters,* p. 454.

65. Yeats, *On Baile's Strand,* in *The Poetical Works of W. B. Yeats* (2 vols.; London, 1907), II, 260.

66. G. B. Saul, *Prolegomena to the Study of Yeats's Plays* (Philadelphia, 1958), p. 52.

67. Yeats, *Strand,* p. 81.

68. Yeats, *Strand, 1907,* pp. 321–22.

69. Yeats, *Poems, 1899–1905* (London, 1906), p. 277.

70. Yeats achieved this plan in a series of plays concerning Cuchulain: *The Golden Helmet* (1908), revised as *The Green Helmet* (1910), *At the Hawk's Well* (1916), *The Only Jealousy of Emer* (1918), and *The Death of Cuchulain* (1938).

71. Yeats, *Controversies,* p. 84.

72. Yeats, *Letters,* p. 482. According to Saul, Lady Gregory's hand was responsible for the conclusion of *Deirdre* and, in his opinion, mars an otherwise fine play. See Saul, *Prolegomena,* p. 46.

73. Yeats, *Deirdre,* in *The Poetical Works,* II, 424.

74. Yeats, *The Collected Works* (8 vols.; Stratford on Avon, 1908), II, 251.

75. See Peter Ure, *Yeats the Playwright* (London, 1963), for a different explanation of the failure of *Deirdre,* pp. 55–58.

76. Yeats and Lady Gregory, *Unicorn,* pp. vii, viii–ix.

77. Yeats, *Works,* III, 220–21.

78. Yeats, *Letters.* In a letter to A. H. Bullen, dated Feb. 12, 1908, p. 503, Yeats wrote: "I planned out *The Unicorn* to carry to a more complete realization the central idea of the stories in *The Secret Rose.*"

79. For a full discussion of the unicorn as a Yeatsian symbol see

Giorgio Melchiori, *The Whole Mystery of Art* (London, 1960), especially Chap. I.

80. Yeats and Gregory, *Unicorn,* p. 47.

81. The Mountain of Abeignos is a symbolic term used in Yeats's occult group, The Order of the Golden Dawn, and means "the mountain of spiritual struggle." See Ellmann, *Man and Masks,* p. 191.

82. Ellis-Fermor disagrees in her *Irish Dramatic Movement,* pp. 103–7. She regards the first version as a more effective presentation of the mystic experience. The revision, she believes, by holding to probabilities, casts doubt on the vision, whereas the improbabilities of *Where There is Nothing* command a more "poetic faith" (p. 105).

83. For discussion of these events see Ellis-Fermor, *Irish Dramatic Movement,* Chap. 3; Lady Augusta Gregory, *Our Irish Theatre* (New York, 1913), especially Chap. IV; Lennox Robinson's *Ireland's Abbey Theatre* (London, 1951), Chap. VI; and Hone, *W. B. Yeats,* pp. 276–77.

84. Ellmann notes that Yeats's interests in the "phenomena of spiritualism" began seriously in 1909. *Man and Masks,* p. 196. It is worth considering whether his increasing tendency to regard subjective experiences as the proper subject for literary exploration is not connected with his tendency to seek for the supernatural in the human mind.

Chapter 4. The Development of the Theatre's Antiself, 1908–1938

1. Yeats, *Essays,* pp. 342–43.
2. Yeats, *Autobiography,* p. 402.
3. Yeats, *Essays,* pp. 302–3.
4. *Ibid.,* p. 314.
5. Yeats, "The Tragic Theatre," *Essays,* p. 296. Yeats's explanations of tragic joy are seldom models of clarity, especially since joy itself became associated in his mind with character, a lower form of dramatis persona. Character, to Yeats, is what divides men, tragedy what links them. Character thrives on what marks men as individuals and is properly at home in comedy. Yet joy is certainly an element in Yeats's notion of tragic ecstasy. The best discussion of this problem is found in Edward Engelberg, "Passionate Reverie: W. B.

Yeats's Tragic Correlative," *University of Toronto Quarterly,* XXXI (Jan., 1962), 201–22.

6. Yeats, "Poetry and Tradition," *Essays,* p. 316.

7. Yeats, *Essays,* pp. 300–1. That Yeats takes his analogies from the static art of painting is hardly accidental.

8. Yeats, *Plays for an Irish Theatre* (London, 1911), p. ix. The preface to this volume is substantially the same essay as "The Tragic Theatre," with some additions and excisions.

9. Yeats, *The Poet and the Actress,* unfinished dialogue of 1915, quoted from Richard Ellmann, *The Identity of Yeats* (London, 1954), p. 105.

10. Yeats, *Letters,* p. 624.

11. Yeats, "Per Amica Silentia Lunae," *Essays,* pp. 523–24. Yeats revealed his indebtedness to Blake for this view of the natural sphere by quoting the latter's "God only acts or is in existing beings or men" (p. 518). This notion, reinforced by his experience with fairy tales, Yeats had echoed long before: "I have been told, too, that the people of faery cannot even play at hurley unless they have on either side some mortal. . . . Without mortal help they are shadowy" *Twilight* (1902), p. 12. Yeats's persistent tendency to locate the supernatural within human nature itself is clearly indicated here.

12. This third state of being was not apparently clear in Yeats's mind during the writing of "Per Amica" for he declared, in a summary statement of the ontological basis of life, that only two kinds of reality exist, the superhuman and human, and neglected or disregarded the "condition of air" (p. 523). In *A Vision* (London, 1937), he made a more extensive analysis of this condition. See especially Book 3, "The Soul in Judgment," pp. 219–40.

13. Precisely how the dead are empowered to affect the living Yeats did not say, although his conception of the relationship between the dead and the living seems to parallel the Jungian theory of the relationship between the racial subconscious—the distilled and typical experience of the dead remaining in archetypal forms with the living—and the individual consciousness. Jung's explanation differs from Yeats's in that Yeats viewed the instincts as supernaturally derived, not accountable by explanations that rely on natural causes.

14. The poet is also subject to this transcendent experience, not, like the hero, through defeat, but through disappointment in the anima hominis: "The poet finds and makes his mask in disappointment, the hero in defeat" ("Per Amica," p. 500). Like Pindar,

Yeats regarded the hero and the poet who celebrates him as performing analogous functions in the world: both offer models of human possibility at its highest.

15. See Earl Miner, *The Japanese Tradition in British and American Literature* (Princeton, 1958), Chap. VIII. Miner has correctly pointed out that Yeats knew of the form when he wrote his essay "Swedenborg, Mediums, and the Desolate Places" (1914). See also Lady Augusta Gregory, *Visions and Beliefs*, 2d series (London, 1920), pp. 295–339). This essay provides a link between the ideas of "Per Amica" and the Nō because it discusses the philosophical ideas of the first and the dramaturgy of the second, though in general terms.

16. Introduction by Yeats to Ernest Fenollosa, tr., *Certain Plays of Japan* (Churchtown, Ireland, 1916).

17. Ernest Fenollosa and Ezra Pound, *'Noh' or Accomplishment* (London, 1916). My discussion of the Nō form derives also from Faubion Bowers, *The Japanese Theatre* (New York, 1952); Donald Keene, *Japanese Literature* (New York, 1955); and Arthur Waley, tr., *The Nō Plays of Japan* (London, 1950).

18. Fenollosa and Pound, *'Noh,'* pp. 120–21.

19. *Ibid.*, p. 121.

20. *Ibid.*, p. 120.

21. *Ibid.*, p. 63.

22. Yeats, *Essays*, p. 274.

23. The relationship between the Nō form and *Deirdre* is lucidly summarized in Thomas Parkinson's "The Later Plays of W. B. Yeats" (an unpublished essay, written in 1958, and lent to the author by Mr. Parkinson):

In *Deirdre*, as in the *Four Plays for Dancers* written with the encouragement of the Noh, the action opens with songs by two musicians. A subsidiary character then enters and with occasional asides to and from the musicians makes an exposition of prior relevant action. The two main characters then enter and take up the action from the point that the expositor has reached, and the expositor remains on the stage as measure and commentator on the action of the principals. Their dialogue moves toward a solution of their problem, and at the moment of climax, the supernatural emerges upon the scene, and with the action brought to completion, the singers conclude with a choral comment. *Deirdre* is a much more cluttered play than any of the *Plays for Dancers*, but seen at such a level of abstraction, the action of *Deirdre* is clearly analogous to that of *At the Hawk's Well* or *The Only Jealousy of Emer* or *The Dreaming of the Bones*—or *Nishikigi*. (p. 5)

24. Yeats, *Controversies*, p. 213.

25. Yeats, *Four Plays for Dancers* (London, 1921), p. 88.

26. The event upon which the plot of *At the Hawk's Well* hinges was evidently fabricated by Yeats and takes place in Aoife's country, a fact which would indicate the action of the play to be during Cuchulain's stay with the Scottish queen, Scathach, with whom in his youth he served as apprentice in arms. See Lady Augusta Gregory, *Cuchulain of Muirthemne* (London, 1907), pp. 32–39. For discussions of the sources of the play, see F. A. C. Wilson, *Yeats's Iconography* (New York, 1960), Chap. II, and Helen H. Vendler, *Yeats's "Vision" and the Later Plays* (Cambridge, Mass., 1963), pp. 204–6, 213.

27. Yeats, *At the Hawk's Well,* in *The Collected Plays* (London, 1952), p. 210. Since the text of this play and most of the later plays remained unchanged, all quotations are from *The Collected Plays, 1952,* except for the early and final versions of *The Only Jealousy of Emer.* For earlier printings of the plays, see G. B. Saul, *Prolegomena to the Study of Yeats's Plays* (Philadelphia, 1958).

28. See Vendler for a different interpretation of the choric function (*Yeats's "Vision,"* p. 208). I generally find myself disagreeing with Helen H. Vendler's view of Yeats's use of the chorus in the dance plays, mainly because of her tendency to give the musicians' words to the principals; so far as I know, Yeats himself nowhere justifies such a practice.

29. Peter Ure sums up his function admirably: "The Old Man has never dared to gaze into the hawk's eyes; he has not risked the curse, and now is cursed with vain senescence. Dramatically, he is Cuchulain's foil." Peter Ure, *Yeats the Playwright* (London, 1963), p. 72.

30. See Vendler for an acute analysis of the meaning of Cuchulain's foregoing of the waters of immortality for heroic destiny (*Yeats's "Vision",* pp. 212–16).

31. Yeats, *Deirdre,* in *The Collected Plays* (London, 1952), pp. 197–98.

32. Yeats, *Essays and Introductions* (London, 1961), pp. 523–24.

33. Yeats, *Waters,* p. 49.

34. Yeats, *Well,* p. 212.

35. See Lady Augusta Gregory, *Gods and Fighting Men* (London, 1919), p. 2.

36. It is no doubt true that Yeats, as Wilson argues (*Yeats's*

Iconography, pp. 52–59), had Morris' "The Well at the World's End" in mind during the writing of *At the Hawk's Well* and that the mythological substructure of the play is an initiation test which the protagonist fails. But heavy reliance on ritual elements on the one hand and a too-ready impulse to equate Yeats's plays with his life on the other lead Wilson to a conclusion about the play that seems to me beside the point. The play, as both Vendler (*Yeats's "Vision,"* p. 206) and Ure (*Yeats the Playwright,* p. 72) assert, is about heroism: it is, as Wilson states on p. 59, "a play of consummate spiritual disillusion" only if one takes it as a figurative comment on Yeats's relationship to his own spiritual development and nothing more. This conclusion denies, in the face of reams of evidence, that Yeats cared anything about the subject of heroism.

37. In the Notes to *Calvary,* a later play modeled on the Nō, Yeats asserted that the hawk and other solitary birds "are the natural symbols of subjectivity," *Dancers,* p. 136. However, this same bird also meant supernatural wisdom to Yeats. In his early story "The Wisdom of the King," the hero is touched with divine knowledge, which is revealed by the hawk's feathers that grow on his head in place of hair. The hawk in Yeats's poem of that title is identified with proud untamed mind. See *The Collected Poems* (London, 1950), pp. 167–68. In another poem, "Tom O'Roughley," the bird of prey is opposed to the butterfly, here a symbol for the same wayward wisdom displayed in *On Baile's Strand* by the fool, Cuchulain's comic double or "shadow." Moreover, in this poem the "gloomy bird of prey" is associated with "logic choppers," the villains who "rule the town" (*ibid.,* pp. 158–59). The inference to be drawn from this shifting and reversal of symbolic meaning is obvious enough: in Yeats's work, the immediate context gives the symbol its specific definition.

38. The Young Man's mask pictured in *Dancers,* p. 12, is crowned with a helmet surmounted by a single horn, undoubtedly that of the unicorn, which Yeats regarded as a symbol for the soul.

39. Yeats, *Well,* p. 215.

40. The first curse, though not clearly applicable to Cuchulain, may be read as applying to his ambiguous relationship with Eithne Inguba in *The Death of Cuchulain;* the second curse is realized with Aoife in the same play; the third in his fight with his son in *On Baile's Strand.*

41. Yeats, *Well,* p. 217.

42. Yeats, "A Note on the Instruments," *Dancers,* p. 90.
43. Yeats, *Well,* p. 208.
44. *Ibid.,* p. 211.
45. Yeats, *Dancers,* p. 9.
46. *Ibid.,* p. 86.
47. *Ibid.,* p. v.
48. Miner, *The Japanese Tradition,* p. 258.
49. Yeats, *Dancers,* p. 86.
50. *Ibid.,* pp. 86, 88.
51. Of the three comedies completed during this last period, one, *The Cat and the Moon* (1924), is strongly influenced by the Nō convention. Though published in 1922, *The Player Queen* was begun in 1908 (see Yeats, *Letters,* to Florence Farr, dated [Sept. ?, 1908], p. 511), and, as Wade asserts, was "planned as a verse tragedy, but . . . at Ezra Pound's suggestion, he turned it into a fantastic prose comedy, exemplifying his theory of the Mask, of the Self and the Antiself" (*ibid.,* p. 521). For an analysis of the play see Norman Newton, "Yeats as Dramatist: The Player Queen," *Essays in Criticism,* VIII (1958), 269–84. *The Herne's Egg* (1938) is a farce somewhat resembling *The Green Helmet* in quality. However, this play, a much-discussed departure from anything that Yeats had ever done before, represents an extravagant attempt to embody on the level of farce and travesty his theory of reality. For a thorough discussion of the play, see F. A. C. Wilson, *W. B. Yeats and Tradition* (London, 1958), Chap. III, and Vendler, *Yeats's "Vision,"* pp. 158–67.
52. For other ways of grouping the last plays see Ure, *Yeats as Playwright* and Vendler, *Yeats's "Vision."*
53. Yeats considered himself a man of Phase 17, see Richard Ellmann, *Yeats: The Man and the Masks* (New York, 1948), p. 240, the phase of Dante, Shelley, and Landor. This phase Yeats characterized in *A Vision* as follows:

Because of the habit of synthesis, and of the growing complexity of the energy, which gives many interests, and the still faint perfection of things in their weight and mass, men of this phase are almost always partisans, propagandists and gregarious; yet because of the *Mask* of simplification [Phase 3], which holds up before them the solitary life of hunters and of fishers and "the groves pale passion loves," they hate parties, crowds, propaganda (p. 143).

54. *Will* and *Mask* Yeats defined as the "Is" and "Ought" (*A Vision,* p. 73). Ellmann defines them as "Imagination and Image"

(*The Identity*, p. 160). These pairs of terms express the Yeatsian relationship between passion and dream found in the earliest work.

55. The 2000-year Christian cycle was regarded by Yeats as objective (primary) as opposed to the classical which was the subjective (antithetical) cycle before it, but each cycle, whether it be objective or subjective, has, like the individual personality, both kinds of phases within it. For an illuminating analysis of *A Vision*, see Vendler, *Yeats's "Vision,"* Chaps. I–V. Her diagrams of the systems of cycles (pp. 62–64, 109, 110) are most helpful.

56. Yeats, *A Vision*, p. 83.

57. There are two versions of this form of the play, one in verse and one in prose. The verse version is the one referred to in the following discussion; it was chosen by Yeats for all the editions of his collected plays. See Saul, *Prolegomena*, pp. 90–91.

58. It could be sensibly argued that both *Calvary* and *The Resurrection* are transitional plays like *The Death of Cuchulain* because both are concerned with the point of transition between cycles. But subjectivity in both plays is a foil for the objectivity of the figure of Christ and, therefore, a subordinated element. It is proper to say here that my categories were chosen for what I regarded as their convenience. The plays, at their best, if it is remembered that they relate to one another a little like Shakespeare's history plays, will stand without anyone's categories or any over-elaborate references to Yeats's system. That system sometimes throws light on the purpose in the plays; it does not explain them. As Peter Ure says: "[Yeats] is ready . . . to weight his style and give strength to his imagery with obscure intimations of the philosophy. He does so, though, only when this is theatrically appropriate . . ." (*Yeats the Playwright*, p. 78).

59. Yeats, *The King of the Great Clock Tower*, in *The Collected Plays*, p. 633.

60. Helen H. Vendler notes that the Queen is at Phase 14 and that the Stroller's kiss brings her to the perfection of Phase 15 (*Yeats's "Vision,"* p. 145). Also see her discussion of the Kiss of Death, pp. 150–51.

61. Yeats, *A Full Moon in March*, in *The Collected Plays*, p. 628. The symbolism of the play's title and the symbolic implications of March in plays like *The Resurrection* are explained by Ellmann:

Yeats, delighted by cyclical rounds, was struck by the fact that both gods [Dionysus and Christ] had died and been reborn in March, when the sun was between the Ram and the Fish, and when the moon was beside the constellation Virgo, who carries the star Spica in her hand. Virgo is usually connected with Astraea, the last goddess to leave the world after the golden age; Virgil prophesied in the Fourth Eclogue that she would return and bring the golden age again, and the passage was commonly read in later centuries as a prophecy of the coming of Mary and Christ, the former as Virgo, the latter identified with Spica as the Star of Bethlehem. (*The Identity*, p. 260)

62. The Queen's fulfillment carries out to the letter the strictures of Crazy Jane who insists:

"But love has pitched his mansion in
The place of excrement;
For nothing can be sole or whole
That has not been rent".
      ("Crazy Jane Talks with the Bishop," *The Collected Poems*, p. 295)

63. Yeats, *The Death of Cuchulain*, in *The Collected Plays*, p. 694. This looks like a comic self-portrait, and it may be Yeats's way of showing his own awareness of how outrageous his views appear in the context of an unsympathetic age. Helen H. Vendler certainly takes the speech too literally (*Yeats's "Vision,"* p. 237). Of course, it is "rant" and is meant to be.

64. The description of the goddess in the play implies that at least she was to be masked.

65. Lady Gregory's *Cuchulain of Muirthemne* provided the subject matter of the play. For further discussion of the sources, see Ure, *Yeats the Playwright*, p. 77, and Wilson, *W. B. Yeats and Tradition*, Chap. V.

66. Aoife says that somebody is coming; "I will keep out of his sight, for I have things/ That I must ask questions on before I kill you" (*Cuchulain*, p. 701). The weakness of Aoife's motive for hiding might have been corrected had Yeats had time, as with his other plays, to revise. The last corrections for the final draft of the play were completed just before his death. See Yeats, *Letters*, to Edith Shackleton Heald, dated [Dec. ?, 1938], p. 921.

67. The souls of the completed dead express their ecstasy in the song of birds, as the Second Attendant in *The King of the Great Clock Tower* asserts after the First Attendant's comment about the immortal dancers of Tir-nan-oge: "There every lover is a happy rogue;/ And should he speak, it is the speech of birds" (*Tower*, p. 633).

68. This passage has inspired sharply different and ingenious

interpretations. See, for instance, Vendler, *Yeats's "Vision,"* pp. 243–46, and Wilson, *W. B. Yeats and Tradition,* p. 186. Perhaps another revision would have cleared up the obscurity.

69. Compare the quoted lines with Yeats's poem "The Statues" (*The Collected Poems,* pp. 375–76), especially the last stanza which, with the same subject matter, embodies much the same attitude. For an extensive analysis of the symbolism of the harlot see Wilson, *W. B. Yeats and Tradition,* pp. 175–89. In the Yeatsian scheme harlot and beggar preserve subjective vitality during an objective age.

70. Apotheosis through beheading appears in three of the mythological plays: *The Death of Cuchulain, The King of the Great Clock Tower,* and *A Full Moon in March.* This ritual act is certainly to be associated with the ritual death of Dionysus; that Yeats knew the available literature on the dying and rising god is made clear by the use of his knowledge in *The Resurrection.* The beheading motif is also connected with the symbolist aesthetic in which the figure of dancing Salome was an ideal representation of perfect harmony of being. For the authoritative analysis of Yeats's use of and connection with this aesthetic ideal see Frank Kermode, *Romantic Image* (London, 1957), especially Chap. IV.

71. Ure, *Yeats the Playwright,* p. 82.

72. Vendler, *Yeats's "Vision,"* pp. 242–43.

73. Wilson, *Yeats and Tradition,* p. 195.

74. E. M. W. Tillyard, *Poetry Direct and Oblique* (London, 1934), pp. 42–43.

75. See Vendler's, *Yeats's "Vision,"* pp. 247–52, for an analysis of the poem "Cuchulain Comforted" as it relates to the play and also for a discussion of Cuchulain's place in the Yeatsian purgatory after his death.

76. Yeats's didacticism—a persistent strain in his work—was based on the assumption of human freedom even in the objective phase. Yet his system appears deterministic. In a last essay, *On the Boiler* (Dublin, 1938), his divided mind on the matter is characteristically revealed:

But we may, if we choose, not now or soon but at the next turn of the wheel, push ourselves up, being ourselves the tide, beyond that first mark. But no, these things are fated; we may be pushed up. (p. 29)

77. For Yeats's own prose exposition of this part of the cycle of being, see *A Vision,* pp. 173–300.

78. Peter Ure acutely notes, and Helen H. Vendler agrees, that

"the play does not attempt to actualize Christ's suffering," but puts, through the device of "dreaming-back," the action at a distance. Ure, *Yeats the Playwright,* p. 117; Vendler, *Yeats's "Vision,"* p. 275, n. 6.

79. Yeats, *Dancers,* p. 136. For a discussion of the sources and symbolism of *Calvary,* see Wilson, *Yeats's Iconography,* Chap. V.

80. Yeats, *Calvary,* in *The Collected Plays,* p. 453.

81. Though associated with subjectivity in the play, Judas is seen in Yeats's *A Vision* as objective man, the man of Phase 26 whose *mask* is "self-realisation" and who

commits crimes, not because he wants to . . . but because he wants to feel certain that he can. . . . If he live amid a theologically minded people, his greatest temptation may be to defy God, to become a Judas, who betrays, not for thirty pieces of silver, but that he may call himself creator. (pp. 177–78)

The explanation of this seeming contradiction is that Judas was born into the end of the old subjective cycle and, therefore, participated in such subjective energies as remained to it, though himself an objective man of its last phases, fallen into sick or criminal divisiveness where there is no longer fruitful relationship between natural and supernatural. Objectivity is the death of fruitful opposition; Yeats asserted in *A Vision* of the coming of Christ and the height of objectivity: "The opposites are gone; he does not need his Lazarus; they do not each die the other's life, live the other's death" (p. 275). See Vendler, *Yeats's "Vision,"* p. 175.

82. Yeats, *Dancers,* p. 137.

83. Yeats asserted in *A Vision* that not only is the being of Phase 15 possessed of the greatest beauty and perfection, but also in this phase "Chance and Choice have become interchangeable without losing their identity" (p. 136). That is, the unqualified capacity to choose and the infinite possibilities among which to choose are both present in the fulfilled being, a state directly opposite to the objective phase where external circumstances impose themselves on individual will and limit possibility by this imposition. Helen H. Vendler, basing her interpretation on Yeats's parable in the Notes to the play (*Dancers,* pp. 137–38), sees the soldiers as standing "outside the cycles of objectivity and subjectivity." They bring Christ to despair by showing him in their dance "the parity of his 'system' with all others." They "have the last word" and the play, therefore, "ends with a shrug of dismissal" (*Yeats's "Vision,"* p. 176).

84. For Yeats's explanation of Christ's divided nature, see *A Vision,* p. 275.

85. Yeats, *The Resurrection,* in *The Collected Plays,* pp. 579–80. Peter Ure regards the choric songs as "completely detached from" the play (*Yeats the Playwright,* p. 127 *n*), but Helen H. Vendler ably defends their dramatic relevance: "The poem in fact parallels the play in using shock tactics to bring about a new awareness of reality" (*Yeats's "Vision,"* p. 179). See Vendler for a discussion of the song's relationship to its sources (pp. 80–81).

86. Yeats, *A Vision,* p. 271.

87. Yeats, *Resurrection,* p. 587. See Wilson, *Yeats and Tradition,* pp. 63–68, for an analysis of Yeats's use of Dionysus in the play.

88. T. S. Eliot, *Selected Essays, 1917–1932* (New York, 1932), p. 97.

89. Yeats, *The Dreaming of the Bones,* in *The Collected Plays,* p. 442. See Wilson, *Yeats's Iconography,* Chap. VI, for sources of the play.

90. The time of the action is 1916, the year of the Easter Rising. It is hard to follow Helen H. Vendler in her rejection of the political nature of the play (*Yeats's "Vision,"* p. 187), unless the surface of things counts for nothing in Yeats's work and everything means something else.

91. The Revolutionist is not masked; the lovers are.

92. The Yeatsian view of purgatory, discussed at the beginning of this chapter, is thoroughly analyzed by Vendler, *Yeats's "Vision,"* pp. 75–92. See also Wilson, *Yeats and Tradition,* pp. 140–47.

93. Helen H. Vendler, so far as I know, was the first to observe the contrast of images of day and night. (*Yeats's "Vision,"* pp. 190–91)

94. F. A. C. Wilson regards the cock as a symbol for the coming of a new age, but the exclamatory tone of the last lines in which the cock appears surely in no way alleviates the dreadful impasse represented in the play. See Wilson, *Yeats's Iconography,* pp. 234–40. Helen H. Vendler, pointing to the contrast in the song between night and day, dark and light, asserts that the address to the red cock that serves as a refrain to the song "is an impatient protest against the night and the powers that inhabit it, those powers that make us remember, relive, and consider the past in all its mixed emotions" (*Yeats's "Vision,"* p. 190). This view makes the songs seem far more pertinent to the play than Wilson's does.

95. Miner, *The Japanese Tradition*, pp. 262–63. For another illuminating analysis of *The Words Upon the Window-Pane*, see David R. Clarke, "Yeats and the Modern Theatre," *Threshold*, IV: 2 (Autumn/Winter, 1960), 36–56.

96. Yeats, *The Words Upon the Window-Pane*, in *The Collected Plays*, p. 615. Yeats on p. 24 in his introduction to the play in *Wheels and Butterflies* (London, 1934) compared Swift to Goethe, "the last typical figure of the epoch," that epoch ending in the Renaissance. Goethe in *A Vision* is a man of Phase 18, in which

the being is losing direct knowledge of its old antithetical life. The conflict between that portion of the life of feeling which appertains to his unity, and that portion he has in common with others, coming to an end, has begun to destroy that knowledge. (p. 145)

Swift is a transitional figure living on the edge of the disintegrating objectivity of the last phases of the great cycle—after him, the Old Man of *Purgatory*.

97. Peter Ure says:

Her voicelessness is significant; she is not present, as Vanessa is, and does not speak, as Vanessa does, through the medium, presumably because her spirit has long ago proceeded to some purer stage of the discarnate life. She cannot pardon or release. (*Yeats the Playwright*, pp. 100–1)

98. Yeats, *Words*, p. 615.

99. Yeats, *Wheels*, p. 7.

100. *Ibid.*, p. 20.

101. It seems no coincidence that a renewed involvement in politics began for Yeats in 1933, a year before this play was published. See A. N. Jeffares, *W. B. Yeats: Man and Poet* (London, 1961), Chap. 10.

Chapter 5. The Climax: Two "Noble Plays"

1. See Eric Bentley, *In Search of Theatre* (New York, 1954), pp. 304–6, for an excellent analysis of the play's construction. Peter Ure finds the characters in plays like *A Full Moon in March* properly abstract. They are "primarily projections of the fable's meanings . . . they have no individuality and no names, except ritual ones. . . .

Everything they do can, and should, be done again exactly as before."
Peter Ure, *Yeats the Playwright* (London, 1963), p. 163. The risk here
is that character can become personification proper to allegory and
lose that richness of suggestion that Yeats always sought in the
dance plays.

2. Yeats, *Letters* (letter postmarked Apr. 10, 1916), p. 612. The
play was completed in January, 1918, published a year later, in *Two
Plays for Dancers*, and significantly revised for the London, 1934
edition of *The Collected Plays*. See G. B. Saul, *Prolegomena to the
Study of Yeats's Plays* (Philadelphia, 1958), p. 57.

3. Yeats's source is partly Lady Augusta Gregory's "The Only
Jealousy of Emer," *Cuchulain of Muirthemne* (London, 1907), pp.
276–93. But a more fruitful source is to be found in John Rhys,
*Lectures on the Origin and Growth of Religion as Illustrated by
Celtic Heathendom* (London, 1888), pp. 458–62. Rhys not only told
the ancient stories but also interpreted them symbolically. Yeats's
Notes to his poem "The Secret Rose" seem very much based on
Rhys's comments, see Yeats, *Reeds*, 4th ed., pp. 103–5. The passage
in the poem concerning Cuchulain certainly prefigures the play:

> and him
> Who met Fand walking among flaming dew
> By a gray shore where the wind never blew,
> And lost the world and Emer for a kiss. (p. 49)

4. Yeats, *Dancers*, p. 105.

5. *Ibid.*, p. 29. All references to this version of the play will be
taken from this volume unless otherwise indicated. The changes
between the version in *Two Plays for Dancers* (Churchtown, Ireland, 1919) and this version are minor. See Saul, *Prolegomena*, p. 58.

6. Emer's drawing of the curtains has permitted a change of
masks from Cuchulain's to the wicked daemon's.

7. Rhys in *Lectures* identified the "story of Cúchulainn's
Sick-bed" (p. 462) with a descent into the underworld and Fand
and her watery home with "the world of darkness and death" (p.
458). Fand, wife of the sea god, Manannán mac Lir, was known,
according to Rhys, for "her brilliancy and comeliness" (p. 463).

8. Peter Ure, however, sees Cuchulain's return as theatrically
weak because Fand tempts Cuchulain with immortal love—the appropriate fate for the dead hero—which is preferable in Yeats's view
to the life Cuchulain is called back to (*Yeats as Playwright*, pp.
76–77). But the point of view in the play is Emer's. It is her vision

that determines value. She states her view of Fand and her temptation most succinctly:

> I know her [Fand's] sort.
> They find our men asleep, weary with war,
> Or weary with the chase, and kiss their lips
> And drop their hair upon them; from that hour
> Our men, who yet knew nothing of it all,
> Are lonely, and when at fall of night we press
> Their hearts upon our hearts their hearts are cold.
>
> *(Emer,* in *Dancers,* p. 40)

9. The choric chant, since it is far "looser" in metrical pattern
than the exchange between Cuchulain and Fand, shows a wider
range of emotion. The recorded performance of the play, however,
proves, I think, that the couplets, like the other kinds of verse in
the play, are well suited to dramatic articulation. *The Only Jealousy
of Emer* (Esoteric Records, Feb., 1951).

10. Yeats, *Reeds,* 4th ed., pp. 90, 72. See Wilson for a detailed
discussion of the esoteric symbolism beyond the sea images in the
play. F. A. C. Wilson, *Yeats's Iconography* (New York, 1960), pp.
92–104.

11. If the white sea bird that the First Musician sang about
reveals the tragic loneliness and uselessness of beauty, the revelation
that Fand was the hawk woman who lured Cuchulain from the
waters of immortality of the hawk's well *(Emer,* p. 42) suggests another side of beauty—its ruthless self-absorption.

12. Yeats, *Reeds,* 4th ed., p. 86. In *On Baile's Strand* wind is associated with the shape-changers who, possessing men, arouse in them
wild destructive passions. See *The Collected Plays,* pp. 261–62.

13. Earl Miner, *The Japanese Tradition in British and American Literature* (Princeton, 1958), p. 259.

14. Yeats, *Essays,* p. 529.

15. Birgit Bjersby, *The Interpretation of the Cuchulain Legend
in the Works of W. B. Yeats* (Upsala, 1950), p. 157.

16. See Wilson, *Yeats's Iconography,* p. 120, and Helen H.
Vendler, *Yeats's "Vision" and the Later Plays* (Cambridge, Mass.,
1963), pp. 218–19, 235. On the basis of Yeats's own revisions of the
play I can hardly see how Peter Ure's judgment can be improved:
"Emer's heroic deed, like Cuchulain's in *At the Hawk's Well,* is an
assertion of her identity, of her name as loving wife, and her only
reward, like Deirdre's, is that the long-remembering harpers shall

have matter for their song" (*Yeats the Playwright*, p. 74). Further, Yeats's own admiration for Emer would seem to confirm this view:

and yet I think it may be proud Emer, Cuchulain's fitting wife, who will linger longest in the memory. What a pure flame burns in her always, whether she is the newly-married wife fighting for precedence . . . or the confident housewife, who would awaken her husband from his magic sleep with mocking words; or the great queen who would get him out of the tightening net of his doom, by sending him . . . with . . . his mistress, because he will be more obedient to her; or the woman whom sorrow has set with Helen and Iseult and Brunnhilda, and Deirdre, to share their immortality in the rosary of the poets." (Yeats, "Lady Gregory's Translations," *Agate*, pp. 9–10).

17. Compare the same speech in *Dancers*, p. 41, with that in *Plays*, p. 291.

18. Helen H. Vendler bases some of her interpretation on the assertion that in the earlier versions of the play the choice between Fand and Emer is left up to Cuchulain (*Yeats's "Vision*," p. 229). In no version I have examined is this the case. Perhaps the flatness of the words spoken by Emer that recall Cuchulain to life in the earlier versions have confused the issue, but in both *Two Plays for Dancers* (pp. 33–34) and *Four Plays for Dancers* (pp. 44–45) Emer's words clearly decide the matter.

19. Yeats, *Emer*, in *Dancers*, p. 45.

20. Yeats, *Emer*, in *Plays* (1952), p. 294.

21. Though Bricriu must speak to Emer in her own voice, blank verse, there is less justification for Bricriu and Fand doing so in their bitter quarrel after Cuchulain is redeemed by Emer. Yeats's revision of the play eliminated this weakness.

22. Yeats, *Letters* [after Sept. 6, 1888], p. 88.

23. *Ibid.*, Oct. 20, postmarked 1938, pp. 917–18.

24. The final chorus, partly cleared up by my analysis of the play's revision, has called forth much ingenious interpretation. Helen H. Vendler typically gives this chorus to the principals, a solution not authorized by anything in the play or any theoretical comments by Yeats (*Yeats's "Vision*," pp. 230–34). F. A. C. Wilson, though I am generally in sympathy with his reading, overpowers the song with explication (*Yeats's Iconography*, pp. 121–27). The fault may be Yeats's and the passage, though generally clear, is inherently obscure in places.

25. A third version, in rather flat prose, entitled *Fighting The Waves* (1929), is admittedly "in itself nothing, a mere occasion for

sculptor and dancer, for the exciting dramatic music of George Antheil" (*Wheels*, p. 70). However, in the Preface to this version, written because Yeats regarded the poetic version as unsuitable for a public stage, he seemed to confirm the view that Emer was meant to be the central figure. For in discussing the modern attitude toward the heroic act, he asserted:

Here in Ireland, we have come to think of self-sacrifice, when worthy of public honour, as the act of some man at the moment when he is least himself, most completely the crowd. The heroic act, as it descends through tradition, is an act done because a man is himself, because, being himself, he can ask nothing of other men but room amid remembered tragedies; a sacrifice of himself to himself, almost, so little may he bargain, of the moment to the moment. . . . So lonely is that ancient act, so great the pathos of its joy. (p. 75)

This definition of the genuinely heroic act perfectly applies to Emer's choice in surrendering her hope of Cuchulain's love in order to save him from oblivion.

26. Miner, *The Japanese Tradition*, p. 259.

27. In fact, the moment an attempt is made to see one-to-one relationships between theory and play, trouble begins and the play suffers because Yeats the theorist could not make Yeats the playwright sufficiently systematic. Those critics who give Fand the play seem to me rather highhanded with Yeats the playwright who, viewing his subject from the human condition, might find Emer's position decidedly "interesting."

28. Yeats, *Letters*, to Edith S. Heald, Mar. 12 [1938], p. 907. See Ure, *Yeats the Playwright*, for a discussion of the play's sources (pp. 103–12).

29. *Ibid.*, to Dorothy Wellesley, Aug. 15, 1938, p. 913.

30. Yeats, *Purgatory*, in *The Collected Plays*, p. 681.

31. Helen H. Vendler acutely observes: "The Old Man's proper function is to forgive his mother and father, since the real consequence in him of their action is his mad hatred of them both, not the coarse son he has begotten" (*Yeats's "Vision,"* p. 200). Like the protagonist of *The Dreaming of the Bones*, the Old Man cannot forgive and accept his past.

32. Both Peter Ure (*Yeats the Playwright*, p. 107) and Helen H. Vendler (*Yeats's "Vision,"* p. 199), for instance, note that the mother of the Old Man takes pleasure in reliving her degradation.

33. Yeats, *Boiler*, p. 35. These remarks appear in the same issue in which *Purgatory* was published.

Conclusion. A Place in the Tradition

1. Yeats, *Boiler,* p. 15.

2. Yeats, *Introductions,* p. 530.

3. In a recent performance of *Purgatory* by a professional company, the play was treated as if it were realistic, but when the actor playing the Old Man, reeling drunkenly around the stage, accidentally kicked over the lantern, it did not go out. What did go out was any sense of dramatic reality that the play to that point had commanded.

4. See, for instance, August W. Staub, "The 'Unpopular Theatre' of W. B. Yeats," *Quarterly Journal of Speech,* XLVII: 4 (Dec., 1961), 363–71; Louis MacNeice, *The Poetry of W. B. Yeats* (London 1941), p. 196; and Helen H. Vendler, *Yeats's "Vision."* Vendler's judgment of every play with which she deals is that it is untheatrical. See her last four chapters.

5. Yeats, *Boiler,* p. 14.

Index